THE UNEXPECTED GAMBLER

A HISTORY OF CASINOS CHEATING THE PUBLIC AND
ONE GAMBLER'S REVENGE

A MEMOIR

ROBERT ASIEL

Robert Asiel/The Unexpected Gambler
The Writers Guild of America, West, Inc.
7000 West Third Street
Los Angeles, California, 90048-4329
Printed in the United States of America

The Unexpected Gambler/ Robert Asiel -- 1st ed.

ISBN 978-0-692-09858-5 Print Edition

Contents

For Kyle, Nolan, and Sofia

A Note to the Reader

In order for readers unfamiliar with casinos to read this memoir more easily, I have placed gambling terms in italics that appear in the glossary. I have changed the names of some casinos and persons to protect former partners from retaliation and for privacy. The names where dates are noted are authentic.

.

Sixteen-year-old Author in back left one week after his arrival in Las Vegas.

PREFACE

When casinos were caught cheating the public, they opened the door for the public to cheat them. Their attitude was, everyone is a sucker, and if you think you're good enough to beat us, bring it on. My partners and I embraced their invitation, and we beat the clueless casinos for over five decades. We didn't consider it cheating though, but a tax for their evil ways.

I began my gambling career as a naïve seventeen-year-old blackjack dealer in Las Vegas. I soon learned that below the surface, a lot of cheating was going on: the house was cheating the public, employees were cheating the house, and some, called *crossroaders*, were sharp enough to beat the casinos and that's what I did. I met people from all sides and learned their secret *moves*.

My youthful innocence led me to risky adventures that I faced with boldness and without fear. They took place throughout the United States, Europe, the Caribbean Islands, and on cruise ships where there's intrigue, danger, and celebrity. Surveillance videotapes of some of my exploits are used to train gaming agents and surveillance personnel and appear on cable and network TV; included, was a feature story on Fox Network's America's Most Wanted.

My innate sense of decency attracted like-minded loyal partners who became close friends and shared in my experiences and belief that the casinos had it coming. They pushed me to write this memoir. It's a story about an unknown chapter of gambling history.

Besides exposing crooked casinos, and how I beat them, I expose various Texas Holdem and Omaha poker cheating schemes and conclude with comments about today's casinos and crossroaders.

I leave this account for my grandchildren to read when they are old enough to understand human nature. They know me well personally, but nothing about my public life and history.

Robert Asiel

CHAPTER 1

WHOLESALE CHEATING

Fifty years ago, most Las Vegas casinos were mob-owned and some, if not all, cheated—they cheated the public, they cheated their employees, they cheated on their taxes—they cheated everybody.

On March 27, 1964, *Life magazine* reported that a math professor named Edward Thorp had devised a winning system for 21 and that he claimed that most Nevada casinos had cheated him. Nevada's chief gaming enforcement agent, Edward Olsen, responded in a letter to the editor of *Life* that Thorp had no evidence that the casinos were cheating, and that Life had libeled the state of Nevada. One week later, the Las Vegas *Review Journal* reported that Olsen closed the Silver Slipper Casino on the Las Vegas Strip for cheating! State undercover agents had found five crooked dice on a routine check of a casino craps game. The agents were in the casino investigating cheating at 21. A *boxman* at the craps game said his boss had given him the doctored dice to put into the game. On May 13, the Nevada *State Journal* reported that the Silver Slipper was the seventeenth casino closed in Nevada in the previous five years for violating state gaming laws.

Since then, state officials have closed numerous casinos for cheating, including the Pioneer Casino in Las Vegas, the Riverside Casino in Reno, the Lake Tahoe Casino at North Lake Tahoe, and Howard Johnson's Casino in Sparks. Blackjack cheating was so prevalent in small towns and rural areas that gaming authorities required casinos there to use multiple decks out of a *dealing shoe* to prevent cheating.

Casino poker games were crooked too. The Las Vegas *Sun* reported that the card room manager and a supervisor at the MGM Grand poker room in Vegas had conspired with two poker dealers to set up winning hands for five confederates. State gaming authorities allowed the cheating to continue for four months while they gathered evidence, costing honest players untold amounts of money. The *Sun* also reported that the Tropicana poker room had closed when the manager and a supervisor were caught putting a *cooler,* a pre-arranged deck of cards, into a seven-card stud game.

When these casinos were caught cheating was it their first attempt at cheating, or had they been doing so for a while? Were any casinos honest? Were they cheated?

The Reno *Evening Gazette* reported that several employees of Harrah's Lake Tahoe Casino, including a casino manager and ten confederates, were arrested for cheating. The casino manager had substituted Harrah's cards for *marked cards* that his accomplices could read using tinted contact lenses.

Renegade dealers stole money from casinos using a *sub,* or they could collaborate with an *agent,* using various moves. Some dealers' agents could *palm* cards in and out of their game, or switch in a cooler. Some dealers' wives or girlfriends, who worked as cocktail waitresses, helped their mates steal chips using the *coffee cup move.* A dealer would palm chips and drop them into an abandoned, half-full cup of coffee or glass of Coke, and set it on a waitress's tray as she came by his table to collect abandoned drinks. She retrieved the chips when she emptied the drink at her station. The crooked dealers swindled honest players to retrieve the swiped money, in order to keep their game percentages up to expected levels.

Some people beat the casinos *on the muscle*—meaning from the *outside*, without *inside* help. They were called *crossroaders* and were modern day Robin Hoods, taking from the rich casinos for their poor selves and some considered what they did honorable. They worked alone or in teams, were creative, and used a variety of moves. On opening day, at a new casino in Atlantic City, a team of crossroaders took advantage of the opening day chaos and set up on a 21 game to switch in an eight-deck *cooler*. Before the card switch, a confederate in the team had posed as a swing shift dealer and slipped into the *pit* to relieve the day shift dealer for the targeted game—five minutes early. The bogus dealer shuffled the eight decks of cards and set them in front of his confederates who swapped them for the cooler. A moment later, the legitimate swing shift dealer relieved the fictitious dealer and unknowingly dealt-off $100,000 to the crossroaders.

After I discovered the diabolical practices of the crooked casinos, and ways to beat them, I became a crossroader. I had read about casinos closed for cheating and I assumed they all cheated. To me they were fair game like the Sheriff of Nottingham was to Robin Hood, and I would be avenging the honest players who were cheated. I felt justified and had no moral issues with it—taking from a thief isn't stealing, and it was fulfilling and exciting.

All questions as to my conduct in life, and all serious thought about right and wrong and self-respect were formed in this period of my life. I reasoned that if I would live a straight life in all my dealings with society, except beating casinos, I would live with a clear conscience.

CHAPTER 2

SIN CITY ARRIVAL

During the summer of 1962, between my sophomore and junior year in high school, I had worked part-time as a delivery boy for Bergen Square Deli and Liquor Store in Jersey City. When I wasn't working, I was hanging out on the corner of Newkirk Street and Summit Avenue. Two of the older guys there had just returned from Reno, where they had worked as busboys at the Riverside Hotel and Casino. They talked about the twenty-four-hour gambling, and how easy it was to find a job.

A friend of mine, Eddie Harrigan, said his uncle knew a big shot in Vegas, and he planned to go there to work. He invited me to go with him and we made a plan to leave in September.

My dad expected me to finish high school and become an electrician like himself and my two older brothers. But two more years of high school, and five years of commuting to Manhattan, for apprenticeship school at night, plus working as an apprentice during the day, didn't appeal to me.

Eddie backed out of our plan at the last minute. I told him I would still go and he gave me the name of Jack Entratter, the president of the Sands Hotel and Casino, and told me to use his uncle's name as a reference for a job.

I was three days late for my junior year at William L. Dickinson High School in Jersey City. I had left home each morning as if I was going to school but I knew the charade would soon end when the school notified my folks I had been absent. I trusted that I could find work in Vegas and I had enough money for a bus ticket and living expenses until I found a job. I was sixteen-years-old with a fake ID so I decided to go to Vegas and let destiny show me the way forward.

My father had left for work and I packed a suitcase and told my mother I was leaving for Nevada and had enough money to live on until I found a job. I told her not to worry about me and to tell my father and brothers not to worry and that I would call home when I arrived. She packed me some sandwiches, and teary-eyed, hugged me and asked me to think of home often.

I arrived in Las Vegas on September 9, 1962, after three days on a Greyhound bus. Vegas was much smaller then—the Strip had one traffic light, and you never saw a sheriff's car that might scare tourists. It only took ten minutes to drive downtown to Fremont Street that had two-way traffic with parking on both sides of the street, and no roof. Most casinos didn't have doors. A sheet of air conditioning in summer and heated air in winter greeted customers at the entrances. You could walk down the street with a drink in your hand and no one bothered you. There wasn't much crime because the sheriff, Ralph Lamb, ran the desperados out of town, or worse. The same Ralph Lamb portrayed by Dennis Quaid in the CBS TV series about Lamb's life.

Vegas was a segregated town where the black population worked at the hotels during the day and returned at night to the West Side on the other side of the railroad tracks. During the Civil War, Northern Nevada, with its mining economy, was sympathetic to the industrial northern states while Southern Nevada was sympathetic to the South. Still today, UNLV sports teams are called, The

Rebels. And Vegas was a male-dominated town—all the dealers, bosses, and bartenders were men.

Vegas was an adult town with adult entertainment, unlike todays expensive shows with lions on stage, knights jousting on horses, and circus acts. The casinos had top name entertainers and floor-shows for the price of a drink or dinner. The Lido De Paris show at the Stardust, featuring topless showgirls, was proclaimed by *Life* magazine as the greatest floorshow in the world. It cost just $7 for the dinner show, which included dinner, and $5 for the midnight cocktail show, which included two drinks. And buffets were cheap; a full buffet at the Silver Slipper Casino cost 99¢. The casinos lost money on food and entertainment back then, but made up for it with gambling winnings.

The casinos had low ceilings, dim lighting, and were quiet. Craps was the most popular game with more craps tables than today and less 21 tables. The Strip dealers made $22.50 per shift, plus gener-ous tips they considered tax-free gifts. Their jobs were competitive, and they acted professionally and kept their games moving quickly, unlike today's dealers who chitchat about their wives, buying new tires, or fishing, and who insult the customers. Slot machines were mechanical and quieter than today's blaring machines and fewer in number. The slot machines and roulette tables were there to ac-commodate the wives of the craps and 21 players.

The bosses treated everyone with respect and knew their big players. A known player would be given credit "on the finger." He would raise a finger to tell a boss or boxman the amount he want-ed. The boss would tell the dealer, "Give Mr. J $500 in chips." The boss would write the amount in a pocket notebook he carried; there were no computers, checks, or counter checks to sign. If a small-time player went broke some bosses would hand him a $20 bill for a bus ticket home.

The customers dressed up instead of down—you wouldn't see someone in shorts and flip-flops carrying a slot bucket through a casino. Men wore suits and women wore their best gowns. When a show let out it was like a parade of beauty contestants.

Vegas was a friendly place where people held doors for strangers, made eye contact, and greeted everyone with "Howdy." It was a new world to me and taught me how to act as an adult, all six feet and 160 pounds of me. I lived hour to hour, with no thought of the future. During my first two days in town, I tried different gambling systems I had learned from an old-timer whom I had met at a lunch counter. After I lost half my bankroll, I headed to the Sands Hotel-Casino to check out my connection for a job.

Jack Entratter, a former bouncer at the Copacabana in New York, was the Sand's president who presented Frank Sinatra, Dean Martin, and a host of other big name celebrities. A casino cashier connected me with Entratter's nephew on a house phone. He asked who I was and I said, "A friend of Bernie Sweeney from Jersey City, who knows your uncle." He said he'd be right down, maybe wondering if I was a gangster.

He asked me what work I could do, a simple question, but it caught me off-guard. I said I didn't know and he responded: "When you find out come back to see me." That was it—I blew an opportunity and embarrassed myself, but it was a wake-up call to reality. I found an employment agency that sent me to interview for a lifeguard job at the Stardust Hotel-Casino.

The Stardust was the newest and largest hotel and casino on the Las Vegas Strip with over one-thousand rooms. It had a huge swimming pool surrounded by manicured lawns and palm trees, a full-service lunch counter and bar, and models from the hotel's shops who exhibited their summer attire.

Daniel, the pool manager, asked me my age, and told me I needed an adult work card from the Sheriff's office, a white shirt, white shorts, white socks, and white tennis shoes for my uniform. The pay was $10 per day and two meals. I'd work ten hours a day, six days a week.

The young secretary at the sheriff's office compared the information on my bogus draft card with my application and issued me an adult work card stamped with the sheriff's signature. I bought my lifeguard outfit, and took a bus to the Stardust.

Daniel and two other employees, Joe, and Chuck, set up chaise lounge chairs with towels for hotel guests while I guarded the pool.

I called home and told my mother about my job and that I was safe and not to worry. She said my dad was sad and would be happy that I called home. Years later, he would tell me he had run away to New York City, from an orphanage in the Catskill Mountains, when he was sixteen. His mother had died when he was eleven and his father had died when he was fourteen.

After several days, Daniel promised me a promotion in one week when he resumed classes at UNLV, and Joe returned to UCLA. I'd work with Chuck earning a full share of tips that averaged $35 per day—I'd be making more than blue-collar workers back home. Another surprise was Chuck told me his roommate had moved back to New York and he invited me to take his place—it was a no-brainer, he was into hot-rods and girls.

I soon experienced a new feeling of independence, and I wasn't going back to the gang in Jersey. I wondered if my good luck would hold.

While gambling at the Stardust after work, a security guard asked me for ID. He studied my bogus draft card and escorted me to the security office. It was cramped with an oversized desk cluttered with paperwork, phones, radio equipment, and walls pasted with mug shots of *crossroaders*. I wondered what my fate would be.

An older man arrived and introduced himself as the head of security. He studied my draft card and asked me where I got it. I said, "My hometown." I was relieved when he asked why I was in town. I answered, "I work here at the pool." He stared at the card for several seconds, handed it to me, and said in a fatherly tone, "Keep your nose clean, son." I knew not to waste any more of his time; I took the card and thanked him. I found out later that he had been the police chief of Las Vegas. I figured he had seen other runaways come to his town and go on to become good citizens, and he gave me a chance. At the time, many people in Vegas lived on second chances including convicted murderers working as casino bosses.

I soon adjusted to the adult world of 1962 Las Vegas. A neighbor was a call girl from Newark, New Jersey, who liked me and told me about her Vegas life. Sherry was twenty-five and had worked as a cigarette girl at the Thunderbird Hotel-Casino where she had turned tricks for high rollers. A casino boss would page her code name over the public address system to tell her a John's room number. The bosses pressured her to lug the Johns back to the casino to gamble after her favors and she grew tired of the pressure and giving part of her money to the bosses and vice cops. She quit and worked on her own having regulars call her and a bellman who set her up with tricks.

Sherry was also a chip hustler. Dressing to the hilt, she'd hang around the Strip casinos to attract a player who'd keep her by his side and give her chips to gamble. She would siphon-off chips into wigs, purses, and clothes she had altered. It was a role portrayed by Sharon Stone in the movie "Casino."

Sherry let me drive her Cadillac, and after two weeks in town, I had learned to drive and applied for a driver's permit. I staggered my place in line at the DMV, waiting for a young clerk to review my application and ID. She took a quick look at my Sheriff Department adult work card and draft card, and compared them with the name and birth date on my application. I was given a permit and eventually I passed my driving test and bought a '55 Dodge on time.

After work, I'd go to the Thunderbird casino lounge to meet up with tourist girls I had steered there from the pool. It was a short walk from the Stardust and was the hot spot in town for young people. It had a dance floor and featured Teddy Randazzo and other top rock-and-roll bands. I soon met several friends as I was sociable, naïve, and no threat to anyone, and I knew several tourist girls. It seems odd now but Vegas had a shortage of girls at that time. There were showgirls, waitresses, and Keno girls, but the casino bosses had the first shot at them.

Most of my friends had come to Vegas from back east to escape the law, or their wives, or to seek adventure and a new life. Marijuana was in vogue and most were potheads. They were in their early twenties, worked as 21 dealers, and were ripping-off the casinos from the *inside*. When we met at somebody's apartment to listen to music or get high, they'd split the money they made and analyzed their plays. I listened as they talked about *tipping their hole card* to their agent, *flashing* the top card, and other moves to beat the casinos. They talked about getting rich and buying a Jaguar XKE, or a sailing yacht to sail the seven seas. Their secret signals and conversation intrigued me and I wanted to learn more.

Don Rolan was twenty-six and the leader of our small group. His father had been a casino boss and had taught him to deal 21, roulette, and craps when he was a teenager. He was a good storyteller and demonstrating how crooked 21 dealers, called *mechanics*, cheated the public. He showed us how they *peeked* at the top card as he nudged the card with his thumb into his middle finger.

The card's corner bubbled up and exposed the index. He said, "The dealer peeks at the card when he checks his hole card for a blackjack, picks up a lost bet, or a variety of other actions. If the peeked card helps his hand, he'll deal the *second* card to a player to save the top card for himself." He demonstrated how to deal seconds as he slid the top card back slightly with his left thumb and pulled the second card out with the tip of his right forefinger. He said, "Mechanics also deal seconds to bust their own hand when their *agent* plays with them, or they *flash* the top card to him, among other moves." He demonstrated the flash as he pushed the top card out with his thumb, exposing the index between the open ends of his first and second finger. He said, "Only the person to my front could see the flashed card as I expose it when I give a hit card to another player." All of his moves were smooth and undetectable and I couldn't imagine a typical Las Vegas tourist spotting them.

He said, "Dice mechanics use sleight-of-hand to switch in crooked dice from the *stickman* position. He hides the rigged dice in his altered *apron* or, a confederate posing as a player stands beside him to feed him the crooked dice. He uses *even splitters* to beat players who bet even numbers and *odd-splitters* to beat players who bet odd numbers. A pair of odd splitters has one die with double aces, treys, and fives, and one die with double deuces, fours, and sixes. They roll mostly losing sevens or two, four, six, eight, and ten, all even numbers. Even splitters have different double numbers to beat players who bet even numbers, and there are field splitters to beat *field* bettors. The players have zero chance to win when splitters are used. Most of the dice mechanics come from the South and Northeast, and most card mechanics come from California. They work part-time or on-call for a percentage or a flat fee of what they steal."

A dealer who worked at the Fremont Hotel-Casino and another who worked at the Golden Nugget told me they needed a fresh face to *agent* for them and asked me to stop by their game on the weekend. I wasn't a bad person, underage drinking in bars, gambling, and one joyride as a passenger in a stolen car had been the limit of my law breaking. The casinos seemed fair game to me so I agreed to agent for the dealers. We had a practice session to go over the signals we would use and the playing strategy. I sat across from them and they flashed me the top card between their middle finger and forefinger. When they checked their *hole card* to see if they had a blackjack, they signaled me if they had a pat hand by slightly raising their thumb. They said to win about $300 and to buy chips from a craps game so they wouldn't have to alert their boss that I was by buying in on their game. If a boss was watching them from behind, they wanted me to alert them by showing them a closed fist.

I sat at the Fremont casino bar to case the 21 *pits*. I caught my dealer's eye and he signaled me to his game. He flashed me the top card just when he gave a hit card to the person on my right. Winning was harder than I previously thought—it was a grind. It was a great move to *double down* on nine, ten, and eleven when the top card was an ace, nine, or ten; but when the dealer had a big card showing, I couldn't stay on small hands without looking suspicious. I'd hit my hand knowing I would bust, but not always. After winning my $300 quota, I left to play at the Golden Nugget. Same outcome there and I waited for the dealers to get off to meet them at Don Rolan's house to cut up our winnings.

Both dealers congratulated me for a job well done and asked me to return the next weekend. Several plays later, they asked me to pull up to give my face a rest.

Don encouraged me to become a 21 dealer so I took a job as a

shill at the Lucky Casino on Fremont Street rather than attend Rod
Morris' dealing school. The pay was $8 per 8-hour shift. I worked
with four other shills; two were in their sixties and two were in
their twenties. The old guys were making another fresh start in life,
or supporting a gambling habit, the young guys hoped to become
dealers. We didn't know how long it would take; one might make it
in several weeks, another would shill for two months and never be
seen again. We played on unoccupied table games to attract a real
player who may be shy to play alone. Most tourists didn't realize the
casinos used shills, but the locals knew and sometimes gave a small
tip when they won.

Twenty-one dealers gave us half-dollars to bet the minimum
fifty-cent wager. We sat in the first seat so we wouldn't appear to
control the dealer's hit cards in collusion with him, and we stayed
on hands of twelve and above for the same reason. We also shilled
on craps tables, one shill on each end. A dealer would pass us a
stack of chips to place our bets. Several players would eventually
arrive and the boxman would signal us to leave.

One day, I recognized a new shill named Ken. He had been the
biggest high roller at the Lucky, and had given me and the other
shills and dealers tips when he won. Someone said he went broke
and couldn't pay for his room so the *shift boss* gave him a job. It was
a common story at the time.

After work, I left for the Strip casinos to watch how seasoned
dealers shuffled and dealt, and I looked for cheating moves Rolan
had shown me. At the time, dealers dealt cards from a hand-held
single deck or double-deck. At home, I practiced pitching cards
into a paper grocery bag and cut chips like the Strip dealers.

The shift boss opened a new 21 game one busy Saturday night
and asked me to deal. I was nervous and experienced sweaty hands

like dealers had told me to expect. The players knew I was a novice and were kind to me so I settled down.

The graveyard shift boss, Leo Bind, asked me to work a double-shift. I accepted his offer and he told me he'd put me on the full-time dealer's list if I transferred to his shift. I transferred the next day but he didn't keep his word and I shilled for another two weeks before I dealt full-time.

Leo was superstitious and mistrusted anyone winning. He had been a casino manager and part-owner of the El Rancho Hotel-Casino on the Strip where he was victimized by crossroaders and crooked employees. He lost his money and credibility and descended from a casino manager and part owner of a Las Vegas Strip hotel and casino to working as a graveyard shift boss on Freemont Street.

When someone was winning, Leo would change decks to look for marked cards and if the dice were hot, he'd change the stickman and the dice. One morning, a player was shooting up a hot hand so Leo had the porter get a saltshaker from the snack bar and throw salt over the player's shoulder to change his luck.

One mob faction or another controlled most Vegas casinos at that time. They avoided paying their fair share of taxes by skimming a percentage of the casinos profits off the top. At the Lucky, two men arrived at the end of each shift to empty and count the moneyboxes in a back room to take their factions share.

Some of the bosses and dealers at the time had worked as dealers and bosses in illegal casinos in Hot Springs, Arkansas; Newport, Kentucky; Steubenville, Ohio; and other venues throughout the U.S. and Cuba. In 1950, Tennessee Senator Estes Kefauver had conducted Senate hearings into illegal gambling and succeeded closing most of the illegal casinos. For some of the dealers and bosses gambling was all they knew so they headed to Nevada, the only state where gambling was legal. They were sharp, and more informal about casino procedures than the bosses who got their jobs rising through the ranks. Some bosses would occasionally take a quarter off a roulette table and give it to dealers who smoked to buy a pack of cigarettes on his break, or if a player lost a lot of money, a boss would take several chips off the winning game to put in the dealers' tip box. A dealer who had friends come to town would ask a boss if he could get a show reservation on the Strip for him and his friends. The boss would make a phone call and get the dealer comped front row seats. Some old-time bosses impressed us young dealers with gambling stories and cheating moves. A rookie dealer at the Lucky asked an old craps dealer from Steubenville, how the dealers there paid the odds for a four and ten. He replied, "No one ever made a four or ten in Steubenville."

We had to follow strict rules to prevent us from cheating the house. Sam Boyd, who ran the Lucky and Mint Casinos, knew about cheating and didn't trust his help; he fired unlucky dealers for that reason alone. There was a joke in town that Boyd would hire dealers at $8 per shift and fire them when they advanced to $12 because by then they knew too much.

Other casinos had less strict rules and procedures to follow, and some allowed dealers to deal any style they wanted. Most casinos disallowed their employees to gamble off-duty where they worked, but Benny Binion, the Horseshoe Casino owner, told his dealers, "If you're gonna gamble your money away, gamble it in my store." And Don Laughlin, the Riverside Hotel-Casino owner in Laughlin, his namesake, allowed his dealers to drink and gamble in his casino while on their breaks.

Card counting was unknown at the time, but when Edward Thorp wrote a book on counting, and beat some casinos, he received national television and magazine coverage and the 21 rules changed overnight; the players could only *double down* on eleven, but not after a *split hand,* and they received one card when they split aces. They used to take as many hits as they wanted on split aces, or any split hand, and could double down on any two cards, including split hands and re-split hands. And we had to shuffle before we ran out of cards—we used to deal to the end of a deck, and even shuffle in the middle of a hand.

My first introduction to cheating was when Leo sent me to relieve the money-wheel dealer. The dealer asked me if I had dealt the wheel before and I said no. He told me not to let anyone hit the $40-to-$1 payoff or Leo would fire me; I asked him what I could do. He spun the wheel, pointed to a chrome bolt on the wheel stand and said, "Use that bolt as a reference point on each spin. Pick a logo on the wheel to intersect with it and you'll develop the right touch to keep off the $40-to-$1 joker logo. When I get back from my break you should have it down pat."

I had good eye-hand coordination and when the dealer returned, I could keep from hitting the $40, $20, $10, and $5-to-$1 payout. He said, "Next time you deal the wheel make it stop on the $40-to-$1 payoff to entice the suckers to bet it."

I had seen cheating of a different kind when I was a shill on craps games. Dealers would pick up *sleepers* that were winning bets players forgot to pick up, and some dealers used sleight-of-hand moves to short-pay players or reduce a winning player's payoff outright.

Dealing at the Lucky gave me confidence to pass as an adult. The legal age to be in a casino was twenty-one and I was seventeen. One day, a security guard asked two young players on my game for their ID. They offered a weak excuse and he escorted them out. Later, the guard bragged to me, "These underage kids think they can fool me."

One day after work, an acquaintance I had met at Sherry's, approached me about *doing business* against the casino. Ricky said he knew some crossroaders and I agreed to meet with them.

I followed him to the Plush Horse Lounge where I met a friend of his. Ricky introduced him as Larry and said he was "with it" meaning he did business. He was a young 21dealer and he showed me some fascinating sleight-of-hand moves and talked about a move called the refrigerator, or *cooler*. It was a bold but simple move—a dealer would set his deck down for the cut, which would be exchanged for a pre-set deck of cards. I agreed to do it and we left to meet the crossroaders they knew.

Oklahoma Jimmy piloted his own plane and beat casinos around the world. The local papers dubbed him "the flying bandit" after he had been arrested at the airport in Alamo, Nevada, with 150 pairs of crooked dice and other cheating paraphernalia in his possession. He was in his mid-forties, was personable, and had a commanding presence about him. He asked me if I would do business and I said I would. He said the easiest move to do was to catch a cooler. His partner J.W. explained the details of the play: "Jimmy, Larry, and Ricky will play on your game until the time is right to switch in the cooler. An agent named Winston, will *take off* the money. He will stagger up to the game with a drink in one hand and some $100 bills in the other. Jimmy will tell you to shuffle and set the deck down for him to cut, and that's when he'll trade decks with you."

J.W. spread some cards on a table to demonstrate how the cooler looked. He pointed to the serial number on the ace of spades and said the casinos keep track of the number. He said, "Casino bosses give customers used souvenir cards which will have the same number since the casinos buy their cards in lots and the same serial number will be in circulation for a month." Eventually, the casinos would cut off the cards' corners and sell them in vending machines or in the souvenir shops.

J.W. continued, "Winston will win the first hand then play two hands. On the second round, you'll get an ace up and ask for insurance, and Winston will insure both hands. You'll turn up a blackjack so the bosses won't suspect a cooler. Winston will get a blackjack on one hand and a twenty on the other. He'll get paid even money for his insured blackjack and a tie for his insured twenty. He wins the next two rounds of hands including a double down and a split-hand. If another player sits down in the middle of the cooler, Ricky will sit out the hand so the player will get a pat hand to play so he doesn't mess up the cooler." It all sounded good. I asked Jimmy when he'd like to do it, and he said Saturday would be best. He said I would get 25 percent of the winnings.

I didn't think what I was about to do had anything to do with Leo personally. After all, it wasn't his money although he acted like it was, and he'd broken his promise to me about starting on graveyard shift as a dealer after I bailed him out.

My pulse quickened and my face felt flushed when Ricky and his friends sat at my game. Jimmy blew cigar smoke in a customer's face to run him off and I settled down. He checked the serial number on the ace of spades and whispered to me to shuffle the cards. A well-dressed man with grey hair stood behind him holding a drink and some cash so I knew he was Winston, our take-off man, who would block the cooler switch from behind. Jimmy whispered, "OK, set it down." I put my deck down and he scooped it up and set the cooler down, cut in half—but he had switched in a red deck, instead of a blue deck. He re-switched it and whispered, "Uh oh, wrong color, be right back."

He left the game and everyone laughed as Winston stepped

back. A *floorman* walked by and said, "Looks like everyone is having fun." In a few minutes, Jimmy was back and said he was ready. I set my deck down and he swapped it for the cooler.

Jimmy left as Winston sat down. He bet the $200 limit and I called out, "*Money plays.*" A boss stood beside me to watch the action. Winston won the hand and spread out to play two hands. The boss left to get Leo. When they returned, I turned over a blackjack and Leo grumbled that Winston had taken insurance. He hurried to the *podium* to get a new deck of cards and yelled at the floorman, "Get Wolfe," who was Leo's favorite dealer.

I finished dealing the third hand when Wolfe arrived. I stood at his dead table to watch the rest of the drama unfold. Leo changed decks and Winston won two hands *on the square,* and staggered to the cashier after losing a hand. I didn't think anyone suspected a cooler because I had a blackjack and Winston had played on the square after Leo changed decks. The Lucky had a bingo room above the casino and didn't have the space for a *catwalk,* and casinos didn't use surveillance cameras at the time. The deck switch was simple enough—no one saw it, so it didn't happen.

The excitement was over except Leo complained to a floorman that I was in a rut again meaning I was on a cold streak. I didn't care what Leo thought and it was neat to put one over on the casino. It did seem I violated an implied agreement a worker has with his employer to abide by the rules, but I got over it.

Later, at JW's house, Jimmy offered me a drink and handed me $350. It was a lot of tax-free money at the time. He apologized for the wrong color slip-up and I said, "That's OK, it was funny and relaxed me."

Ricky asked Jimmy to show me his dice switch. He picked up a pair of red dice and tossed them toward me; the dice were now green. I didn't see anything, and I asked him to show me again and asked how he did it. I was naïve to the ways of the world, not realizing that crossroaders, like magicians, were secretive about disclosing their tricks. Jimmy knew it was an innocent response and he showed me in detail the mechanics of his switch. He even showed me some fascinating 21 moves to beat the casinos on the muscle—he was like a baseball coach teaching a rookie "inside baseball" tricks-of-the-trade.

I had spent many hours on games at the Lucky and I knew Jimmy's tricks would get over on the bosses there. On my way home, I stopped at a souvenir store to buy some dice and cards to practice the moves Jimmy had shown me.

I asked Leo if I could go home for the Christmas holidays. He said to remind him one week before Christmas.

Frank Wolfe, the dealer who relieved me on the cooler play, who I'll call "The Captain," approached me and said he was quitting dealing and driving home to Washington, DC, for Christmas. He heard I was going back to Jersey and asked me if I'd share the driving and expenses with him. I agreed and we made a plan to leave on December 20, to drive straight through.

Cap had packed a cooler with sandwiches and beer and we headed out. He asked me if the big money play I had dealt had been a cold deck play. I said, "Yea, how did you know?" He said, "A player on the game acted suspicious, and I know about cooler plays because a guy back home I know would put them into poker games. He wore black pants with a black handkerchief on his lap, and after he switched in a cooler he'd drop the square deck into the handkerchief and fold it over to conceal it, and put it in his jacket."

I was impressed with his insight and knowledge, and that he'd kept his suspicions about the cooler to himself. I told him about the

people I'd met in Vegas, and the information I knew about employees cheating the casinos, casinos cheating the public, and crossroaders beating casinos.

You can learn a lot about someone on a cross-country drive and
I found Cap to be special by the way he told interesting stories about
any number of subjects. He spoke clearly and thoroughly and I had
no doubts he knew what he was talking about. Personally, he was
kind and honest, and in two-and-a-half days of straight driving, we
formed a friendship that has lasted over fifty years to this day.

We arrived at my grandparents' house in a small town between
Philly and Trenton. After some hot tea, conversation, and a sand-
wich, Cap wished everyone Merry Christmas and left to backtrack
to Washington. My grandfather said, "You won't meet many friends
like him."

Next day, my dad drove down from Jersey City to bring me
home. It was Christmas Eve and the first time I'd been home in
fifteen months. My three brothers were there and everyone asked
me about Las Vegas.

I spent New Year's Eve at Molinari's Bar in Union City with
two of my brothers and some friends, like I had two years earlier.
Not much had changed and I thought of the previous New Year's
Eve with Chuck and our dates at the Dunes casino lounge show. I
missed Vegas and looked forward to returning.

CHAPTER 3

CROSSROADING 101

I flew back to Vegas in early January 1964, where Ricky and Larry invited me to make a payday as a shill on a cooler play at the Riviera. I'd play two hands and be a lookout. Larry and his friend would also shill up the game. The bettor was a known high roller at the casino, and the dealer previously did business with Ricky. A friend of Ricky's named George Bentress would kick in the cooler. After the play, I'd hover around the game to hear what the bosses would say then meet Ricky at the A&W restaurant. The play was set for noon on Saturday.

When we set up on the game, Larry signaled me to follow him outside the casino. He said the serial number on the casino's ace of spades was different from ours and he'd have to palm it out of the game to use for our cooler. He wanted me to distract the players when it came time to steal the ace.

Larry played two hands and when dealt the ace of spades, he palmed it and left to give it to George. They came back and sat in the middle of the table. The dealer shuffled the cards and set them in front of George. He swapped in the cooler, cut it in half, and left the game. When our bettor placed his bet our dealer called out, "Money plays." A boss approached and chatted with the bettor. After the cooler ran out, he played on the square until he lost a hand then left to cash in. The boss told the dealer the player was one of their big suckers and he'd be back. I told Ricky what I had seen and heard. He handed me $50 and said he'd be in touch with me. George thanked me and said I did a good job.

It felt good to work with another crossroader crew and I was impressed how they operated. Ricky met me after work the next day and asked if I wanted to do some more business at the Lucky. I agreed and followed him to George Bentress' house.

George was middle-aged and lived in Vegas with his wife and daughter. Ricky said he'd been a capable craps dealer and 21 mechanic. George suggested switching-in a cooler marked with *juice*. He said juice was a solution to mark cards, seen by a trained eye and he could see it. He demonstrated as he read several cards as either big, medium, or small. He said the nines, tens, and aces were marked in one place, the sevens and eights in another place, and the deuces through sixes were unmarked. I looked at several cards and couldn't see anything.

George would sit in the last seat where he could read the top card and send subtle hand signals to Ricky, and when possible he would leave a bust card for my hand. We would split the winnings three ways and we'd play in one week when Leo was off.

I was dealing on the main game when they sat down. I felt my temples pulsate as I set the deck in front of George and he exchanged it for the cooler. Ricky bet $100 and I called out, "Money plays." The shift boss stood beside me to watch the play. I won the first hand to allay any suspicion of a cooler. The boss left and came back every few minutes.

Ricky was up over $1,200 in thirty minutes and the shift boss brought a new deck to the game. As I shuffled, George surprised me when he rubbed his chin—he wanted to kick in another cold deck! The boss stood next to me, but looked at the bar when Ricky asked him for a cocktail waitress as George switched-in the cooler. After I lost two hands, the boss called to another dealer to relieve me.

The boss brought a *fill* of chips to the game when Ricky was ahead over $2,000. He was tired of losing so George ended the play.

We split the winnings and George asked if there was any *heat*. I said I didn't think so. He said no one followed them when they left the casino. I asked how far the Lucky would go to check the cards for marks. He said, "I don't know, but I made several juice plays in other casinos and no one found my juice. The beauty of it is the closer you look at the cards, the harder it is to see anything, the farther away it is, the easier it is to see."

George introduced me to a 21 mechanic who worked at the Golden Gate Casino. He was practicing a new false-shuffle move and he asked George to look at it. He appeared to shuffle the cards, but he had passed the riffled top half of the deck over the bottom half as his hands covered the action. It was a deceptive move that evolved into the *sky-shuffle* years later.

I practiced the shuffle at home on an ironing board. At work, I did it with two customers on my game—but I forgot about my back. The shift boss appeared beside me quaking and said, "You're false-shuffling and you're fired." He called to a floorman to get another dealer to relieve me and I left out the back door, never looking back.

I knew I had dogged-it, but I was consoled that the boss had too. He let the two players know what happened and they could have caused bad publicity, claiming I cheated them. The boss wasn't from the old school, but had come up through the ranks starting as a dealer in Vegas. Another boss might have told me to practice my moves at home and given me a pass.

I wondered if I could find another job, and was concerned I'd be *blackballed*. I only had five months dealing experience and it was wintertime. I felt better when George told me it was an occupational hazard and I could find another job.

I checked and rechecked with the shift bosses in every downtown casino over the next six weeks with no success. George said my chances would be better in the summertime. In the meantime, he invited me to go with him and Ricky on a *daub* play. The daub was a colored waxy substance contained in a dime-sized metal disc and used to mark cards. George concealed it inside his shirt cuff with adhesive. He'd rub the daub with his fore finger enabling him to mark several cards before he re-loaded. He wanted me to sit in the first seat to play two hands and to slow the game down while he daubed the cards. When the deck was worked-up, he'd leave to wash his finger with bleach then stash it along with the daub. He would return when Ricky arrived to take off the money. He would signal him how to play his cards as he had done on my game at the Lucky Casino.

I met George at Denny's restaurant and he looked different. He had cotton stuffed up his nose and in his mouth behind his cheeks. It changed his looks and voice. He also wore glasses and a fake mustache. He said we would play at the Tropicana, and that he had to duck some employees there whom he'd had worked with in the past.

George sat on an end game and I sat down a moment later. I did my best to slow the game down while he did his work. After twenty minutes, he left to hide his daub. When he returned Ricky sat down. George used hand signals and made sounds with his chips to tell Ricky how to play his cards. He played his own hand to leave a bust card for the dealer; if the dealer had a big card up and a little one in the hole, he'd leave him a ten to bust. Ricky won several hundred dollars and the boss changed decks. Ricky and George left as I watched the boss study the cards then put them in a card box and into a drawer with other used cards.

I told George what I saw and he surmised that the boss looked for bent or marked cards and said it was routine for a boss to change decks when a player won. He invited me to meet a friend who dealt 21 at the Thunderbird who needed a new face to take off some money.

Johnny was a middle-aged 21 dealer who wanted to use the *pat and pay* move and he explained to me what to do. "When you put your cards under your bet, put the bigger of your two cards on the bottom. When I turn them over, I won't spread them apart and expose the smaller card, but will show the bigger card and pat your cards like a tie hand, or pay you like you won. If you have a winning hand, signal me and I'll spread your cards to expose them when I turn them over. If a boss is watching me, close your fist, if it's safe leave it open. Sit in the first seat since I turn your cards over last while the players are busy making new bets." He said the casino didn't have a catwalk, but had mirrors on the ceiling that the bosses use to watch the games. I would play on Friday night.

I stopped by the Thunderbird on day shift to see what the bosses could see in the ceiling mirrors. I looked at them from several angles to get a birds-eye view of all the 21 tables. I was surprised how effective they were—it was as if I was on a ladder looking straight down on the games. I'd have to watch the bosses closely.

I knew the Thunderbird well and arrived early to get the props I needed. I bought chips at the craps *pit* so I wouldn't attract attention by buying-in on Johnny's game. I stopped in the Keno lounge to pick up a Keno ticket. I would use it pretending to check the numbers on the Keno boards that hung from the ceiling as I scanned the casino for outside men or anyone checking the ceiling mirrors.

Johnny rubbed his chin and I sat down in the first seat. Some of the players bet $25 chips, so that was my first bet. I had nineteen and Johnny had seventeen so I signaled him I won the hand. Next hand, he dealt me a ten and a five that I tucked under my bet with the ten on the bottom. I opened my fist to let Johnny know his back was safe to move. He turned my cards over exposing the ten and payed me while the other players placed new bets. The boss was busy with a fill on another game and didn't notice me. During the shuffle, I scanned the casino and went south with the chips I had won. After ten minutes, Johnny *brushed* me out. The boss never knew I was there.

As I left, I saw Don Rolan who told me two of our 21 dealer friends at the Mint Casino were fired for *flashing* and were *blackballed.*

I met with George to give him Johnny's 50 percent of the win and George's 10 percent of my end that was a standard bird-dog fee for introductions. Johnny told George I did a good job and he wanted me to play again in one week.

George invited me to meet an old-time crossroader named Mike Markis. He was married and had two daughters and two grandchildren. He was practicing card tricks and he showed us a new hop move; it was a move to nullify the cut by manipulating the top half of the deck to its original position after the cards were cut. George told him that the daub he had made for him worked well. Mike said he used beeswax, glycerin, rosewater, and a new aniline dye he had ordered from Germany to make it.

Mike said he worked as a shift boss at a new casino on Fremont Street called the Carousel and would call George to do some business once he was established there. He said his picture was in the *Griffin Book* at the pit podium there and he tore the page out and tossed it.

George said he wanted to go downtown to switch in a couple of blackjack hands and he asked Mike to accompany him to distract the dealer. He'd use a *slick-sleeve* to make the blackjack. It was a jacket with an oversized sleeve, lined with mohair so a card easily slid in and out of it. He would sit down with an "ace up his sleeve," and when dealt a ten, he would slide the ace into his hand with a slight downward move of his arm as he flicked the random card up his sleeve with his right middle finger as his left hand covered the action. The move was so subtle that even though I knew what he did, I couldn't see it—the hand is indeed quicker than the eye. The bad part was the deck would be dirty with an extra ace and a random card missing. George told me it was a *heat score* and asked me if I'd be the wheelman for them.

They would play in the Mint so I parked across from the casino and kept my eyes glued on the entrance. After several minutes, they hurried out and I eased my car out. They hopped in and were out of breath from the short run.

George said, "When I turned up a blackjack, the dealer called to a boss so we hit the door." Mike said, "The dealer was counting aces. Some bosses tell their dealers to *selectively shuffle* when the deck is rich in aces and face cards to take away the player's advantage for the blackjack bonus payoff. Conversely, he'll deal to the end of the deck if the aces are gone early." Mike said another move some dealers use is to cull the small cards and keep them on the bottom of the deck as they shuffle. The small cards are brought into play when the deck is cut, making it hard for the dealer to bust.

George invited me to make a payday using a move called the *slug*. It consisted of a clump of ten cards that a dealer keeps on the bottom of the deck when he shuffles. He creates the slug when he picks up the discards from a previous hand. He arranges three small cards followed by two ten value cards, three more small cards, and two more tens—it's a mini-cooler.

We would know the succession of cards whereby we could control the game by making our best hands and busting the dealer; if he has a five showing and a ten in the hole, George would leave a ten to bust him like a daub play. The first card of the slug was the key card. We would spot it and know the next nine cards' values.

George was in disguise and led me to a 21 game at the Flamingo Casino. I sat in the middle, he sat in the last seat, and we each played two hands. A boss stood at the game when I sat down and our dealer built a slug right away. He shuffled the cards, leaving the slug intact on the bottom of the deck. He offered me to cut the cards and I cut them deep enough to insure the slug would show on the first hand. The key card showed in one of George's hands, and we knew the dealer's hole card and the next eight cards. George signaled me to hit, then took two hit cards and left a ten for the dealer to bust. The boss watched the shuffle, the cut, and the first hand of the slug. He walked away unconcerned and wandered to and from our game. After I won several hands, George brushed me out. It always felt good to leave a casino after a play.

Ricky and Larry would work with George for the remainder of the busy weekend and I'd play the next weekend.

After two more slug plays, George said the dealer decided to pull up for a while. He asked me to accompany him to Gardena, California, to play poker. He wanted me to distract for him while he used his slick-sleeve. He would steal a card while playing and use it as needed. He went over the signals we'd use to communicate and said, "We have to be careful giving signals or someone will pick us off. Before we give a signal, our eyes should meet for an instant, look away, and look back for the signal. By the way, never get caught looking at a boss in Vegas. It makes them paranoid if they're doing business, or they'll be suspicious that you're doing business."

George told me some code words for card values that we'd use, and he told me some rhyme-speak words that crossroaders use that they picked up from Australian crossroaders. He said, "Australia had been a penal colony that the British had populated with prisoners and indentured servants from England who invented their own lingo to covertly communicate. Some of the jargon they use is: Nits and Lice for dice, Jack and Jill for shill, Bees and Honey for money, Tommy Tucker for sucker, Twist and Twirl for girl, Storm and Strife for wife, Near and Far for bar, Grumble and Groan for loan. They only use the first word when conversing, they'll say, 'Thanks for the grumble.'"

I followed him into the Normandy Club, and we put our names on the wait list. The poker casino spread lo-ball and five-card draw. George prowled the floor and after a while, he brushed me out to meet at his car. He said, "There's two thieves on every game, and someone I know from Vegas told me there was heat."

It was the same at the Horseshoe Club. George said, "I spoke to a scuff who said it had been that way for about a week. Every hustler in the world came out of the woodwork and thought they had a license to steal. When the *eye-in-the-sky* sees someone cheat, he comes down and runs his fingernail down the cheats back to let him know he was busted. The hustler leaves the joint and goes to another club." George said the California card rooms didn't prosecute card cheats but would sometimes bar them for trespassing and arrest them if they returned.

On the drive back to Vegas, George shared some secrets about moves that poker rounders and crossroaders use. He said, "To overcome the poker fee for playing, hustlers use a sticky substance called *check-cop* to steal chips from the pot. They will push the winner the pot appearing to help as they cop a chip which sticks to the check-cop that's applied to their wrist; or they'll make change from the pot and cop a chip." You make check-cop by heating waterproof tape with a cigarette lighter, and then scrape off the sticky substance with a sharp knife, or you can buy it at *T.R. Kings* or another crooked gambling supply store.

He said, "Lo-ball hustlers mark the face cards with daub to see when an opponent draws a losing big card. Some hustlers use superfine sandpaper glued to a finger to remove the microscopic fibers that cover the backs of plastic cards. They sand the northeast and southwest corners of the tens and can feel them with their thumb as they deal. You buy the super-fine sandpaper at a billiard supply store. The top-of-the-line hustlers palm cards in-and-out of a game and are called *hand-muckers* or holdout men. Some will use a slick-sleeve, or an oversized paper clip fastened to his bi-cep under a short-sleeved shirt. After he steals a card, he'll park it under the clip until he needs it. Some park the card in the crock of their knee and some will keep the held out card in their hand and will even reach out with it to scoop in a winning pot in front of the losing players. Muckers are gutsy and win a lot of money fast. Other top-line hustlers are shuffle artists who stack the deck with winning hands for their agents. Some dealers can cut an exact number of cards to preserve a *slug* of cards. They practice the move for hundreds of hours, or they'll file a fingernail a certain length as a guide to cut to an exact number of cards."

He said when the poker rooms in Gardena close at four a.m., the hustlers get in the cashier line with the players to lure them to a private game. He alerted me to be careful about whom I did business with. He said, "Many crossroaders and hustlers were scoundrels and untrustworthy and they gossip and knock everybody. Some need crooked dealers and bosses to get by because they have no talent and are afraid to take risks, and if you do business with them they hold out money on you, and if you're busted with them they'll turn on you."

He said he knew a young craps dealer working at the Riviera and doing business with a crossroader who told the dealer he knew the guy working in the *eye* who would tell him if the dealer had heat. The dealer agreed to pay the eye ten percent of what they stole. They were using a handoff move where the dealer palmed several $25 or $100 chips and handed them across the table to his agent under cover of making change for his agent's $20 dollar bills. It was a new move at the time that evolved into the *pitch*. George said the crossroader told the dealer the eye said there was no heat and to go stronger. They eventually were caught and arrested for embezzling. The dealer found out the crossroader lied about knowing the eye and got even with him by copping out to the District Attorney.

George said, "The best move is to find a grind move you can do on your own. Daubing and bending are OK if you keep a low profile. The best move would be a move beat craps since you don't stand out like on a 21 table, and craps game losses are spread out amongst a lot of players."

I made another play at the Thunderbird and phoned George to give him Johnny's end. He said we could make another payday with another crossroader he knew.

Bill Douglas had moved to Vegas from Palm Springs. He'd been a protégé of Titanic Thomson, who was an underground legend as the premier golf and card hustler in the country. George said Douglas's specialty was beating other poker and gin rummy hustlers and crossroaders.

Several years later, Douglas was accused of being the master-mind of the Friars Club cheating scandal in Beverly Hills. The Las Vegas *Sun* reported on December 4, 1968, that five men had rigged gin rummy games at the elite club. Douglas and his partners had drilled holes in the floor over the card room, and used WWII bombsights to spy on the player's cards below. They signaled the cards' values electronically to their confederates. Phil Silvers, Tony Martin, and a host of other celebrities fell victims to the scam. No one volunteered how much money he lost.

George said, "Douglas will give us each $1,000 in cash to buy $1,000 in nickels from the casinos. He'll pay us $25 for each $1,000 in nickels we buy. The casinos can't buy enough coins from the banks for their slot machine players because the U.S. Mint doesn't produce enough coins and there was a shortage due to the prolifer-ation of vending machines throughout the country. Douglas found several Strip casinos that paid him $50 for every $1,000 in nickels he brought them to accommodate their slot players. It takes about three hours to buy the nickels. Ricky and Larry were out there right now buying nickels."

Douglas looked to be in his mid-forties and in good shape. He was cordial and offered us a drink. His wife and two toddlers were on the floor breaking open rolls of nickels into bank bags. After a cup of coffee, Douglas gave us each $1,000 and wished us luck. We left in separate cars and would meet at the Horseshoe casino bar.

George said, "Buy at least $20 in nickels from each change girl on the floor and in the slot booths and hit every casino on Fremont Street." I was enthusiastic about this new hustle. I wouldn't get rich, but I would get some exercise, it would pay my *nut,* and was legal.

I asked the first change girl I saw for $20 in nickels. She said, "Good luck," as I spun away in the opposite direction to seek another girl. After I hit several casinos, I had half of my quota. I crossed Fremont Street to cut through the Golden Nugget casino to my car to unload the nickels.

After another coin-run, I hurried back to Douglas's house to unload the coins and get another $1,000. In two days, I bought $6,000 in nickels and decided to give my feet and face a rest.

Next day, George told me one of the Douglas's kids left a Mint Casino coin wrapper in a bank bag and a Tropicana cashier found it. They figured out what happened, let the other casinos know, and the trick was over.

Over the next several weeks, George and I made some daub plays, and he shared some other secrets with me. As I dealt to him, he bent certain cards as he picked them up and put them down. He put subtle concave waves in the big cards, convex waves in the little cards, and left the medium cards flat. For a different bend, he bent the cards' corners up or down. I could barely see the bends and waves that he made and he quickly read them off to me and never made a mistake. Next, he put a bubble in a big card as he pressed his thumb into the center face of the card and forced the back of the card between the tips of his fore finger and middle finger. It produced a bump that I could see when light reflected off the card at a certain angle. He said, "Some hustlers file a fingernail to a point to indent a card that a ceiling light will glare off of." He next used a sliver of sandpaper glued to his middle fingertip to mark cards by sanding their edges that he read from the side and the front of the deck. Next, he used a gold-colored daub to *shade* the sevens and eights on one corner of the card as he picked it up to look at it; he marked the opposite corner as he put the card down. He marked the big cards in the middle using his index fingertip. He said, "I use *check-cop* to hide the daub button inside my collar, or cuff. Some crossroaders rub daub in their hair or mustache instead of carrying the button."

After he daubed several cards, he mixed them up and recited the value of each card. He gave me the cards to look at and pointed to where the marks were but I couldn't see anything. He handed me a deck of marked cards and said, "Take these home to practice with. Take your eyes out of focus and just glance past the mark without staring at it and after a while you'll see it. It's like reading someone's handwriting, at first it's not legible but with practice it's easy to read."

I took my eyes out of focus and looked for the marks each night before I fell asleep. After one week, the marks jumped out at me and I felt like I found a hidden treasure.

George showed me some moves that he used to switch dice when he worked as a stickman on craps games. He kept his crooked dice in his altered apron, and removed them as he bent over to collect the square dice with the stick. He hid the *baloneys* cupped in his hand at the base of his folded last three fingers. He secured the square dice with his forefinger and thumb, and released the baloneys out the back of his hand when he passed them to a shooter. He showed me a move that boxmen use to switch in crooked dice. He secured a pair of green dice at the base of his fingers and pinky and laid his hand over and in front of a pair of red dice, securing them with his thumb and heel of his hand just below his pinky. In a sweeping motion, he released and pushed the red dice out the side of his hand. He said, "A stickman sets up the boxman's move by pushing the square dice next to a proposition bet as an excuse for the boxman to move the dice away from the bet."

He showed me a *second* that he used as a 21 mechanic, and a move called "rolling the deck." He dealt out several hands to imaginary players; his hand totaled sixteen. He said, "I'm looking for a four or five in a losing player's cards that I'll place on the bottom of the deck when I pick up his busted hand." He showed me a five that he placed on the bottom of the deck and said, "As I reach out with my deck hand to move an ashtray, or for some other reason, I roll my hand over the top of the deck. When I pull it back towards me I roll it upwards so that the bottom of the deck is now the top. He turned over his hand of sixteen and hit it with the five.

He showed me a *sub* he had worn to steal chips when he worked in the casinos. It was a nylon pouch that attached to the inside front of his trousers with grommets. The back of the pouch was held to his stomach by an attached elastic band that he latched around his back. When he pulled his stomach in, the top of his pants opened slightly and he dropped some chips into it—the opening closed when he relaxed his belly. He said some dealers wear "Sansabelt" slacks for their sub. They're popular slacks because they're stylish and they have a wide elastic band around the top to keep a shirt tucked in and neat. He said, "A stickman secures a chip under his thumb as he picks up losing proposition bets. He slides it into his Sansabelts when he bends over to retrieve the thrown dice with the stick. He lines chips up side-by-side across the front of his waist and retrieves them on his break. The move is undetectable from anywhere."

He said, "Some dealers go to work 'clean' but make a sub in their car while on a break. He wears two pair of undershorts and duct-tapes the bottoms around his thighs. He tapes the top outer pair to the top front of his slacks; the inner pair he tapes to his belly and tucks his shirt between the shorts. When he slides a palmed chip into the top of his pants, it drops into his secured underwear. He'll empty the chips and remove the tape on his break."

George said, "A dealer at the Dunes had been stealing $100 chips by putting one in his mouth just before he left the table to go on his break. When he was caught and in the back room, the casino manager asked him, 'How did those dirty chips taste in your mouth?' The dealer answered, 'Like New York steaks.' Security roughed him up, and he wound up with an undisclosed settlement after his lawyer threatened to sue the casino. Another 21 dealer who had dealt downtown for forty years, left work one night, had a heart attack, and died on Fremont Street. When the coroner undressed him at the morgue, he found a sub in his pants with $45 in it." George said the casinos didn't miss the money the dealers and bosses stole because the dealers made up for it by cheating the customers.

He said, "The eye-in-the-sky is a network of catwalks behind one-way mirrors or plate glass, above the casino floor. Some casinos hire ex-crossroaders to work in the eye, or as *outside men*— they walk the casino floor and pretend to be customers as they spy on dealers and players. Sometimes, a boss goes up to the eye to watch a dealer, or another boss. And some people who work in the eye do business with dealers, bosses, and crossroaders." He said he had done business with some poker hustlers who were putting in coolers in the Dunes Casino poker room when no one was up in the catwalk. The entrance to the catwalk was through a door on the roof that the observer climbed to from a ladder. He sat in Denny's restaurant next to the Dunes to watch when the observer took his breaks, and notified his confederates. The simplicity and effectiveness of all his moves, and his interesting stories, fascinated me, and I felt privileged that he confided in me.

He told me he was going to England with Bill Douglas and a professional card counter, to challenge the newly opened casinos there with Thorp's card-counting system. He said I could go to work for the re-opened El Rey Casino in Searchlight that needed 21 dealers. He said it was a *flat store,* meaning it cheated the public. He said some of the dealers were mechanics, and some couldn't find work in Vegas, like me. I would find out the casino had its gaming license revoked on two separate occasions in the early fifties for cheating.

I made a beeline for Searchlight. It was a ghost town in the middle of the desert about seventy-five miles from Vegas. The El Rey Casino had slot machines, 21 games, and a craps table. The customers were flown in on *junket*s from California and Arizona, to drink and gamble.

I walked into the pit, introduced myself to a floorman, and said I needed a job. His name was Jack and he was the casino manager. He said I could start that night. The pay was $25 cash, and tips that the dealers pooled, and there was no application to fill out.

The waitress told me that the casino security guard had taken a bus to pick up the customers at a landing strip one mile from the casino.

Soon, thirty men came rambling into the casino heading to the tables. Several sat on my game and were eager to play. As the night wore on, the players became rowdier as they drank and lost their money. A huge security guard who wore a sidearm and handcuffs on his belt, paraded up and down the aisles to keep them in check.

I started losing and Jack sent a relief dealer in to give me a break. When I returned, the players complained that the relief dealer made twenty or twenty-one on every hand. Must have been a mechanic, I thought. Just before midnight, a dealer put an envelope in my back pocket and said, "Your tips, and pay."

After work, I counted down $50, which was more than most dealers on Fremont Street made. I stopped at the bar adjacent to the casino with the other dealers. It opened at nine p.m., for any stragglers from the casino, or any nightriders on the Laughlin Highway.

It had been popular before the original casino and bordello had burned down in 1962. Now it was a trap for the dealers, where their gossip would stay in Searchlight. The slot machines were tight, the pull-tab cards already had the big bonuses pulled off, and the bartender booked football bets, but the main entertainment was listening to the dealers talk about their past lives. One had worked in Cuba and another had worked in Hot Springs, Arkansas. The dealer who had given me my envelope said, "We average $30 in tips. The craps dealers put us up on eleven on every come-out roll. The owner allows it because the players never win and the dealers need to make decent money to endure the commute from Vegas."

At home, I practiced dealing seconds and peeking at the top card as Rolan and George had taught me. I had never thought of being a mechanic, but now I felt I needed to protect my game and make my share of tips. After a few days of practice, I felt ready to try it.

As I prepared to deal a second, my heart rate jumped and my hands quivered. I had calmly peeked at the top card several times but I didn't have the nerve to deal the second. When I realized none of the players paid attention to me, I dealt one, then several more to bust my hands. The players made bets for me, and when it was time to get the casino's money back, I busted them out. Two guys continued to tip me even though they were now losing. I helped them get even and finished the night dealing on the square. Beating casinos seemed fair to me, but busting out unsuspecting innocent players wasn't my style. I was done working for the crooked casinos and told Jack I quit.

I felt relieved because it wasn't right beating a casino from the *inside*, even though they were the bad guys. To beat them from the outside was different; it was risky, challenging, rewarding, and left no guilt feelings.

I got a notion to try a blackjack move that Oklahoma Jimmy had shown me. I would bring a blackjack hand to a 21 game and switch it for the two cards dealt to me. The blackjack hand will be secured in my palm that I'll slide sideways under the two cards dealt to me. The dealt cards will curl up into my palm as I simultaneously turn over the blackjack. I had practiced the move for many hours in front of a mirror and had confidence I could move on any dealer. It would be my maiden voyage on the muscle, single-handed. The deck would be dirty, but I'd leave after one hand. As a precaution, I parked my car with the wheels turned out and the doors unlocked.

I picked the Las Vegas Club because it had several exits and I found a dealer I liked. As I approached the game, a friend of the boss came by to visit with him and they parked at the game I intended to play on. I moved to another game and put a $50 bill in the betting circle and the dealer called out, "Money plays." The boss nodded as I waited with the blackjack palmed in my sweaty hand. I was nervous, but determined to make the move. I exchanged the blackjack for the two cards dealt to me, but I forgot paper cards curl up like potato chips from sweaty hands. The dealer reached for the cards to straighten them and when he turned them over, we both woke up that they were the wrong color. I reached for my $50 bill but the dealer beat me to it. I said, "Let go of my money." He called out, "Cheat! Cheat!" I hit the back door and sprinted through the parking lot and down the sidewalk. Voices behind me shouted, "Get that guy." When I looked over my shoulder, a dealer, a security guard, and two parking lot attendants pursued me like a pack of wolves. It was noon, and the tourists stopped to watch the spectacle as I scrambled into my car and sped away.

I recovered my wind and laughed at myself for swapping the wrong color cards like Oklahoma Jimmy had done on the cooler play at the Lucky—another occupational hazard, I thought. I needed to tell a friend and headed to see Cap who had just returned to town and was dealing 21 at the Sands.

I told Cap my latest adventures as I downed a shot of his whiskey. As always, he offered me some good worldly advice and boosted my morale.

Oklahoma Jimmy had told me the blackjack switch was a heat score to use when leaving town. I had been anxious about doing something on my own, but I should have been more patient. My next move would be Jimmy's safer 21 *press move,* where I would slide a $25 chip under my bet when dealt a 19 or 20. I would make the play at night in case of a *runner.*

I stopped at the Sahara craps pit to buy chips for the move. I didn't want the 21dealer to notice the amount of chips I had—I needed to surprise him.

I found a happy game with a talkative dealer and a few players betting $25 chips. I sat in the last seat and bet four $5 chips stacked slightly like the Tower of Pisa leaning toward the dealer to conceal my press move and make it easier for the cards and chip to slide under my bet. I won the hand and he paid my bet like a robot and kept his conversation going; so far, so good. I bet another four chips and was dealt a twenty. I had a $25 chip hidden between my thumb and forefinger that I slid, with my two cards, under the four $5 chips. When I pulled the cards back out ostensibly to re-check their value, the four $5 chips settled on top of the $25 chip in a neat pile. I put my cards back under the five chips. It was a clean move that someone could look at and not see. When the dealer paid me, I asked him where the men's room was as an excuse to leave the game. I didn't want to push my luck and I was happy with my work and winning $65. I had learned a valuable lesson that when a dealer conversed with someone, or looked at their eyes in response to a question, he wouldn't notice how much they were betting or if they were marking their cards or anything.

After another successful play, I quit for the night. Jimmy had told me the move wasn't well known, and I didn't want to burn it up.

The next day, I was out pressing bets and ran into Larry's friend Ronnie Catlin whom I hadn't seen since the cold-deck play at the Riviera. He was staying at the Desert Inn Hotel-Casino on an RFB *comp* (free room, food, and beverage) and he invited me to the lounge for some drinks. He said he would meet Oklahoma Jimmy in a few days to make a craps play.

Ronnie said his dice switch was rusty and he asked me to help him practice. We left for his room and I asked him to go over the mechanics of the move; he did the same switch that Jimmy had shown me called "the suicide switch." He picked up a pair of dice using his three middle fingertips and rolled them up into his palm where he secured them. He picked up another pair the same way, and as his hand moved forward, he released the first pair he had picked up. They came out of his hand like a normal dice throw as he rolled the other pair into his palm. He turned his hand up to show me they were secure in his palm. It was a beautiful move and awkward for me, but I soon did it right. We crouched down at opposite ends of the room about the length of a craps table and switched dice back and forth to each other. After an hour, my hand was sore and I had two indentations in my palm from the sharp corners of the dice.

Ronnie suggested a break and he ordered some free sandwiches and drinks from room service. He showed me a dice shot called "the blanket roll" where he rolled a pair of dice on the bed to control which numbers rolled and couldn't roll. He held two dice together with the sixes facing each other and said, "This is how you set the dice if you want them to pass. They'll roll every number except for craps and eleven, and they'll roll one less seven. If you want to roll a lot of craps you face the four on one die with the four on the other one." He rolled them end-over-end like a wheel on the bed. He said, "A shot for playing craps on the beach or a sandlot is the spin shot. You set the dice and spin them as you release them and they'll stick and stay on the set number when they land." After another practice session, we made plans to meet the next day. At home, I practiced the switch in front of a mirror and fell asleep with a pair of dice duct taped to each hand.

Next day, I met Ronnie at the swimming pool where we played gin rummy and had some drinks. He won every hand and he showed me a clever move. He had a small convex-shaped mirror glued to his palm that he called *the light* or lamp. He could see my card's index as it passed over the mirror as he dealt to me. He said it was best to play under a bright light and over a white tablecloth, to reflect the card's index. He used waterproof glue to secure it, enabling him to remove it and park it to show his opponent he had a clean hand. He said, "In poker games, I glue it to a $100 bill that I keep on the bottom of my money stack. Just before I deal, I nudge my stack forward to expose my light. After dealing, I nudge the stack back to conceal it. I wear a baseball hat so my opponent can't see my eyes as I spy the card's index." He also showed me several clever sleight-of-hand moves for gin and poker. He said he rubbed Corn Huskers Lotion into his hands to facilitate palming cards. After lunch, we practiced switching dice for several hours and I left for home to practice on my own.

Ronnie woke up with the flu and was not up for meeting Jimmy that night. I said I was confident in my switch and I volunteered to go in his place. He thanked me and told me where to meet Jimmy.

Jimmy sat with two other men and I joined them. I told him Ronnie was sick and I volunteered to take his place. He asked if I ever switched dice on a live game. I said, "No, but I had been practicing and was ready to try." One of the men, Dan, owned a bar that had a small craps table and we drove there for my audition.

Jimmy said the best place to stand was at the end of the table where there was less of a chance for a dealer or boxman to see a *leak,* and it was the best place to spy the employee's eyes. He pushed me a pair of dice and I rolled them up into my palm. He pushed me another pair and I made the magical mid-air switch. I did it several times, as they looked at it from different angles. He said my move looked good except for a small *leak,* but if I worked to keep my thumb pressed to my hand, I would fix it.

He handed me some chips to put into my jacket pocket and said they were my excuse to go into my pocket to get the dice. He said, "When you come out of your pocket with the palmed dice secured and the chip, you set the chip in the field or toss it to the stickman to bet the eleven or a hard way bet." I switched the dice several times making the pocket moves.

Jimmy said we would play at the Flamingo and he showed me a pair of *loaded dice* and pointed to the logo on the deuce. It was a picture of a flamingo in three colors of white, pink, and yellow. He said, "They look the same as the Flamingo dice except the colors on the logo are placed so we can identify our dice from the casino dice. The dice are weighted to favor the five to come up more often than normal dice and they're called *dead fives.*"

I was impressed when he said, "Everybody was in for an equal share of any profits, or losses, and if anybody gets in trouble we're all in on bail money and legal expenses."

On the way to the Flamingo, He said, "After you switch the dice leave the casino to hide the casino dice, and come back to bet the *weight*." He explained the various bets to make and said we'd abandon the dice after the play as it was unlikely they'd be discovered. He went over the same signals we used for the *cooler* play at the Lucky—if he touched his chin, everything is OK; touching his eye means he wants to see me in private; brushing off his sleeve means to leave the casino; a quick brush means leave quickly. He said to check the casino exits before I make the play and if I felt nervous to have a shot of brandy.

I felt butterflies in my gut for the first time, but a shot of brandy at the casino bar cured them. From there Jimmy led me to a craps game. When the shooter next to me shot a losing seven, I wiped my damp hand on my slacks and eased it into my jacket pocket to palm the loaded dice and a chip. The stickman passed me the five dice. I set the chip in the field, picked up two dice, threw my hand forward, and switched the dice. I felt relieved it happened so quickly and that everyone on the game looked normal. When I rolled a losing seven I left for the pool, hid the casino dice in some shrubbery, and returned to bet our dice. After thirty minutes, Jimmy called the play off.

On the way to the meet the others, Jimmy told me I did well. He said he was leaving town for two weeks and asked me if I wanted to work with him when he returned. I said I did, and he said to continue practicing and to check the craps games on the Strip to find dealers and *boxmen* who were lax checking the dice.

He said, "An alert stickman occasionally rolls the dice over with his stick looking for tees. Tees have duplicate numbers on opposite sides and can't roll a losing seven. Square dice have numbers on opposite sides that add up to seven. A four has a three on its opposite side, a five has a deuce, and a six has an ace. The opposite sides of two dice add up to fourteen. So if a stickman is looking at a total of eight, he wants to see a total of six on the bottom of two dice when he turns them over with his stick. If you ever shoot *tees,* you have to be selective when you pick a game to play on." We split our winnings over a few drinks and I left to tell Ronnie about the play.

Next day, I drove Ronnie to the airport then stopped at the Strip casinos to check the dice crews. Unlike today's employees, the dealers and supervisors were serious and professional about their work. However, most didn't check the dice—they were satisfied seeing the shooter pick up the dice and toss them. I was surprised they were so vulnerable. I couldn't anticipate Jimmy's plans, but I would practice my switch and be ready for anything.

CHAPTER 4

TEES

I held a pair of dice taped to each palm as I fell asleep. Eventually, I held them without tape and woke up still holding them. And I held a pair in each palm while steering my car with my fingertips driving around town—I was becoming a serious *crossroader*.

Jimmy was back in town after his road trip to Oklahoma. I told him I'd been practicing and checking the casino dice crews. He opened a custom-made suitcase that he called his dice kit. It had compartments containing various dice and explained how to identify crooked dice that he called *baloneys*. He said, "These are six-ace-flats; they're more brick-shaped than square dice and tend to land more often on the flatter, bigger surfaced side of the dice, like if you rolled a brick on the ground, it would likely land on the flat side. They'll roll more aces and sixes to make more craps and sevens. They're what the Silver Slipper Casino was caught using and shut down. These other flats are shaped to make different numbers." Next, he showed me loaded dice he called *weight*. He said they had thin heavy tungsten discs placed beneath certain painted spots that he pointed out. He said, "These discs aren't noticeable unless a person is suspicious and knows what to look for." He showed me several pairs of dice he called t*ees,* or tops, that came in a variety of sizes and colors. They had duplicate numbers on the tops, sides, and bottom and can't roll a losing seven. He said, "Shooting tees was hot work."

He said, "Some crossroaders use the *sail shot* rather than risk shooting tees. One member of a crew throws one die and slides or scoots the other as another crewmember leans out to block the stickman's vision as the die slides by. The shooter slides a six and his crew bets the field, and the numbers ten, eleven, and twelve, for a huge advantage." I told him I felt ready to go to work and he showed me a pair of four-five-six tees. He said, "These are called 'snowballs' because of all the white spots and they're the strongest tees to win with, but the riskiest. They'll roll eight, nine, ten, eleven, and twelve—all field bet winners except the eight. Mathematically, eight will show once in nine rolls, but you can place the eight, and when twelve rolls it pays double in the field plus thirty to one on boxcars which offsets an unlikely eight." We made a plan to meet his bettors on Friday night at a lounge near the Strip.

Dan, the bar owner whose craps table I auditioned on was at the meet as well as Jimmy's girlfriend and a guy named Barry; they were in their mid-forties. After an introduction, Jimmy explained to them how to bet the tees and how to set up on a game. Dan would place the eight, nine, and ten and the others would bet the field. He told them to hover around the game where I set up and pick a spot to play when the man beside me is shooting the dice. He said a game could be too crowded to get a spot, but a person could reach in to make a bet. He said, "Bobby will put a cigarette in his mouth when the tees are coming in; when he removes it, they're coming out. He might get two or three rolls with the tees, then shoot the square dice one or more rolls, and come back in with the tees so watch him closely."

We would play at the Sahara and meet back at the lounge after the play. Jimmy told everyone to check they weren't followed after the play. On the way to the casino, He told me, "You always want to make sure you're not followed after making a play. You wouldn't want to lead a gaming agent or *outside man* to the rest of the crew. When I arrive at a meeting spot, I find a place where I can watch from in case a careless partner is followed."

Before entering the casino he said, "Try to find a game with a lot of action so if the tees are picked up, our bettors won't come under immediate suspicion and might get away. And watch other player's hands as someone could reach out to make a last minute bet and collide with your hand causing you to *spill* the dice. And if the stickman starts turning the dice over, throw some chips to him for proposition bets to distract his attention away from noticing the tees. Prompt him to send the dice back to you by reaching out for the dice. Watch that dealers and bosses don't see the dice in the table mirrors where they'll see both sides of the dice. You have to be good at reading people; you have the *floormen*, *boxmen*, and dealers to contend with who can check the dice at any time. You need a sixth sense to know when to take the tees out before someone reaches for them to check. You hope to get two or more rolls with them. The dice mechanic always picks the game to play on and checks that the tees' color and size matches the casino dice. They could be cherry, or tangerine-colored, and light, medium, or dark. And always look for a trap, and check all the exits before you set up."

The Sahara dinner show let out and filled the casino. I liked it that way, in case something goes wrong I could get lost in the crowd. I checked the casino exits and observed the craps *crews* and the action on my way to get a shot of brandy.

I found an action game with room for everybody, and the dice were the right color and size. The shooter was next to where I stood as I wiped my sweaty hands on my slacks and was ready.

My heart and pulse pounded when the shooter next to me rolled a losing seven. I lit a cigarette, set it in the ashtray, and put a $1 chip on the *pass line*. When the stickman passed me the bowl of five dice, I picked a pair, tossed them for a point of six, and put the cigarette in my mouth. I reached in my pocket for the tees and a $1 chip as my partners made their bets. When the stickman passed the dice back to me, I threw him a chip with my loaded hand and said, "This is for a *hard way* six." I picked up the dice and threw my hand forward releasing the tees as I rolled the casino dice into my palm. A ten rolled and nobody flinched or looked at me. I carefully watched the employees and customers' eyes as I dropped the casino dice into my pocket. I came out with a chip, set it in the field, and rolled a nine for another field winner. I looked at my partners and they were smiling.

I pulled my cigarette and set it in the ashtray as my partners were paid and took their bets down. I reached in my pocket for the casino dice as the tees sat in front of the world. I watched for a box-man or boss to pick them up, or see them in the mirror that lined the inside perimeter of the table. If they saw the dice in the mirror, they'd see only fours, fives, and sixes on the dice and would make a knee-jerk grab for them as I would hurry away from the table and out the door. The stickman pushed me the tees and I switched them out and brushed-out my partners.

Jimmy said, "Boy, you did good work." He asked if I wanted to go again and I said yes. When our partners arrived, they congratulated me. We had a drink and headed to the Sands.

The craps pit was located near the cashier where a huge security guard sat in a *shotgun chair*. The games were crowded and I had to muscle my way into a game as the players grudgingly allowed me a little of their space. The dice were two players away from me, but when the shooter shot a losing seven, the player beside me passed the dice and it was my turn to roll. I stalled by making change to give my partners time to get in position as I wiped my moist hands. After getting a point, I rolled twelve with the tees and my partners won double in the field. I rolled another twelve and yanked my cigarette. I switched the casino dice back in and rolled twelve again! A boxman reached for the dice to check—one roll too late. Jimmy was right; shooting tees was hot work. I brushed-out everyone and left.

At the meet, everyone commented about the three successive twelves. Jimmy said if I continued shooting four-five-six tees, I would see it again. He suggested we quit for the night and he asked everyone to square-up their starting money and to give him the rest. He made five piles and asked everyone to pick up a pile, count it, and trade stacks with each other and count it again. Each stack had over $500 in it and everybody seemed happy. Dan said, "Bobby, I couldn't see any leaks in your switches and they all looked natural." Barry said, "It was exciting watching you work Bobby." I thanked everyone and felt good at my success and being the center of attention to people who were more than double my age.

I told Jimmy I had a hard time squeezing in on the game. He said, "When I shot tees I would spill drinks on players or step on their feet to make room for myself. One time I put a lit cigarette in a guy's pocket to move him, and another time in Reno, a man wanted to fight me for a little space on a game. When the stickman passed me the dice, I switched in the tees and passed them to the smart ass telling him, 'I don't shoot.' My partners and I bet the tees to the hilt and as we left the casino we watched a security guard tackle the smart aleck who was still shooting the tees."

For two weeks, day and night, we used a variety of tees and played in all the Strip casinos. Some casinos brought in VIP junkets, that were good for us because the players bet big, and most played on credit that kept the boxmen and bosses busy. They flew to Vegas free and had "the power of the pen" to sign for free food and beverages. They came to gamble for two or three days. Some would start playing as soon as their limo dropped them off at the hotel. They'd tip a bellman to take their luggage to their room and would head straight to the tables. Some stayed at the tables for their entire visit, never sleeping or unpacking their suitcases. And some were lucky to get out of town with their suitcases.

I felt comfortable in the casino environment and confident with my switch. It was undetectable and so bold and unexpected. At the time, the Strip casinos had two boxmen and a floorman or two on every game, but none checked the dice. Each boxman and boss thought the other boxman and boss checked the dice, and both boxmen thought that both bosses checked them and vice versa. And they all thought the stickman checked them since it was his job to do, but he thought no one would attempt to switch the dice with so many eyes on the game—especially a kid like me. Looking back, I'm surprised I didn't realize the danger I was in; it must have been the innocence of youth.

I switched in the four-five-six tees at the Sahara again for two rolls and signaled my partners to take their bets down. I picked up the tees and moved my hand forward to switch in the casino dice but all four dice flew out toward the end of the table. Before they landed, I was gone and into my exit ballet looking at my watch like I was late for an appointment. Jimmy had told me never run from a play because it was an admission of guilt.

At the meet, Dan said, "The stickman pushed the four dice to a boxman who told him to give the next player new dice to finish out my roll. In the excitement, no one observed our bettors or asked the dealers who had made a recent bet. A boss brought a pack of new dice to the game and had another dealer take out the stickman. The stickman told the boss the guy shooting the tees was middle-aged and heavy-set!" I was eighteen and thin so we all had a good laugh to close out the night.

I told Jimmy I felt fine when I picked up the dice, and I didn't know what happened. He said he never found an explanation for the *spill-shot* other than it was an occupational hazard. He said, "At home, I practiced spilling the dice deliberately, then recovered before losing them. It helps me control the dice and gives me confidence." I asked him if the town would be steamed-up and he said that the casinos competed with each other, and they wouldn't want it known that somebody shot tees on them, suggesting they were a weak store. He said, "If the town's steamed-up, the stickmen in the other casinos will be turning over the dice checking for tees." He suggested we quit for a while.

When the others left, Jimmy told me he'd be going to Puerto Rico in two weeks and he invited me to go. Our bettor Barry would be going, and another crossroader from Reno. It sounded too good to be true: an adventure to the Caribbean in a private plane. He said he was flying to Los Angeles in a few days to renew his passport and to buy some dice, and he asked me to go.

Next day, I checked every casino craps pit on the Strip. None, except the Sahara, was checking the dice for tees.

Jimmy owned a Cessna 195 four-seater. We cruised over mountains and desert on the way to Burbank airport where he parked his plane and rented a car. We special ordered our passports, and drove to Kingsley Manufacturing Company in Hollywood, where Jimmy bought an embossing machine to monogram his dice As the sales rep explained how to use it, Jimmy cut him off and said,

"How much is it and I expect you to throw in a variety of colored rolls of tape." He paid for the machine and put it into a small gym bag and we left for Jimmy's dice maker in Fontana.

Dale Jones made dice in his garage. He had a drill press and other machinery to cut and shape dice as well as an oven to bake the enamel spots on them. Jimmy ordered several sets of *dead fives*, *dead aces*, and tees. Jones would send them to Vegas via American Airlines, the next day.

Jimmy taught me how to use the new machine to stamp dice. It had a temperature gauge and control knob to heat up a brass die that stamped the casino logo onto the dice. Jimmy said he gets the brass dies from an engraver in Florida who also made the dies for various casinos. He gave me some old dice to practice with and showed me how to center a die before I stamped it. With the die in place, and without using colored foil, he pulled down on the handle lightly to put a faint colorless logo on the die. After checking that it was centered, he put a permanent logo on it using colored foil. I practiced several times then monogrammed a die perfectly.

Soon we were packed and ready to leave for Puerto Rico. It would take a few days to fly to Miami, with stops along the way. Jimmy would store his plane in Miami, and we would fly to San Juan on Eastern Airlines.

One of the guys who came with us was Larry Doss, a crossroader who went all routes meaning he could beat all casino games including switching dice. His specialty was beating slot machines with a variety of homemade tools and gadgets. He was Jimmy's age and a licensed pilot who had worked with Jimmy flying around the country beating illegal gambling casinos, Monte Carlo Nights at fraternity clubs, and smokers, or anywhere there was gambling. Barry wasn't a crossroader, but somehow got involved with Jimmy as a bettor. He was a cheerful guy in his early forties and recently divorced. He worked in Vegas as a bartender and was a 32nd degree Mason.

To break up the trip, Jimmy and Larry talked about other cross-roaders and gambling stories from their past. Larry told Jimmy, "Glen Graystone had been arrested shooting tees in Macau. He escaped jail and was caught and beheaded on the spot." I asked Larry who he was and he said he was the "King of Crossroaders," and double tough. He said, "One time, a friend of Glenn's was caught cheating at Harrah's Lake Tahoe, where two security guards worked him over before they called the police to arrest him. Glenn and a friend of his waited for the security guards to get off work and put a bad hurting on them. No witnesses from Harrah showed up at the preliminary hearing and the cheating charges against his friend were dropped."

Jimmy told Larry he was hoping to make some money to finance a scientific project. A chemistry professor he knew in Oklahoma had discovered a laboratory phenomenon while working with some cobalt and ceramic magnets. He told Jimmy he could apply the process to control what numbers would roll on a pair of dice, but he needed money to buy the cobalt to continue his work. The story fascinated me and I hoped to play a part in it someday.

In Santurce, Puerto Rico, we rented a sixth-floor, three-bedroom condominium by the month. Larry rented a car at five cents a mile, and after one week, he disconnected the odometer. He also reversed the condominium's electric meter that he found outside the condo—just another crossroader trick. Our electricity and car mileage would be free.

I jogged to the beach every day to stay in shape in case of a *runner*, and to check the hotel and casino exits and surrounding areas. I wanted to know where every door led and where all the taxi stands and alleys were. I finished by swimming in the ocean, then jogged the several miles home.

Jimmy showed me how to test for loaded dice. He held a dead five obliquely by opposite corners between his thumb and forefinger. He gently spun the die upward with his forefinger and the die wobbled and settled on the five. Next, he set the die down, lifted it on its edge and let it fall forward. It rolled over onto the five like a Mexican jumping bean. Then he dropped it into a glass of water and it settled on the bottom with the five up.

He said the casinos in Puerto Rico put a secret mark on their dice that I could find if I stood beside the stickman and bent down low when I made my bets.

Our first play would be at the Caribe-Hilton in San Juan using dead fives. They were the same type dice I had first switched at the Flamingo, but this time I'd swap all five dice into the game. It was a scary thought and I hoped that Jimmy and Larry would help me, but they remained silent and I realized I was the sole mechanic in the crew.

Jimmy demonstrated the move explaining, "When the stickman passes you the dice, pick up two and set them aside like this and say, 'Not this pair,' as you switch them for two dead fives. With the casino dice secured in your palm, you pick another square pair and throw them for your point. Then drop the casino dice in your pocket where you palm two more dead fives. After another switch, there will be four loaded dice in the game and one square die. If you roll craps, you could ask for new dice and switch out the one square die for the fifth piece of weight, or we'll get by with the four pieces. We'll distract the boxmen and dealers as you make your moves."

I did the move exactly as Jimmy had explained. After an hours practice, we left for the Condado Beach Hotel-Casino where we had a successful "Off-Broadway" dry run. I was satisfied that I could repeat the move under pressure, trusting that my partners would distract the employees for me. We would play at the Caribe-Hilton in San Juan, the next night.

The secret mark on the Hilton's dice was a pinprick on the "o" in the word Hilton. Jimmy gave me his metal scribe and I headed to the men's room to mark our dice.

Back at the game, everyone was in place. The stickman pushed the five dice to me, as Jimmy threw five $100 bills on the table for change as Larry and Jerry asked their dealers for change. I calmly picked up two dice and switched them for two dead fives as I set them aside saying, "Not these." While holding the palmed pair of casino dice, I picked up a second pair and threw them for my point. I reached in my pocket to drop the square pair and get the second pair of weight as my partners made their bets. I switched them in and made my point. When I rolled craps, I asked for new dice, and switched in the fifth loaded die and felt relieved it was over.

When I rolled a losing seven, I left to hide the casino dice. I rejoined the crew and they flashed me the *George* sign and smiled, but after one hour we were dead even and Jimmy brushed us out and told me the dice weren't worth retrieving—I felt good hearing that.

Jimmy said we would use dead aces on the next play, saying they were stronger than dead fives. He pointed out the twelve discs inside the transparent dead aces compared to the eight discs in the dead fives. He said, "We'll make our next weight play after Christmas when all the merchants up north close their shops and head here to do some gambling. In the meantime we can make some tee plays.

We drove to the Dorado Beach Hilton and won several bets then beat all the casinos in and around San Juan.

The weight play was at the San Geronimo Hilton in San Juan. I found the secret mark and marked our *dead aces*. I switched four of them into the game and they did work, but a suspicious floorman took one die to the podium, dropped it in a glass of water, and discovered it was loaded. We took our bets down and left unnoticed.

We discovered the next night that all the Puerto Rico casinos were checking for loaded dice, so we flew to Miami Beach, then to Freeport, Bahamas, on New Year's Eve.

Jimmy had high expectations of a big score and he invited another bettor for our play. Jack Dunley flew in from Junction City, Kansas. He was an old friend of Jimmy's who was born in the 1880s and was now in his 80s. Jimmy said as a young man Jack had held up stagecoaches, banks, and trains, but "reformed" to become a crossroader after he married a religious girl who bore him several children.

Jack was soft-spoken and cheerful. I asked him if he had been to Vegas and he said he dealt 21 at the Golden Nugget in 1946. He said he came through "the desert" with a crew of crossroaders that he had been on the road with in California and Oregon. When he saw the dealers handling chips, and no one watched them, he decided to stay and his crew headed back to Kansas. I asked him where the term crossroader originated and he said, "In the Old West, there was a restaurant and saloon with gambling located at major 'crossroads.' Travelling gamblers tied their horses up there and preyed on the square gamblers and became known as crossroaders."

The Lucayan Beach Hotel-Casino was the casino in Freeport. At the time, the Bahamas were a British possession and the licensed casino owner was a Canadian who was a front man for Meyer Lansky, the mobs' gambling czar.

The casino was as elaborate as any casino in Vegas. Two boxmen were on each game and a boss sat in a shotgun-chair overlooking the huge Cleveland-type craps tables.

I couldn't find a secret mark on the dice so I intentionally threw a die off the table and watched a boxman examine it. He gave it a quick look and balance spin, and set it on the table. I was satisfied there was no secret mark.

It was business as usual to switch the five loaded dice into the game. They worked at times then cooled off. After two hours, we were even and Jimmy called off the play before we lost—another loaded dice play gone bad.

We returned to Miami, where Larry, Barry, and Jack chilled and decided to go home. Jimmy and I flew back to Freeport to make a play with tees. It was New Year's Day, 1965.

Everyone looked relaxed so it seemed no one had found the loaded dice from the night before. I checked the game and was surprised to see that our dice were still in action so we decided to make a tee play on another game.

I checked the dice color on a table closest to the casino entrance and left to pick out matching tees from the several sets I brought. I hid the extra tees in an ashtray stand outside of a hotel elevator.

I couldn't stand in my regular spot so I stood beside the stickman to make a switch. I faked a switch on my first shot to test the boxman. He seemed OK so I put a cigarette in my mouth and Jimmy made his bets. When I switched the dice, the boxman flinched—he had nailed me. Jimmy was right: the end of the table was the best place to switch dice from and I should have waited for an end spot to open. The stickman was unaware of what happened and he pushed me the tees. I switched them out and hurried toward the exit as the boxman jumped up and yelled to the door bouncer to grab me.

I weaved through the crowded lobby and was tackled to the floor and tossed the tees. Two men in suits stood me up and another one picked up the dice. One guy said, "Hold him while I hit him." Another said, "Wait a while," and they walked me back through the lobby to the casino. An older woman asked, "Where are you taking that poor boy?" I put on the saddest look I could muster up for her.

They brought me to a back room and sat me down at a long table with the bouncer and left. He asked me where I was from and when I said Jersey City, he said he had lived and trained at the YMCA there when he was boxing. His name was Joey Maxim and he had been the light-heavyweight boxing champion of the world. He was impressed that I knew who he was, and that he'd beaten the legendary Sugar Ray Robinson. He scolded me and tried to scare me by saying they had just caught a guy cheating at 21 and dumped his body in the bay.

Frank Ritter, a.k.a. Red Reed, arrived with another man. Ritter was a fugitive from New York wanted on bookmaking charges who ran the casino for Meyer Lansky. He said they had my partner from Detroit, which meant Jimmy got away. Jimmy had told me never plead guilty to anything. He said he was arrested over fifty times and had never been convicted. I was on my own on foreign soil and handled my predicament my way.

I said, "I came alone and I don't know anyone from Detroit." Apparently, they had questioned a guy on my game who was betting big. Ritter said I had only been betting $5. I said, "I planned to bet more as my confidence grew." He asked where I got the dice and who put the casino's logo on them. I said, "From a guy in a Miami poolroom who said he was an artist and had painted the logo." He grabbed my jacket collar, shook me, and asked for my ID. I handed him my passport and he handed it to a tall, well-dressed man and they chuckled about something—my age I had hoped, I had just turned nineteen. They kept my passport and left.

Maxim tipped me off not to worry. I would surprise him twenty years later when I re-introduced myself to him in Las Vegas at the Frontier Hotel-Casino where he was working, and we had a good laugh.

Ritter returned, handed me my passport, and warned me not to come back and to tell my friends to stay away. Maxim told me someone would drive me to the airport and he wished me luck.

I was relieved to be free, and not roughed up and had learned a lesson about being patient; it would be the only time in my career that I was caught "in the act" of making any move.

I phoned Ritter from Miami so he could *clean up* the dead aces and the hidden tees before the law found them. At the time, Scotland Yard had administered the law in the Bahamas. When I told him about the loaded dice still in action from the night before, he threatened me but I cut him off and said my crew didn't make any money with them and they were beating the square players. I told him about the tees hidden in the ashtray stand and he thanked me for the tip-off and wished me good luck.

Jimmy said he knew an Argentinian crossroader in Puerto Rico, and he was flying his plane there to work with him. They were going to hustle the winter tourists playing gin and poker at the hotel pools. He invited me to go but I declined. I planned to go back to Vegas to put my own crew together.

CHAPTER 5

VETERAN CROSSROADER

After a visit home, I headed to Vegas. Bill Douglas's wife told me George and Bill were still in London playing 21. She said Clint Bell was home and would like to see me.

I had met Clint before I left for San Juan. He was a 21 dealer and had done business with George. I told him I wanted to put a dice crew together and I needed a partner to help me buy some equipment. He was interested and we made plans to drive to LA.

Bell was a thirty-year-old Korean War veteran who grew up in Culver City, California. After he left the marines, he got married, and worked as a stunt man in western movies. He was arrested for armed robbery of a Robert Hall clothing store and spent two months in the LA county jail. When another man confessed to the robbery, he was released. He sued LA County, and moved to Las Vegas to await the outcome. He rented a house beside Bill Douglas and became his protégé.

I had learned a lot about Clint and other crossroaders on our trip to LA. Clint was a gossip and had told me inside information about the top poker players and crossroaders in Vegas, and a variety of plays that he and Douglas were involved in. He showed me a device called "the periscope" that he'd been using to 21 games. It was a flip-top cigarette box with a prism inside that revealed a

21 dealer's *hole card* when he put the card under his up card. An opened pack of matches glued to the back of the box covered the prism. A cutout in the matches exposed the prism and looking into it exposed the dealer's hole card. Several cigarettes stuck out of the flip-top box for show. He said he'd used the device successfully with card counters and poker players in Vegas, and he had enticed a rich sucker with it and lugged him to the Cal-Neva Casino at North Lake Tahoe to scam him. He said the formerly Sinatra-owned casino was a steer joint that would pay hustlers 20 percent of whatever money any sucker lost whom they had steered there. His sucker lost over $8,000 before he quit. Bell said they were comped to the Shecky Greene show and during the show, the drunken comedian told the audience the casino was cheating everybody, including himself. Green said the casinos paid big money to entertainers who gambled, because they'd gamble the money right back to the casino. The casino fired him and he returned to work at the Riviera in Vegas.

Carlo, a dealer I had worked with at the Lucky, would later tell me that he had worked at the Cal-Neva at the time and the casino was indeed flat. He had dealt craps there with Clayton Gatterdam who would switch in *splitters* to cheat the customers. Carlo also worked with Gatterdam at the Lake Tahoe Hotel-Casino, where state authorities caught him switching splitters into the game from the stickman position and closed the casino as was reported in *Time* magazine on October 27, 1967. Carlo said the casino was owned by the Teamsters Union and was *flat*. The teamsters front man brought in junkets to gamble and carloads of young hookers from Reno for them. Nobody won except *shills* working for the flat casino. The shills flew on the junket flights posing as players to advertise to the losing players that they had won.

I was impressed with the periscope and the stories and information Bell had told me, but I should have quit him for *dumping* his player and for being a gossip. I would learn the hard way that leopards don't change their spots—Bell would become a police informant, turned on me and sixteen others, and was involved in several Las Vegas' scandals including testifying that he and an FBI agent had burglarized convicted Federal Judge Harry Claiborne's house looking for evidence. His testimony was never proven.

We bought a stamping machine at Kingsley Manufacturing in Hollywood, and drove to *T.R. Kings* gambling supply store to buy some tees. We stopped at Oklahoma Jimmy's dice maker to order some weight. I ordered two sets of dead aces and asked him to make them stronger than the weight he had made for Jimmy. He said he would put a bevel on them and insert heavier discs. I phoned Jimmy's engraver in Florida and ordered the brass dies for the Strip casinos' logos.

We needed another partner and Bell suggested Gary Mills. He said Mills had dealt poker at the Fremont and Golden Nugget casinos and he was casino smart. His wife had died recently and left him some money and he wanted some adventure.

When our dice arrived, we drove to Mills' house. He was Bell's age, mild-mannered and on the quiet side like me. I told him whom I was, and showed him my dice moves and the different types of tees, and ways to bet them. We rehearsed the signals we'd use and would meet that night at the Algiers's lounge.

I had told them about some previous dice plays in Vegas and Caribbean casinos, but I wondered what they thought about me, and if I could switch dice on the casinos. They would soon find out.

At the meet, I told them to check the casinos' exits in case of a runner, and if we were separated to meet back at the lounge or my motel room. I said our main concern while playing should be a boxman or floorman seeing the tees in the table mirror, or a stickman rolling them over to check for tees. I said, "If that happens, I'll throw some prop bets to the stickman to distract his attention away from the dice, and you guys should do the same."

The Johnny Carson Show at the Sahara had let out and the casino was packed. Players were receiving chips on credit that distracted the bosses. I would shoot deuce-trey-six tees. Each die had two deuces, treys, and sixes, and would roll a four, five, six, eight, nine, or twelve, and they looked more like square dice than four-five-six snowballs. My partners would place the six, eight, five, and nine from opposite ends of the table from each other.

I rolled a four for a point and put a cigarette in my mouth. My partners had their bets placed and I made my switch. I looked at them and they smiled back. We had the unique perspective of knowing we couldn't lose as we watched the anxious players and employees wondering what would roll.

After three winning rolls, I removed my cigarette and my partners took their bets down. I brushed them out and left for the meet.

Mills and I talked about the play while we waited for Bell who hovered around the game to notice anything unusual—maybe a guy in the *eye* saw something and would come downstairs to look for me, or an employee or customer might say something. We'd be coming back and didn't want to walk into a trap.

Bell arrived and said it was *Jake* and we left for the Flamingo. After three winning rolls, a relief boxman sat down just as I replaced the casino dice. He reached to check the dice as I smiled at my partners and lit a new cigarette. My partners made new bets while the new boxman checked the casino dice. I switched the tees back in for three more winning rolls and left.

We set up on a game at the Tropicana with an old boxman on my end who looked bored. When I got a point, he closed his eyes to take a little nap. Mills and Bell smiled as they "quietly" placed their bets. After a few rolls, the boxman opened his eyes to watch a dealer make a payoff to Bell, and dozed-off again. After three more rolls, I yanked my cigarette and my partners quietly took their bets down and left the game as the boxman continued his nap.

We had a good laugh on the sleeping boxman. Mills and Bell liked what they saw and for several weeks, we worked the Strip day and night. We knew when the sharper dealers, boxmen, and bosses took their breaks and for how long. We knew the time when each casino's shift changed and when the *count* took place, which we took advantage of.

During the count the outgoing and incoming shift bosses, or their assistants, counted every chip on each game in the casino. The casino owners wanted to know the bosses whose shift held the highest win percentage and would reward them with bonuses accordingly. The count was done quickly because the game would stop for the actual count. Each boss counted the stacks of chips and tallied up their totals to compare before they moved to the next table. Two security guards followed them and changed out the cash moneybox for an empty one for the new shift. The count put pressure on everyone involved and we took advantage of the seriousness of it all.

At the Sands, I was ready to remove my tees as the count team arrived at the game beside ours. There was a delay on our game because a new fill of chips had arrived and the boxmen and floorman hurried to get them stacked for the count. The stickman passed me the dice just as the count team arrived at our game. I had the added pressure of everyone waiting on me to throw the dice so they could begin the count—I had to switch out the tees or they'd sit in plain view until the count team finished. To distract the bosses, Bell and Mills complained they hadn't seen a cocktail waitress for an hour. I made my move and when the count team left, I lit a new cigarette—the employees relaxed after the count because any money won or lost after the count was the responsibility of the new shift coming on shortly. After three rolls, we left for the Thunderbird where their count would begin.

After the Thunderbird, we set up on a game at the Stardust where Sonny Liston was playing. A few players made a fuss over the former heavyweight-boxing champion but the employees weren't impressed since Sonny didn't bet much money and he was a regular there like us. He made my job seem more exciting and I slipped him some money and told him how to bet.

One afternoon, we set up on a game at the Flamingo where Robert Goulet was playing. The star singer played craps there in the daytime and appeared in the showroom at night. I stood next to him as he lost several big bets and looked upset. I quietly told him to place the six and eight again and I'd make him some money. After a few winning rolls, he looked at me and smiled. I told him to take his bets down and when I sevened-out I wished him luck as he waved to me—he had no idea he'd been betting on tees.

I wanted to try the dead aces that Dale Jones had made for me and I stamped them with the Thunderbird logo. Mills recruited several friends to help us take off the money; Gentleman Jim was a poker player, Chuck McGilery was a poker dealer, and Frank Peltro was a gigolo. Bell said Bill Douglas was back from England and knew a casino boss who would like to be in on the play. I met the boss, explained how to bet the weight, and said that we had a small edge. Douglas told me that George had married an English dealer and stayed in London. I would never see him again.

We arrived just before the dinner show let out and we were the only players on the game. I was able to load the dice bowl while my partners bought into the game and distracted the employees. When Mills threw the dice, one bounced off the table and he said, "*Same dice!*" so the boxman would quickly examine it and return it to the game. Asking for the same dice is a superstition about not changing dice in the middle of a hot roll.

He looked at the logo, did a quick balance-spin for show, and set it back down. The weight didn't work as it was supposed to, so I left to get the deuce-trey-six tees. I conveyed to the players my intentions so they could sweeten their bets for sure winners on my roll. Before I had a chance to shoot the tees, Douglas came up to the game to see how his bettor was doing. A boss recognized him and hustled to the dice bowl to check the dice. He woke up to the loaded dice and rushed to the podium for new dice. Everyone got away clean and we finished breaking even. Bell told me Douglas was barred from every Strip casino. Douglas apologized and I told him it was no big deal and it might have been a blessing in disguise. I would never use weight again—tees worked 100 percent.

We took a road trip to Reno and Lake Tahoe. There was no speed limit in rural Nevada, and Mills averaged 90-mph. Most of the landscape between Vegas and Reno was desert with a few small towns, a ghost town, and several bordellos. We stopped in Beatty, a small town about two hours from Vegas. There was a restaurant with a bar, slot machines, and a 21 table. There was one 21 player who looked like a shill, and an old dealer who looked like he was at his last stop in life and he beckoned us to play. We had a coffee and left.

We passed two cars on the 430-mile trek; one was a wooden dummy police car with a dummy cop who glared at us at the sharp turn in the road entering Goldfield.

The Mizpah Hotel in Tonopah had a few casino games that looked flat. The mining town was known for its past history of silver mining where a sign there read more silver had been extracted there than anyplace on earth, and gave Nevada its nick-name, "The Silver State."

We stopped in Hawthorne at the El Capitan Casino to eat and pick up some road money. It had the best food between Reno and Vegas, and was the center of activity for the townspeople, military personnel, and the hookers, ranchers, and miners from the surrounding areas. The craps crew looked weak and so did the boss. We met in the car and made a plan. Bell would bet on the four-five-six tees if Mills could distract the boss. Mills said he'd buy-in for $500 at a 21 game and draw the boss into a conversation.

The two-man craps game was dead. The dealer closest to me emptied the bowl of dice in front of my bet as Mills bought in at the 21 game and talked to the boss. I signaled Bell to the game, he put $200 in the field, and the dealer called out, "Money plays." The boss didn't hear him as I switched in the tees for a field winner. Bell's dealer trembled as he paid him while my dealer was busy answering my questions about the best way to play craps. The boss still catered to Mills as I next rolled twelve for a two-to-one payoff. Bell's dealer tried to call the boss over, but he stuttered and couldn't speak. He wanted to tell the boss that $400 was going out as Bell scolded him for not paying him fast enough. My dealer called the boss as Bell gathered up his chips. I switched the casino dice back in, rolled a seven, and left to start the car as the boss arrived at the craps game. Mills left the 21 game and headed to the cashier with Bell behind him.

As we backed out of the lot and pulled away, the boss stormed out of the casino. He pointed at us and shouted, "You cheated me."

I headed south toward Vegas, and turned onto the first "crossroad" to head back north to Reno and felt like we were bank robbers in a Wild West movie.

In Reno, I wanted to do a quick check of the Virginia Street casinos so we split up and would meet at the Golden Casino in one hour.

Harrah's had the biggest action in town and several craps pits under one roof. Most of the dealers, and some bosses, were women, something that didn't exist in Vegas at the time. Reno was the divorce capitol of the country and there was no shortage of divorcees, who had stayed in Reno after their divorce. They learned to deal, and when the men left to fight in World War II, they took their places dealing and the tradition stuck.

I checked the exits and the dice color and sizes and left to meet the crew at the Golden Casino where Bus people from the Bay Area had packed the casino. Bell was excited to tell me he nailed a twenty-one dealer cheating. He led me to the game where I spied on the dealer. She was a skinny fifty-year old, who joked with the players while she cheated them by peeking at the top card and dealing *seconds*. Bell found another deuce dealer whose seconds were sloppy, but the customers had no clue what was happening. They were betting one or two dollars a hand. I was surprised the dealers cheated for such small stakes. Mills said they were probably making an extra $20 a day like snatch game poker dealers made.

The craps tables at Harrah's didn't have sit-down boxmen. Roving bosses would watch the craps games and twenty-one games. Mills and Bell both bet the $200 limit in the field and I switched in the tees for two winning rolls. I brushed them out so the boss wouldn't get a free look at them—we'd be back.

We moved to another craps pit and made another play. After

dinner, we made two more plays at Harrah's, two at Harold's Club, and left for South Lake Tahoe. Oklahoma Jimmy had told me not to play at the North Shore of Tahoe because the casinos there were *flat*.

South Lake Tahoe was a playground for the San Francisco Bay Area. The main casinos were Harrah's-Tahoe, the Sahara-Tahoe, and Harvey's. We split up for one hour to check the casinos exits and would meet at the State Line Bar.

We made several plays at each casino and stopped at Harvey's Casino lounge to unwind before we left for Vegas. It was 1965, and go-go girls were on stage doing their bump-and-grind in their flapper-like costumes. The small dance floor below the stage was crowded with intoxicated dancers where Mills and Bell had met two girls and they weren't leaving anytime soon. I said I'd be at Harrah's and would meet them later.

I found a craps game with no boxman and left to get my tees. When I returned, there was one player on the game and no boss in sight. I felt frisky and switched in my four-five-sixes and bet $200 in the field. I won my bet as Mills appeared on the game with a big grin. I lit a cigarette and he put $200 in the field. After two winning rolls, I pulled my cigarette and shot a spill-shot—all four dice flew out of my hand. I hurried out of the casino and crossed the state line just 20 yards away. I scrambled behind some motels then made it to the car and waited. Mills arrived and said he sent Bell to Harrah's to check if it was *Tom*. Bell arrived and said there was no commotion in the craps pit and we left for Vegas.

Back in Vegas at the Hacienda Casino, a boxman picked up my tees. I quickly turned to leave but hesitated as Bell called out for a cocktail waitress. The boxman looked at the logo on one tee and set both tees down. Bell and Mills looked at me and we laughed. I left the tees in for two more rolls and we left for the Tropicana.

A boxman at the Tropicana saw my tees in the table mirror and grabbed them. Clint and I got away, but Mills was stopped by a boss and a security guard and asked for his ID. The shift boss accused him of betting on the tees, that he denied. There was no proof so he was warned not to play there again and let go. We met and decided to wait a while to see if anything was said on the grapevine. Two days later, Bell phoned me and asked me to meet him at Mill's house.

Mill's face was red and swollen, and he had two black eyes, but he smiled as usual. He had gone back to the Tropicana to play 21 with his girlfriend. Two security guards dragged him from the table to the back room where a boss read him the trespass act. The two guards worked him over and threw him into the back parking lot. He was OK, but he wanted to pull up for a while. Bell said they never lost a bet in any casino, their faces were familiar to the casino employees, and he wanted to pull up. I agreed with them. We had had a good run and made over $12,000 each in ten exciting weeks.

I didn't spend much time wondering what I'd do next. A friend named Don Jordon who I had worked with at the Lucky met me and wanted to do some business. He was dealing 21 at the El Dorado Club in Henderson and wanted to make some money before he moved to LA. I suggested that I switch in a cooler, bet it myself, and we would split the take. He agreed and I said I'd be in on Friday night.

I had been on several cooler plays, including dealing-off a few as a dealer at the Lucky Casino. I had never put one in, but I did know how it worked—when nobody is looking you switch decks; if nobody sees it, it didn't happen.

Henderson was a small town outside Vegas. A factory there processed titanium and employed many of the town's residents who went to the El Dorado Club to eat, drink, and gamble away their paychecks.

I drove to the casino on day shift and asked a boss for several decks of souvenir cards. Besides matching the color and serial number on Don's cards, I would match the wear of the cards I would switch. Before I left town, I drove into a mobile home park to familiarize myself with the area in case I needed a cover story.

I set up the cold deck similar to the one that Jimmy put in at the Lucky, except I would lose the last hand so the boss wouldn't think he witnessed a cooler play.

At home, I practiced the switch in front of a mirror. I used the technique that George had used by inserting a pack of matches to divide the break in the deck where I would put my forefinger before I cut the deck. I put a rubber band around the deck to keep it intact.

I waited near the entrance of the casino as two couples approached. I greeted them, walked in with them, and talked all the while. I wanted to give the impression that I was with them rather than stand out by walking in alone. I quickly got lost in the slot machines.

After I checked the color, the wear, and the serial number on Don's cards, I stopped at the bar and ordered a double Scotch on the rocks. I told the bartender that I lived in Henderson and worked as a chemical engineer at the titanium plant. I downed my drink and ordered another to give the impression that I was a lush. I poured the drink on the floor and ordered another double. I left a $3 tip so he'd remember me. I noticed Don's game was dead on my way to the bathroom where I replaced the scotch with water.

I had Don's cards matched up, and staggered up to his game with my half-filled glass of water and sat down. I scanned my front and reached into my jacket for the cooler. I removed the rubber band

and put my forefinger in the break that divided the deck and I let the matches drop to the floor. Don shuffled and checked my back. I whispered, "OK, *George.*" He set his deck down and I scooped it up, set my cooler down, and cut it into two halves. I put the casino cards in my pocket and stood up.

I bet $100 and Don called out, "Money plays." I won the hand and spread out to two hands. Don asked for blackjack insurance with his ace up and I insured both hands. When he turned over a blackjack, I turned over a 20 and my blackjack. The boss seemed happy Don had a blackjack even though I won my insured blackjack bet. I ordered a double Scotch from the waitress and won several more $200 limit hands before losing a hand. I counted my chips while Don shuffled. I was $1,000 ahead and played on the square until I lost a hand. I gave the waitress two $5 chips and said, "Give one of these to the bartender and bring me another double, please." When I lost a hand, I gave Don a $25 tip and left for the dead two-man craps table.

I bet $100 on the pass line and $100 in the field and made a bet for the inexperienced dealers. The boss watched thinking I'd blow my winnings back by making field bets. After I lost a bet, I headed toward the men's room, but left out the back door to hide the casino cards and to get my four-five-six tees.

When I arrived at the craps table, I bet $100 on the pass line and $100 in the field as before. I switched in the tees and rolled an eleven for a field and pass line winner. I let both bets ride and rolled a nine for another field winner as the boss approached the game. I felt like I owned him and the two dealers. My adrenalin was high and an idea came to me. I let the $200 go in the field, and when the stickman passed me my tees, I set an additional $25 chip in the field and said, "This is for the dealers." I handed the tees to the boss and said, "Sir, why don't you roll them for us." The bewildered boss rolled twelve for a two-to-one payoff in the field. I scooped up the $600 and dealer's tips and handed them to the boss to distract him. He put the tips in a dealer's shirt pocket as the stickman pushed me the tees. I swapped the square dice back in and eventually rolled a seven and cashed-in. The boss seemed in shock. Handing him the tees to shoot was the crowning achievement in my career, although a future bold move beating 21 games would match it.

I had advanced from a rookie to a journeyman dice mechanic in just over a year. When I set up on a game, I was on automatic pilot and never hesitated to switch dice when it was my turn to roll. It is a mystery to me now how easy it was for me to get over on the crooked casinos, and I wondered where my aggressiveness or what-ever it was came from. It came uncalled and seemed normal to me.

Don said the bartender told the boss I was a drunk and worked as an engineer at the titanium plant. The boss told Don I got lucky and would be back again. We split over $900 each.

I visited the Captain to tell him about my adventures, including what happened to Mills. I said I was thinking of going back to Jer-sey and he said he planned to drive home for Christmas. We made a plan to leave together as we had before. I showed him my dice switch and the tees, and asked him if he would like to go out with me to bet them. He said he would and suggested we invite Carlo who had worked with us at the Lucky.

At the Desert Inn, my new partners made their bets and waited as I switched the casino dice out for my tees. I rolled an eleven and as they picked up their winning bets, they smiled at me that same smile I had seen from past partners surprised that the dice could be switched on professional dealers and bosses so easily. I rolled another eleven and removed my cigarette and the tees. My partners picked up their bets and watched with me as I rolled another eleven with the square dice. The boxman looked at the stickman and waved his hand in a circular motion for him to roll the dice over with his stick to check for tees as I brushed out Cap and Carlo.

At our meeting place, my partners said everything at the game was Jake. I thanked them and told them I had shot three consecutive twelves before and they shook their heads and laughed. I asked them if they wanted to go out again and we headed out.

After two successful rolls at the Sahara, we packed it in and had a couple of beers. Carlo was twenty-five, Cap was twenty-three, and they thought I was close to their age since I had dealt 21with them at the Lucy Casino. I was nineteen and hadn't revealed my true age to anyone, not even to Cap, who I considered my best friend. It was a self-preservation habit I picked up when I arrived in Vegas.

They both liked betting the tees and we hit every Strip casino for several weeks with a few close calls. At the Flamingo, a stickman rolled the tees over and I tossed two chips at him and said, "Eleven for the dealers and me." My partners did likewise and the stickman grabbed the chips by force of habit and placed them on eleven saying, "Thank you sirs." I reached out to show him that I was anxious to shoot and he pushed the tees to me. I switched in the fronts and finished my roll. At the meet, we agreed that the stickman saw the tees subconsciously, but the bets we tossed at him disrupted his thinking.

At the Tropicana, I switched in a pair of tangerine-colored tees that I realized were too light-colored when they left my hand. I threw some proposition bets to the stickman that he placed, then passed me the dice. I swapped them out and the stickman said to his boxman, "Those last two were a little light." The boxman didn't want to hear it and told the stickman, "Move the dice."

A floorman at the Desert Inn saw my tees in the table mirror. I left before he realized I was gone. Cap and Carlo said he squeezed the tees in his fist and looked angry, and that one of the regular customers called to him by name and asked why he took the dice off the game just when he was winning. He answered, "Some kid just shot these tees to see if you were awake." It was the first time someone described me correctly.

One week later at the Sands, one of my tees bounced off the table as I hurried away. At the meet, Carlo and Cap laughed saying the customers kept yelling, "Same dice! Same dice! Same dice!" as a cocktail waitress picked up the tee and handed it to the boxman. He discovered it right away and yelled back at the players, "We can't use the same dice!" and he called to the boss. The boss asked him and the stickman to describe me and they said they hadn't noticed me.

The next day, Cap and I met at the Fremont Casino bar. Mills' friends, Chuck McGilery and Gentleman Jim approached us and said that the Sands had some people out looking for whoever shot tees in their joint. A hi-roller there won over $30,000 just before our tee play and the mob owners were mad.

Cap suggested we leave town the next day. I said goodbye to some friends and gave my car to McGilery. Bill Douglas showed me some card tricks and strategies that he used playing cards. He said, "Bobby, if you master these moves, you'll never have to work again." Then he said, "When I play someone, I feel him out slowly to see what he will ride. First I play the *bend* on him, then the *light,* and if he rides that I'll pull *strippers* or *hand muck* on him." I said goodbye and to tell George I left town.

I moved in with my folks and registered for the draft. I soon received my draft notice and reported to Newark for a series of tests.

One week later, I boarded a bus for Fort Jackson, South Carolina, to fill a new basic training company. From there I went to Fort Sam Houston, Texas, then Vietnam.

In Vietnam, I worked as a messenger, a clerk, and base security among other duties in an artillery unit of the First Infantry Division at Phu Loi. That period of my life wasn't the best of all worlds for me or anyone who served there. I was awarded two army commendation medals and two bronze stars, one with a V device for valor that others deserved more than I did. At the time, 1967-68, the 1st Division suffered a lot of casualties and when a lot of people died they gave out a lot of medals. I believe every GI would trade his medals to have those casualties back.

After the army, I bought a car with money I had saved from my combat pay and Vegas days. I passed a GED exam and attended Prince George's Community College in Largo, Maryland, but it didn't pan out for me.

I was twenty-three, and for several months, I partied like most young people at that time, and played and dealt poker in Washington and Alexandria, Virginia.

I got a notion to call Carlo who was living in Reno with his wife and son. He knew of a casino where I could go to work for the summer to do some business. He said the casino was semi-flat and the owner was stealing most of the dealer's tips. I didn't think I would work for a casino again but a new Nevada adventure and dealing craps appealed to me. It was just what I needed to pump up my spirits and bankroll. Carlo said I'd have to get there by Memorial Day Weekend to cinch the job—I left that night.

CHAPTER 6

THE PITCH

The Nevada Lodge was located at North Lake Tahoe's Nevada-California state line. Today it's called the Tahoe Biltmore Lodge and Casino. The owner was a former gangster named Lincoln Fitzgerald who also owned the Nevada Club in Reno. He came to Reno from Detroit where he'd been an associate in the notorious Purple Gang. Three years after he opened the Nevada Club, he was extradited to Michigan to face charges of illegal gambling and bribing public officials. He paid a fine after a conviction for the gambling charges. Three months later, he was maimed in an assassination attempt when he was shot-gunned down in his Reno driveway. I wondered how he and other gangsters like Moe Dalitz, owner of the Desert Inn in Vegas, and Harvey Gross, owner of Harvey's at South Lake Tahoe, obtained gaming licenses. It doesn't say much for Nevada lawmakers where prostitution is also legal. It's not that I have an ax to grind with the state—it has been good to me. It would have been better if "What happened in Nevada, had stayed in Nevada," rather than have legalized gambling throughout the country draining their citizen's resources.

The casino manager at the Lodge was Ed Bates who did all the hiring and enforced Fitzgerald's policy of stealing dealer's tips and not hiring anyone with previous dealing experience or whose name ended in a vowel (Italian). Fitzgerald had put a $15 limit on the dealer's tips at the Lodge and the Nevada Club in Reno, and he took anything over that. After years of the diabolical practice, everyone in Northern Nevada knew about it, but I wondered if anyone tipped off the IRS. And Bates had a 21 mechanic working for him. Years later, Bates would testify at a Reno 21 cheating trial, and when asked if casinos cheated, he answered, "If you're in the gambling business you have to protect your games."

I approached Bates and said I wanted to learn to deal craps. He said to see the slot manager. After several days of making change for slot players, the manager told me to report to the pit boss. The boss handed me a sheet of paper listing the craps payoff odds and describing how to call out the dice from the stickman position. He pointed to a craps table and said to stand there and take instructions from the dealers.

I had never dealt craps, but I knew the game well and could handle chips. The dealers explained the fundamentals and rules to deal the game: the first move was to take the losing bets, then pay the winners, and lastly place the new bets. The stickman said, "Never take your eyes off of the dice so no one can switch them." I had to bite my lip on that one.

I could take chips or cash from a player's hand to book their bets any time prior to the dice settling—the hand-to-hand exchange was the main part of the *pitch* and the reason I was there. The casinos eventually realized they couldn't stop the pitch and required the players to "mail their bets in" by placing them on the *layout*.

I rented a room two miles from the casino in Kings Beach, California. On my day off, I met with Carlo in Carson City, and we drove to his friend Freddy's house where I met my future partners and learned the pitch on Freddy's craps table.

Freddy was forty-years old and married, and had worked at Harrah's in Reno as a boxman. Carlo said he had been falsely accused of stealing there, was fired, blackballed, and became a crossroader.

Carlo acted as a dealer to demonstrate how the pitch worked. Freddy stood at the end of the table close to him acting as a player. Carlo palmed several chips with his left hand from the stack of chips in front of him. The chips were concealed in his hand that looked normal as it hung limp. Freddy held a chip in his right hand lodged between his thumb and forefinger—it stood up like a flag. He reached out as if he were shaking hands with someone and said, "*Hard eight,* please." Carlo's hand reached out in a backhanded motion pressing the short stack of chips into Freddy's palm. Simultaneously, Freddy dropped his chip into Carlo's upturned empty hand who put the chip on the hard eight logo in the center of the table.

It was a simple move. I looked at it several times from different angles and it looked normal with no *leaks.* Carlo said the best time to do it was when the dice were in the air going away from us when all eyes were on them to see what number rolls. I traded places with Carlo and began pitching in slow motion and then speeded up; it was an athletic move. We practiced for one hour and took a break to rehearse the signals and tactics we'd use. I would touch my chin to call Freddy to my game. He'd watch my back and vice-versa. When it was safe to move he would bring his hands together on the table rail. We had signals to standby, to leave and come back, or to go home.

Carlo said Freddy needed to keep a low profile to return to my game throughout the summer. He wouldn't shoot the dice, pick up a die that flew off the table, or do anything to cause an employee to remember him. He'd talk to the other players on the game in order to turn his face away from the employees. Freddy called it, "Giving them the back of your head."

Wesley Reese would be my other agent. He was a rodeo cowboy from Washington state and Freddy's age. He had a pleasant personality, good common sense, and Carlo pointed out his large hands. I pitched small stacks of chips to him in slow motion then increased the speed and number of chips.

After another practice session, we were ready. Freddy and Wesley would alternate working with me from week-to-week throughout the summer. The Lodge had two craps games so they wouldn't always play on the same dice crew.

Freddy was playing a slot machine and I signaled him to my game. He put his hands together to let me know my back was clean as the player beside him picked up the dice to throw. I secured a short stack of $5 chips and when the dice were in the air Freddy reached out with his $1 chip and said, "Hard eight please." Our hands met halfway and I exchanged my chips for his dollar chip that I put on the hard eight before the dice settled. I looked at the players and could see they weren't aware of us. Freddy placed a $1 bet in the field with his left hand as his right hand slipped into an inside jacket pocket where he dropped the chips I pitched him; it was a misdirection move like a magician uses. His hands were together again and I locked up another stack and waited as the stickman pushed the dice to the shooter. When he let the dice go Freddy reached out and said, "Hard six." and we made another exchange.

The beauty of the move was its simplicity and I could pitch as many chips as I thought wouldn't put heat on the game—the bosses and dealers were asleep to the move and we'd leave them that way.

A boss approached the table and stood where a boxman normally sat. The Lodge was one of several Northern Nevada casinos that didn't use full-time boxmen. Freddy reached out with a $1 chip and said, "Hard way six." It was a dry run to test the boss—he watched the dice settle like everyone else. To me most bosses weren't any smarter than the players. On the next roll, Freddy asked for a hard way eight and I pitched him a load and put his bet on the hard eight as the boss turned to follow the dice. A seven rolled and Freddy moved straight to his pocket with the chips as the players groaned. The boss helped to stack the losing chips then walked away to chat with a young 21 dealer.

After several pitches, the two $5 chip bettors on the game left so I pitched Freddy several stacks of the metal dollar coins. He signaled me he would leave and return. He avoided heading directly to the cashier's cage that could mark him as a winner to anyone who looked at him. Cashing chips without taking recognition was an art and Freddy had mastered it. He played the slots as he spied the cashier's cage and then glided to the cashier with the shortest line. He couldn't cash all his chips because the cashier could remember him so when he left the first window, he did a subtle about face and stood in the other line. Before he left the casino, he bought $30 in quarters at a change booth using $5 chips. Whatever chips he didn't cash he'd cash on his return trip to the casino or his wife would cash them. He kept 40 percent of what I pitched him and Carlo got 10 percent. My end was 50 percent that Carlo held until the end of summer.

Freddy came back and I pitched him several more loads before he left for the night. I had no idea how much I had pitched to him.

After one week, we met at Freddy's house for a strategy session with Wesley who would catch me the following week. Carlo told me I had pitched over $1,500 (1969 dollars) in the last six nights—it looked like it could be a good summer.

Wesley stood on my game and his hands were together so I secured a stack of chips. He asked for a hard eight and his large hand was an easy target. He wore jeans with strong, deep pockets, and a windbreaker with extra pockets.

The agents could hardly keep their pants up when I pitched them the iron $1 tokens. They left my game slowly and carefully, fearing a pocket would break and their chips and tokens would splash over the casino floor. After several catches, Wesley left to unload his chips and would return later.

On my night off, I drove to Carson City, to agent for a 21 mechanic named Henry who was a friend of Carlo's. He worked at the Carson City Nugget and was doing business with two bosses there. They were busting out the public and having friends and relatives come in to take off the stolen money. My job was to bet as Henry dealt me winning hands, or busted himself. I kept 25 percent of what I won. It was a unique experience watching Henry setting up hands and dealing seconds in front of the world. When he brushed me out, one of the crooked bosses shook my hand as if he knew me as a regular player there and said, "Good to see you again Mister Johnson, let me buy you lunch." He escorted me to the restaurant and whispered, "That's all for today."

As the summer moved along, the bosses talked about the craps games losing. They must have thought it was a bad run of luck because they spent most of their time watching the 21 games. Ironically, the 21 games were winning because the relief dealer was a mechanic who would relieve a losing dealer to get the casino's money back and more.

I soon realized that Bates was rifling our tips. A high roller had made numerous $25 proposition bets for us that we won. I estimated that each dealer should make at least $50 in tips for the shift. When I picked up my tip envelope at the cashier's cage there was $15 in it. Bates's cashier had stolen most of our tips again for Fitzgerald.

Other shenanigans happened at Tahoe that summer of '69. A crew of crossroaders set up on my game to shoot the sail shot; they made big bets on the hard ten and eleven. The player beside me was shooting a sail shot that enabled one die to stay up on a five. It gave his partners a huge advantage. As the die scooted and spun down the table, his partners distracted the other dealers and the boss who didn't know he was alive. I whispered to the shooter he was putting heat on my game—he never blinked, but quit sliding the dice. When he rolled a seven, he and his crew left.

Oklahoma Jimmy had told me about the sail shot years earlier, and I assumed it was well known and burned up. Apparently, it was so old and forgotten that it was new again, outliving the older generation of bosses. Years later, two men were arrested for shooting the sail at the Wynn Casino in Vegas. Steve Wynn, the owner, claimed they won over $700,000 during an eight-month period as reported in the Las Vegas *Review Journal* on October 10, 2011.

While on a dead game, the shift boss told me and the other dealers that someone had cheated a 21 game at the North Shore Club for $3,000 the night before. The casino found extra face cards and missing small cards in the dealing shoe after the players left the casino. He said they knew that one of the crossroaders was "Freddy the Filipino." I laughed to myself because I knew whom he was talking about and his name was Filipino Freddy. I'd find out that it wasn't Freddy after all, but another Filipino-Mexican crossroader named Bobby Anrino.

A boss finally convinced Bates that someone was using crooked dice. Next night the dice were multi-colored; it was an omen to pull-up. My summer would end after Labor Day Weekend, in one week.

I left for Reno to pick up my money from Carlo who handed me an envelope with over $10,000. He opened a bottle of champagne and we drank a toast to Bates and Fitzgerald—it had been a good summer.

I stopped in Vegas before heading to Jersey. My old dice partner Clint Bell was going to Houston to make a "peek score" and he invited me to go with him. I volunteered to take my car and we left the next day.

Bell told me about the peek store in Texas and other stories to break up the trip. He had a partner in Houston who would steer high rollers to play gin rummy with him under a peek. His partner had rented two upscale apartments, one above the other, and had them furnished with classy furniture. Bell chiseled out a foot-wide diameter hole in the floor of the top apartment and cut out a hole in the ceiling of the bottom apartment. He covered the ceiling hole with an air-conditioner vent that he could see through to peek at players' cards below. He would signal his partner electronically using a *stinger*. Bell said he'd been hustling top-notch chess and backgammon players in Vegas. He put a peek in a popular nightclub where expert chess and backgammon players hung out and gambled. Bell matched them up with his agents who were known weaker players. He used a former U.S. Chess Champion and a backgammon expert in the peek to electronically signal Bell's agents what moves to make.

In Houston, I looked through the peek with opera glasses at a gin rummy hand that Bell's partner held. He sat at a large round table under the peek. Bell and his partner practiced using the stinger as I watched. He would signal his partner what card to throw or not throw. It was like a scene in the James Bond movie, "Goldfinger."

Bell showed me a special telescope that enabled him to see an ink that was invisible to the naked eye. A friend of Douglas called "The Mad Professor," had made it for Douglas to beat 21 games. Douglas had a friend who worked in the eye at a Strip casino who would smuggle it up to the eye to use it to read marked cards on a twenty-one game below. He would use a stinger to signal Douglas' agents what card was coming off the top of the deck. They were looking for a way to smuggle the marked cards onto the casino floor to complete the caper. Meanwhile, Douglas loaned it to Bell.

It was a Starlight Scope; a night-vision telescope like one I had used in Vietnam. Apparently, someone had stolen it from an Army base and filed-off the serial numbers and "Property of U.S. Army."

Bell dipped a Q-tip into a bottle of liquid solution and painted a figure eight on the back of a card. The mark was invisible, but when I viewed it through the scope, I could see the figure eight in bold black. He said he'd use it in the peek for poker games. It all seemed like it would work but I wasn't interested to stay there to find out. It was a long drive to New Jersey and I was anxious to get home.

I had been home for one month when Bell phoned to ask me to fly to Sacramento. A bookmaker there had beaten Jack Prince, a friend of Bill Douglas, out of $20,000 playing gin. Douglas wanted to beat the bookie before other hustlers around the country heard about him. He had a friend in Sacramento who owned a poker club where the bookie played.

Bell picked me up at the airport and we headed to the poker club to meet Douglas and his friend, Charley.

Charley said that Jose, the guy who beat Prince, was a successful bookmaker and bar owner in Sacramento. He played cards and bar dice games for high stakes and I was there in case Douglas needed me. He said the bookmaker shot dice out of a cup and used the *dump shot,* to control one die. He gave me a pair of drug store dice that Jose played with. I told them I could get some magnetic dice and tees made to match them. I phoned Tex at his store in San Francisco to tell him what I needed.

Charley said Jose had used marked cards to beat Prince who was a champion gin player and had played location on Jose by false shuffling groups of cards. But he couldn't overcome Jose's advantage and luck. Douglas said he would play him any card game and would use the *light,* hand muck, and make *strippers* while playing, or whatever it took to beat him. Strippers were specific cards sanded, cut, or shaved on the sides and were located by feel, pulled to the top of a deck during a shuffle, and manipulated to beat an opponent.

Clint told me that Douglas had beaten a champion gin player a year earlier. The player had won the top prize of $99,999 at the annual gin rummy tournament at the Sahara in Vegas. He was from Knoxville, Tennessee, and his bookie there knew Douglas and told him that the gin champion was going to the Bahamas for a vacation. The bookie told Douglas the flight itinerary and Douglas "coincidentally" sat beside him on the plane trip to the Bahamas. The player "hustled" Douglas to play gin with him on the plane and later at his hotel room where Douglas busted him for the cash that he'd brought with him.

I drove to San Francisco to meet the man who would make the baloney dice. Oklahoma Jimmy had given me his name and phone number. He had a thriving business making gambling equipment for casinos worldwide and a variety of rigged devices for owners of illegal gambling joints, carneys, charity fund-raisers, and crossroaders.

I gave Tex the drug store dice to match up with tees and magnetic dice. He said he had the tees and had blank dice to make the magnetic dice that he would drill, plug with magnetic discs, and paint; it would take him two hours. He showed me several ceramic bar magnets to use with the dice. He said many hustlers had been buying the magnets and dice on their way to Alaska that was booming because of the new oil pipeline. He was giving me a tour of his shop when a priest walked in and he asked me to go outside for a cigarette. When the priest left, Tex said he had made him some crooked bingo equipment.

I drove to Fisherman's Wharf while Tex made the dice. When I returned, he demonstrated how to use them. He secured a ceramic magnet to his arm with an Ace bandage and said to wear a baggy-sleeved jacket to conceal it. He shook the dice in a dice cup and turned it over next to his arm. He moved it away from his arm before he exposed the five dice—all sixes. He said before lifting the cup I needed to slide it away from my arm or the dice would cling to the magnet. He said I didn't need to use all five dice to win the money, two or three was strong enough, and he gave me some matching *fronts*. He said, "If you play on a table, strap the magnet to your leg and lift it up close to the bottom of the tabletop and dump the dice over it to bring up the sixes, but lower your leg before lifting the cup. If I wanted to roll aces reverse the magnet to reverse the polarity."

He invited me to share a pint of whiskey and we shared stories about other crossroaders we knew. Tex was born in Dallas in 1900, and had been a crossroader all of his adult life before he squared-up and went into business. He said that crossroading had been good before movies and television woke everybody up to what was happening. He said, "I settled in California because the laws are so liberal here. The liberal politicians and judges are descendants of the original settlers, most of whom had been runaway convicts and criminals from other states and territories." He said he visited Reno periodically with his wife who liked to play the slots and eat at the grand buffets. He played the *bend* on 21 games to pay for the trip. He said, "The new generation of casino bosses didn't know they were alive and if they died they wouldn't realize anything had happened." I asked him where the term crossroader originated and he said, "When crossroaders beat a game they met at the first "crossroad" and headed back in the opposite direction from where they left in case someone called the sheriff."

When I got back to Sacramento, other hustlers had arrived. Bobby Anrino, a hand mucker, had flown in from Phoenix, and Ken Lundy, a poker world-beater, had driven up from Vegas.

Douglas was set to meet Jose at Charley's club later that night. I demonstrated to him how the magnetically charged dice and magnet worked. Bell told me Charley would put Tex's dice in his dice cup and for me to wait with the tees by the phone in my motel room next to Charley's club.

Bell woke me in the morning and gave me my expenses and $1,000 for the dice play. He said that Douglas had beaten Jose playing gin and Jose quit and suggested they play bar dice. He lost $5,000 and melted down the dice to find the magnetic discs and the play was over.

Anrino and Lundy were going to Lake Tahoe to hustle the casinos there and he invited us to go. Bell and I would go and Douglas went back to Vegas. It was the last time I saw him. He was shot dead three years later in a poker game in Tennessee, trying to stop three stickup men heisting the game.

On the way to the Lake, I mentioned that I had dealt craps at the North Shore the previous summer. Anrino said that he and a partner had beaten the North Shore Club there out of $3,000. I told him a boss at the Lodge had told me about it and that Filipino Freddy took the heat for it. He laughed and said Freddy was his uncle and he'd tell him. He said, "The North Shore Club had dealt 21 *face down* out of a shoe and Jess Pierson and me had palmed out most of the fours and fives and replaced them with face cards. It gave us a huge advantage and we passed our winnings off to our wives to cash in as we played. When the boss brought new cards to the game, we left."

Anrino would shoot the sail at Harrah's Tahoe and he explained what he wanted us to do. He'd stand beside the stickman and slide one of the dice. The other die would bounce alongside of the sliding die and hit the end of the table to come up random. The sliding die would be a six. Betting the field, the eleven, and twelve, would give us a big advantage. An ace or deuce on the random die would be a loser in the field; any other number would be a field winner and Harrah's paid triple odds in the field for twelve and 30-to-1 odds to bet it straight up; the eleven payed 15-to-1 odds. Anrino would lay his hand on the *layout* to let us know when he was sliding a die. We'd make our bets at the last second to surprise the help. Lundy and Bell would each bet $200 in the field and I'd bet a $25 chip on eleven and twelve and lean out to block the stickman from seeing the sliding die. Anrino would try to get more than one shot. After the play, we'd meet at the Stateline Bar across the state line.

Anrino set up on a game next to the stickman's right side. There were several players and no boxman. He laid his hand on the layout and we were poised to make our last minute bets. He held the die he was sliding in the base of his pinky and spun it along the surface in a whipping motion as he opened his hand and released both dice. The sliding die looked like a sailboat gliding down the layout while the random die bounced off the end stopping on four for a field winning ten. It was a simple and effective move. Anrino brushed us out just as a boss walked up.

He wanted to go back to Harrah's to play 21. He'd steal a card while playing to use it for several hands. He would be playing with three cards to the dealer's two cards. He schooled us what to do; I'd sit on his left and play two hands and wouldn't hit a hand that would go over 21 so that the dealer wouldn't take my cards. He said, "I might need to clean up the held-out card in one of your two hands." Bell would stand behind us as a blocker and lookout, while Lundy would play in the last seat to distract the dealer or a boss.

Anrino pranced through the casino like a lion prowling for prey with its cubs following. He found a dealer he liked and broke two twenties for chips after we took our seats. He bet $20 and *scratched* his cards on the table for two *hit cards*. He said to the dealer, "I'm good," as he appeared to put his two dealt cards under his bet. He had tucked only one of his cards under his bet, palmed the other one, and put it behind his knee. When the dealer busted her hand, Anrino picked up the one tucked card and laid it over the two hit cards as if that helped him figure what he had. All the while, Lundy distracted the dealer.

Anrino added $20 to the $40 in his bet circle as the dealer dealt out a new hand. He tucked one of his dealt cards under his bet as before and palmed the other card. He reached under the table with the new held out card to exchange it for the ten behind his knee. A boss walked up to the game just as he put the ten under his bet to improve his hand to twenty. His moves were bold, smooth, and unexpected.

Two hands later, Anrino palmed the ace he had behind his knee and waited for the next hand to begin. As the dealer dealt the new hand, Anrino picked up his cards, brought both hands together for an instant, and turned over a blackjack. He had exchanged one of the dealt cards for his ace. It was obvious to me what he'd done but when I glanced at the boss, she never changed her expression.

Another boss came up to watch as Anrino bet the $200 limit. He scratched for two hit cards and put his two dealt cards under his bet. He reached behind his knee to fetch the held out card that he had switched for his ace on the previous hand. Lundy asked the new boss if he could find him a pack of matches as Anrino slid the held out card under his two tucked cards simultaneously turning them over. He mixed up the five cards and asked the boss if he'd busted. She added up his five cards and told him he had twenty-one. She wished him luck as he picked up his winnings and left.

I waited on the game to hear if anyone said something and to give the eye-in-the-sky a chance to come down if he saw something suspicious.

I was impressed with Anrino's boldness and his "one-handed" palm move that he did in front of the world. I thought of it as a million dollar move and if I could learn to do it, it could be like shooting tees again, where I could play when and where I wanted, and choose the partners I liked.

Anrino split the money—50 percent for himself and 50 percent for Lundy, Clint, and me to split. I would find that some mechanics kept the majority of any money won, and some split their winnings evenly. I had learned the latter way is best because it promotes loyalty, friendship, and a better job performance; and everyone involved in a play has equal legal jeopardy.

Anrino said he had *heat* in the other casinos at Lake Tahoe but he could play in Reno. At Harrah's, he let his scoot shot go on his first roll and the random die came up a three for a field winner. He left his hand on the layout and we won again. We hit another *pit* for two rolls and left. Anrino said Harrah's was the softest casino in the state but they prosecuted to the hilt when they caught crossroaders.

At the Primadonna Casino, we set up on a crusty old boxman. When Anrino let his shot go, Bell bet $200 in the field and said, "It all goes," but the boxman didn't turn and he saw one die sail by. He called out, "No roll!" and jumped up. Anrino bolted and I picked up my money and said, "What kind of place is this?" as I hurried away from the game and out the door. The boxman left the game to tell the floorman as Bell and Lundy left.

On the drive to Vegas, Anrino told me he found the one-handed palm move in a book written by a magician named Walter Gibson and he got the idea to use it for 21. He'd previously used a two-handed palm move called the *chop* to steal a card.

We got down for one sail shot at the Las Vegas Club and met at the Mint Casino. Anrino slid a winning shot down the layout but the boxman refused to pay me saying that my bet was late. The dealer had called out "Bet," when I set my money in the field but he denied he said it. I shouted, "The dealer is wrong!" as I looked at the players on my end for support. Two of them said the dealer acknowledged my bet and I was paid.

At the Fremont Casino, Anrino slid a winner down the layout and the boxman called a boss over to the game to verify where the $100 chips had gone. The boss was suspicious and had his antennae up. Another boss called to him and he turned his head as Anrino slid another shot down Broadway. The shot hit a chip and flopped over onto the ace. The random die also landed on an ace. The suspicious boss watched as the dealers paid us double in the field for the two aces. He knew no one would slide an ace and bet the field, so his suspicions turned to confusion as we left.

We found out there had been heat in the Fremont craps pit because of a recent incident. A drunken field bettor got winner there over $4,000. A woman came up, stood beside him, and held his arm. She told the boss that she was his wife and she asked him for two racks to put her husband's chips in. She walked away with the drunk toward the cashier. Later, a boss saw the drunken player asleep in the Keno lounge and asked where his wife was—he said he didn't have a wife.

Anrino left town and I flew home to Jersey. I found a bookstore and ordered the Walter Gibson magician book to find the one-handed palm move Anrino had used.

After Christmas, Carlo called from Reno and said he wanted me to shoot some tees on his craps game at Harold's Club on New Year's Eve. I phoned Tex to make up the tees I'd need. He would send them to Reno on a Greyhound bus.

Carlo and I went out for some drinks and sat down on a 21 game at the Palace Club. I had practiced the one-handed palm move and felt brave enough to try it. I'd palm one of my cards and exchange it for one of Carlo's cards. He'd seen me practice at his house and knew what to expect. The palmed card was a seven that I would exchange for one of Carlo's big cards. As the dealer hit her hand I slid my card under Carlo's cards and asked, "What do you have?" as I dropped my seven and palmed his face card. I was surprised how easy it was.

On the way home, we made a plan for New Year's Eve. I'd shoot four-five-six tees, and my old pitching partner Wesley would bet them as well as Henry, the 21 mechanic from the Carson City Nugget.

When Carlo was on the stick, we set up on his game. After two winning rolls, an older dealer on the game saw my tees in the table mirror and grabbed them. I left before he had time to look up at me. Henry and Wesley left too. I told them I'd wait for Carlo at his house. I felt so low and hoped Carlo didn't come under suspicion. I picked up a pack of cigarettes and a six-pack of beer at the 7-11 for the long wait. I was surprised the dealer discovered my tees. I had shot tees hundreds of times before and no dealers had ever nailed them. I thought maybe he had worked in a flat casino before and sensed what was happening after Wesley's and Henry's sudden big bets.

Carlo told me that he told the boss that it happened so fast that he didn't get a good look at me and it ended there. I was relieved and told him I needed a break and was going to Europe.

I bought a six-week Eurailpass that was good for unlimited first-class travel by train in seventeen European countries. I wanted to learn to ski in Innsbruck, Austria, and to visit the main European cities.

After landing in Luxembourg, I travelled by train to Innsbruck. The train stopped in the center of town where I checked-in to a hotel. I would find that in most European cities the main train station was in the middle of town with a variety of hotels to choose from within walking distance. The European train systems were efficient, with reliable schedules, and were comfortable. It was early spring, 1970, so the trains weren't crowded and sometimes I had a first-class compartment to myself.

In Innsbruck, I was fortunate to draw a nineteen-year-old ski instructor who had been a member of the Austrian national ski team. After a two-hour lesson, I felt ready to ski at Lake Tahoe the next winter.

After Innsbruck, I stayed a few days in Salzburg, Austria, to do some sightseeing then left to Venna to the city's main attractions by foot or guided bus tours. The tours were available in all the main European cities and were a great way to relax—the purpose of my trip. I avoided newsstands or conversations with Americans.

After Vienna, I travelled on an overnight sleeper train to Rome and Naples, then to Palermo, Sicily, for some warmer weather. After Sicily, I travelled up the western coast of Italy where I stopped at a few places for a day of sightseeing, and then on to the French Riviera. The Casino de Monte-Carlo was impressive in style and formalities. It was quiet and formal like the Vegas Strip casinos were in the early 60's. The main games were roulette and Baccarat. There was an "American Room" where they spread several 21 games and a craps game as well as roulette and Baccarat. The craps dealers were typical of Nevada dealers as far as not watching the dice closely.

Paris was my next venture with many sights to see like Rome, but I missed communicating in English and looked forward to London.

I crossed the English Channel on a train ferry. The train slowly drove onto the ferry in Calais, France, and drove off in England to continue on to London.

I felt more at home in London and stayed there ten days. I was twenty-four years old, and after some sightseeing, I was feeling my age and looked for some company. I met a girl at a nightclub who had worked as a nurse in San Francisco and loved Americans. We shared several days and nights together and did some sightseeing. Eventually, I visited the casinos.

To get into any of the several London casinos, a person had to become a member by filling out an application and paying a nominal fee. I joined the Curzon Club Casino and waited the required twenty-four hours before I could enter.

The casino spread roulette, 21, and Baccarat games like at Monte Carlo. While touring the casino, I noticed someone following me and I couldn't imagine why. I played some 21 and roulette and the man continued to observe me. Eventually, I saw him talk to a boss and felt sure he was an *outside-man* so I left the casino and watched my back for a while.

The attention I picked up puzzled me. Years later, a crossroader named Florida John, would inform me that some of the London casinos had subscribed to the Las Vegas Detective Agency, which became the *Griffin Detective Agency.* The agency gave the subscribing casinos a book with pictures, histories, and mug shots of known crossroaders. I was in the book thanks to my old partner Bell. He became a police informant after being arrested in a drug bust, and finked on everyone he knew that did business.

After visiting Holland, Denmark, and Sweden, I finished my trip visiting Berlin then headed back to Luxembourg to fly home. It was a relaxing vacation, and a bonus to visit a few of the casinos there. At the time, I thought there was no future for me in Europe.

CHAPTER 7

THE THREE MUSKETEERS

My father met me at the airport and invited me to live at home. My brothers were working and living on their own and I had no plans so I decided to stay awhile. I dated a girl from Bayonne who had grown up there with her parents and two siblings. Karen and I spent all of our free time together and when she became pregnant, we were married and had a baby girl, Sierra Ann.

I applied to the Local 3 Electricians Union and passed all the tests and interviews, but I needed a waiver since I had passed the 25-year-old age limit by several months. I commuted to Manhattan to attend apprenticeship school for several days until the teacher told me that the union executive board turned down my waiver. My father was hurt but I told him it might turn out to be a blessing in disguise. I got a temporary job dealing poker in Union City.

When Sierras was a year old, we moved to Reno where we rented a house. I called Carlo who said, "Bobby, there's a ton of business going on in Northern Nevada. Henry still dealt 21 in Carson City and needed agents and I know a craps dealer at the Mapes Casino who needs an agent to pitch to." It was 1974, and the casinos wouldn't wake up to the pitch for several more years. The dealer's nickname was Rabbit and Carlo had done business with him when they dealt craps together in Las Vegas.

Rabbit was ten years older than I was and had to do business because he had a bad gambling habit like many dealers. He told me, "I can't pitch you much Bobby because everybody at the Mapes is stealing. Sometimes more agents are in the casino than customers."

Rabbit pitched me $130 and it was obvious he had a lot of dealing experience and was aware of everyone in sight. Not only did he pitch to me, I saw him palm a $25 chip and slide it into his waistband. Carlo would cash in Rabbit's stolen chips for the standard 10 percent commission. As I set my $5 chips in front of a cashier, she pulled them toward her to count and paid me $125—she had palmed one of my chips—Rabbit was right, everybody at the Mapes was stealing.

I continued to catch Rabbit on weekends and made several trips to Carson City to agent for Henry. On one trip there, a boss whispered to me to meet him in the bathroom. He said, "Henry told me you can switch dice and if you want, you can take off some money right now. A sucker just lost $1,200 and we want to win $1,000 of it. The stickman will be in on the play." I said, "I'd love to," and he handed me a pair of four-five-six tees and said, "After the play, meet Henry on his break."

I headed straight to the craps game and bet the $200 limit in the field. After several rolls, I won $1,000 and cashed-in. I met Henry on his break and gave him the money. He said the boss would like to meet me and we made a plan to meet when Henry was off work.

The boss' name was Glen Graystone who Larry Doss had referred to as "The King of Crossroaders" on our trip to Puerto Rico. I wondered how he could he be working in the biggest casino in the state capital; just another Nevada anomaly, I thought. Henry introduced me to Graystone who asked me if I wanted to do some future craps business. I said, "Sure," and gave him my phone number. I said, "Glen, I was on a trip with Larry Doss and Oklahoma Jimmy and Larry told Jimmy that you had been caught switching dice in Macau, had escaped jail and was caught and beheaded on the spot." He laughed and said, "I had heard that rumor too when I got back to Nevada. I was arrested in Macau, and lost over one-hundred pounds in jail. A lawyer from Vegas named Mike Hanz eventually flew there and sprung me." Glen invited me to come back to play with Henry anytime I passed through town. Three bosses and a craps dealer at the Nugget now knew my face that I wrote off as an occupational hazard and hoped it wouldn't come back to bite me someday.

While on a "two-man" craps game at the Mapes waiting for Rabbit to come off his break, I noticed a $25 chip on eleven and an eleven had rolled. My first thought was the man who made the bet had *past-posted* the game, meaning he bet after the eleven had rolled, and maybe a dealer was in on the play. The man stood in front of the proposition bets where an outside stickman normally stands. One of the dealers paid him $375 and the bettor left after one more roll. I realized I learned a new trick: I could past-post two-man games that didn't have a boxman. I would bet the two aces, two sixes, ace-deuce, or eleven. It was a matter of placing a chip on the winning proposition bet after it rolled. I would bet a $5 chip, which drew less attention. Harrah's would be an ideal place to play because they had plenty of two-man games and the customer was always right there in case of a beef.

After catching Rabbit, I left for Harrah's. I checked the exits and bought twelve $5 chips at a 21 game to bring to the craps game. I pretended to be a beginner as I fumbled with my chips and bet the field. When the dealer on my left collected the dice with the stick, I'd have a split second to make a late bet. The dice had to be thrown toward him, and the dealer on my right had to be distracted making change or moving bets around.

The shooter picked up the dice to roll and a player next to him asked the dealer for change. The shooter rolled an eleven and my hand struck out like a rattlesnake dropping a $5 chip on eleven. I said, "I hit it!" and pointed to the fifteen-to-one proposition bet. The dealer payed the pass line bets and pushed me $75. Both dealers went about their business and I left after the next roll.

The next day at Harrah's, I picked a game with a young girl on the stick. The shooter set down $12 and asked his dealer to place the six and eight. He rolled two aces and I swiftly placed a $5 chip on the aces. I saw the stickgirl look back to see my bet. I shouted, "All right!" The dealer on my right said, "We can't pay that bet Sir, it was late." I shot back, "I bet before the dice landed." The stickgirl said I had bet on time and the bluffing dealer gave me $150. After another roll, I left.

I past-posted Harrah's and two other casinos several times for several weeks then took some heat. A dealer at Harrah's saw me bet late and said, "No bet on that!" I tried to look dumb but he said "You tried to past-post me!" as he turned around and called to a boss. I picked up my bet and said, "BS, what kind of place is this." I glided through a maze of slots and headed to my car. I would have to retire the move for a while.

Rabbit knew a boss at Fitzgerald's Casino who wanted to do some business. Lincoln Fitzgerald, my old patron from the Nevada Lodge owned the newly opened casino bearing his name. I thought of Anrino's million-dollar move and I told Rabbit I could *hold out* on 21 if he could distract the dealer for me.

I set up a mirror at home to brush-up on the one-handed palm and technique I would use. I would explain to Rabbit the next day what he could do to help me.

We met with the boss and I explained what I could do. He suggested we come in on Monday night when no one would be in the eye. He said to win about $900.

We entered the casino through different doors and looked for a trap. The casino was half-busy and the 21 games were half-full. I found a rookie dealer with three players on her game. Rabbit played two hands beside me and chatted with the dealer and players to distract them. I bought in for $200 and bet $20. I was dealt a ten and a deuce and scratched my cards for a hit, then another, and said, "I'm good," as I palmed the ten while sliding the deuce under my bet. The dealer looked past me to Rabbit who scratched for a hit. When the dealer busted her hand, I turned up the deuce under my bet, mixed it in with my two hit cards, and placed the held out ten behind my knee. My leg quivered so I pinched and squeezed it but nothing worked. Above the table, I was calm so I ignored it. I felt like a duck that glides calmly on a pond, but with its feet moving violently under the surface.

I increased my bet to $100 and was dealt a ten and a seven. With my right hand, I palmed the seven as I tucked the ten under my bet and said, "I'm good." My hand dropped below the table surface where I exchanged the seven for ten held behind my right knee as I checked my back. I waited to see what hand the dealer would make. She made eighteen so I slid the ten under my bet to make twenty. Our boss approached the game and said something to the dealer and she laughed. I bet $200 and got a blackjack on the square. On the next hand, I moved to make a twenty. After two more hands, I was ahead over $900 and I returned the held out card by mixing it in with my hit cards.

I tipped the dealer a $25 chip and left. Rabbit met me at the Eldorado Club and said it was *Jake* and the boss, whose name was Mark, was happy with my work. I told Rabbit we needed a code name for Mark to protect him when we talked about him. I said, "Let's call him *George* since he was so George turning the dealer for us and staying at the game." We chopped the winnings three ways and celebrated with a couple of beers.

After the next play, George escorted me to the cashier and gave me a ticket for a comped meal as an excuse to talk to me. He whispered, "Meet me at the Safeway food store tomorrow at noon."

George said there was a craps dealer on his shift who would do business. I said I could shoot tees on his game and Rabbit could take off the money. He gave me the dealer's phone number and said his name was Wally.

I showed Wally my tees and dice switch and explained that when I had a cigarette in my mouth I'd switch in the four-five-six tees and leave them in until my partner won $1,200. I told him to wrap the stick around the tees so no one could see them in the table mirror, and if a boss reached for them to push them back to me so I could switch the fronts back in.

George was in the craps pit, and the other bosses were watching 21 games. I walked past George and he touched his chin. Rabbit and I set up on Wally's game and I put $2 on the line when he passed me the dice. I scanned the casino and it looked OK so I lit a cigarette. Rabbit made his bets and I made my move. Wally protected the tees with the stick and we finished the play in a few minutes.

Rabbit asked me if I wanted to make a payday at Lake Tahoe. He knew a dealer at the Sahara-Tahoe who invented a new move for *mini-baccarat* and he needed agents to take off some money.

We met the dealer's partner at the Stateline Bar. His name was

Bobby McBride who Rabbit called Mack. He had done business with Rabbit while working at the Golden Nugget in Vegas. Mack explained our part in the play and the game rules. He said, "Baccarat is a mindless game with no decisions made by the players. The dealer uses six decks of cards dealt face up from a dealing shoe. A player could bet on the bank, or the player's hand, and/or a tie. Two cards go to the player's betting box, and two to the bank-betting box. The cards' values determine if a hand needs a hit card. The new move is a mini-cooler consisting of a *slug* of about thirty cards. I'll know in advance the winning hands for the first six hands dealt out of a newly shuffled shoe. When the dealer sets up the slug, it takes a half an hour to finish dealing the rest of the shoe giving me time to compute the winning hands. The casino rules help set up the slug of cards. Dealers pick up the played cards in the order they lie when a hand is over just like 21 dealers do. That way, the dealer can retrieve the cards and display the hands if a customer claims he won his hand. I'll write down the cards played in the first six hands played from a new shoe and will know the order they will be dealt out of the newly shuffled shoe. I'll compute the winning hands and signal you what bets to make from across the pit."

He said the dealer keeps the slug intact by not shuffling it. He puts a crimp (bend) in the first card of the slug to mark the start of it. Rabbit will ask the dealer for change for $200 when the dealer begins to shuffle. After the shuffle, Rabbit will cut the cards at the crimp. Mack said for us to win about $1,600 on the slug, then play on the square until losing a hand. After the play, we would meet back at the Stateline Bar.

Mack signaled us that the dealer had set up the slug. We sat down on the half-full game just as the dealer finished the last hand of the slugged shoe. He set the six-decks of cards in the middle of the table and made four piles to shuffle. Rabbit asked for change and the dealer turned to a boss and said, "Change, $200," as he picked up the 30-card slug and set it in front of him without shuffling it. When the boss arrived, he shuffled the remaining cards and set them on top of the slug. Rabbit cut the cards at the crimp and the boss said, "Go ahead and make change." Making change was a ruse to have the boss at the table to think he witnessed a legitimate shuffle and cut. We won ten hands including four on the square before losing a hand. Our total win was over $2,500. It was a beautiful move and years later would evolve into a more sophisticated move using a laptop computer.

My old pitching partner, Wesley, was working with a *hand mucking* crew and a slot machine gang. He asked me to collect a slot jackpot at a casino in Fallon, a small town an hour's drive from Reno. He said, a partner of his had a key to a slot machine there and he'll line up a $500 jackpot for me to collect.

I arrived at the casino at five p.m., where Wesley and another cowboy were playing slot machines. Two other cowboys stood next to Wesley who said they were his partners and he handed me some quarters to play the machine beside him. One of the men hovered around to distract any onlookers or employees, while we encircled the slot man as he opened my slot machine door. I could hear the reels crank as he turned them to line up three sevens. The jackpot bell rang and the mechanic closed the door and left with the others. I moved in front of the blaring machine acting excited as if I won the jackpot on the square. I called to a change girl and said I think I hit a $500 jackpot but not many quarters fell into the coin tray. She said a boss would come by in a few minutes to pay me the rest. It felt like a long lonely wait, but in just a few minutes a boss showed up, paid me, and handed me a quarter and said to play the machine to erase the jackpot.

At the Safeway parking lot, I jumped into Wesley's car and met his partners. Bill Price was a full-time crossroader and flew his own plane. Kevin was Wesley's brother-in-law, and Freddy-the-Cat was Bill's partner. They were all ex-rodeo cowboys in their mid-forties.

Wesley asked me to collect another $500 jackpot at the Safeway store. We followed Bill and Freddy into the Safeway several minutes apart. Bill brushed us out and said it was no good because a change girl was there. He said, "We'll come back later and I'll put a laxative in her coffee to send her to the bathroom." He was another serious crossroader.

We drove to a drug store where Bill bought what he needed. When we arrived back at the Safeway, the change girl was on a break. We set up on the $500 slot but Bill aborted the play because his key didn't work. He said, "The locks on all his machines must have been changed after my girlfriend picked up two $500 jackpots there in the last two months." Wesley said they'd be in Reno later in the week and he asked me to pick up a jackpot at a Safeway there.

When I claimed the $500 jackpot at the Reno Safeway, the slot manager checked the machine for drill holes and paid me. We split the $500, and Price asked me if I knew any slot bosses or slot mechanics that would do business. I said I would let Wesley know.

Wesley asked me to shill-up a 21 game at the Silver Spur Casino. Two crossroaders named Fat Charley and Florida John were going to do some hand mucking there and Wesley wanted me to play two hands in the last seat to distract the dealer. Wesley would block Charley's back.

Florida John *chopped* out a card and went south with it. Charley took the card and moved it to his knee. He raised his bet and played several impressive hands using Anrino's one-handed palm move. After several moves, John took the card from Charley's knee and cleaned it up in his hit cards.

After the play, Wesley handed me $50. I was happy to be in on the play and surprised to see Charley use the one-handed holdout move.

Rabbit and I made another 21 play at Fitzgerald's and I asked George if he had access to the slot machine keys. He said he could get a key that opened all of Fitz's machines.

I told Wesley and he said that if Price could have the key for about ten seconds he could make an impression of it.

George told me he didn't want to expose his identity to anyone, but he would pass me the key under a stall in the casino bathroom to make an impression of it. We agreed that everyone involved in a slot play there would get an equal share of any money we won.

Wesley and I met Price who said the slot machines at Fitzgerald's have Abloy locks that used keys with a code that he could decipher. He held up an Abloy key and taught me how to read the secret code. He said, "Each cut in the key represents a numerical code: the top edge of the key represents a zero and any cuts between the top edge and the centerline represent the numbers zero through five." He loaned me a key to practice reading the code.

George passed me the key that I deciphered and wrote down. I passed the key back to him and left to meet Wesley and Price.

At Price's workshop, he proceeded to cut a key. He disassembled an Abloy lock and removed the thin steel wafers inside. The first number I had written down was a four. He picked out a number four-sized wafer, transcribed the measurement with a metal scribe onto a half-round brass rod held in a vice, and measured it with a micrometer. He used a Swiss file to make a cut in the rod and held the wafer up beside it to check it for accuracy. He made the remaining cuts the same way. He sawed off the end of the rod and cut a slit into it to fashion a handle. He inserted a dime-sized washer with quick-drying metal glue into the slit to complete the key. He reassembled a lock to correspond to the code on the paper. He tried the new key in the lock and said, "Presto!" when it opened the lock. We left for the casino to try it.

We found a slot machine in a secluded spot and the key worked. I told George who said, "Let the large jackpots be for now and to take off ones of $3,000 or less, at a rate of one a week."

Wesley and Rabbit had some friends we would use as collectors. They, along with Rabbit, Wesley, and his brother-in-law, Kevin, would close around Price's back as he put up a jackpot. I would hover around them to head off anyone who happened by.

After taking off a few jackpots, George said to take two weeks off and then take off a "progressive jackpot" in the $10,000 range. The progressive jackpots increased exponentially with each coin played and several were in the $10,000 range.

In the meantime, Price was caught putting up a jackpot at the Sparks Nugget Casino. Wesley told me the casino had no material evidence, but Price had hired a lawyer to fight the case and he wanted to quit working until his case was over. I told Wesley I would put up future jackpots if Price would teach me how.

Price agreed and taught me his method. We would take a part of our future shares for consideration money for Price. He opened his machine and said, "You play a machine on the square until a seven shows up on at least two of the three reels." When two sevens came up, he inserted a quarter and said, "After you open the door and insert a quarter, move the two sevens to the center line and hold them in place as you pull the handle halfway down where it stops." With his right hand, he searched for the third seven by manually turning the last reel. When he found it he said, "Hold the three sevens on the centerline as you complete pulling the handle all the way down."

Each reel clicked into place and the jackpot bell rang. He handed me some quarters and I played his machine until two sevens came up. I inserted the key, opened the door, and awkwardly put up the jackpot. It took me about thirty seconds. Price said with practice, I could do it less than ten seconds. After two hours, I could put a jackpot up in less than ten seconds. He said, "Before you go out on a play for a big jackpot, you should paint clear nail polish on your fingertips to fill in the grooves because some casinos dust the reels to check against crossroaders fingerprints when someone hits a big jackpot."

While waiting for the OK from George, I bought two Abloy locks at the Reno Lock and Safe Company to make another key. At Commercial Hardware, I bought a packet of Swiss files, a micrometer, a metal scribe, a vise, and a half-round brass rod made for toilet reservoirs.

After disassembling the lock, I put the brass rod in the vice and proceeded to cut a key as Price had done. I tried it in the reassembled lock and it worked—I was beside myself with joy and as usual my fertile imagination took-off. I chanced on the idea that I could secretly photograph other Abloy keys hanging from the belt loops of slot employees. I'd have the photos blown-up to read the coded cuts and could make keys for casinos worldwide.

I bought a miniature spy camera and drove to South Lake Tahoe to scout the casinos there. The Sahara-Tahoe Casino's machines used Abloy locks and I followed two slot employees around the casino for two hours without any luck. I put bent coins in several machines to jam them up so the mechanics would stop to fix them but they left their key ring in the lock when they opened the door. I followed a mechanic into the men's room and occupied the stall beside him but I couldn't get a fix on the keys that hung from his pants. I found the slot employees workshop and tried to think of an excuse to enter to look for a spare lock to take home. I could then decipher and cut a master key. Finally, I decided it was too risky and left.

George gave me the OK to take off a $10,000 jackpot. The collector was a friend of Wesley's who was a blacksmith from California who had competed with him at rodeos. Wesley and I formulated a plan that we explained to everyone. Wesley, Kevin, and the collector would play machines on either side of the slot that I played while Rabbit hovered around us looking out for employees who he could block and distract when I had the slot door opened. When I said, "George," everyone would surround me facing outward as I opened the slot door and put up the jackpot. When the jackpot bell rings, they'll disperse except the collector who will stand in front of the jackpot to claim it. Wesley will hover around the area to see if everything was OK and to alert the collector if anyone was following him.

We went to Harrah's to do a mock play and then to Fitzgerald's to take down the jackpot. At the meet, Wesley said the slot boss checked the slot machine for drill holes and tampering, and told the shift boss it was clean and the boss paid the collector.

Over the next three weeks, we took down two more big jackpots. The collectors were friends of Wesley who were from out of town and were solid people. George said there was no heat but to take off for two weeks. He said slot teams had been fattening up the progressive jackpot machines by playing them around the clock. Jackpot brokers would find progressive slot machines that mathematically paid more than the odds against hitting the jackpot. They paid people $10 an hour and gave them the coins needed to play the machines continuously with a promise of ten percent of the jackpot if they hit it. The casino manager thought they were the reason more jackpots than usual were hit.

The Captain was in town visiting Carlo and I filled him in on my adventures, including the slots and the million-dollar move. The 21 move appealed to him and he said if we could find the right partner, we'd be in control of when and where we played like in the old days when I shot tees. I told him a friend of mine was working with a hand-mucking crew and he suggested we visit him to learn how he operated.

Wesley explained to us how his crew worked. "My partner sits beside me and steals a card for me that I use for several hands. When I'm done playing my partner cleans it up for me in his cards. Let's go to the Primadonna casino and We'll show you."

We followed Wesley and Kevin to the casino and stood behind them at a 21 table to block their backs. Kevin sat beside Wesley, scratched for two hit cards, palmed one of his original dealt cards and put it behind his knee like Anrino and Fat Charley did. Wesley took the card and used it to play several hands before Kevin took the card from behind Wesley's knee and cleaned it up in his hit cards—the young dealer had no idea what had happened.

Wes said his favorite place to play was Harvey's Casino at Lake Tahoe. He said there was a 21 pit there where you can see if anybody was up in the eye. He said, "You can see a light bulb behind the one-way mirror unless someone's up there blocking it out." The next day, Cap and I bought a jigsaw, some plywood and felt, and made a regulation-sized 21 table to practice Wes's 21 moves.

George asked me to take off another jackpot. Wesley had to be in Las Vegas so Cap would take his place and Rabbit recommended a young guy named Jesse to collect the jackpot. Cap and I found an $8,000 jackpot in a safe spot. After a mock play at Harrah's with

Rabbit and Jesse, we took off the $8,000 jackpot and invited Jesse to have a few beers.

Jesse was twenty-five-years old and had gambled since he was sixteen. He said he had been a successful pool player but would lose his money in crooked card and dice games. Cap told him we wanted to put a hand-mucking crew together to beat the casinos and we needed a partner. He said he'd like to join us.

After taking off another jackpot, George phoned me for a meet. He said the slot department installed a new alarm system on all the progressive slot machines and asked me to check the new alarm.

At Fitzgerald's, Cap and I put bent coins in a couple of machines to jam them up. A slot mechanic opened the jammed machines and we saw the new alarm. When a slot door was opened, a small, spring-loaded chrome button protruded from a steel sleeve. When the door was closed, the button pushed back into the sleeve and tripped a switch that blacked-out the machine. The mechanic put a coin in the machine and pulled the handle to restart the machine, which would erase a jackpot. I told Wesley about it and he said he would check with Bill Price.

Slot manufacturers and slot hustlers waged a constant battle. The manufacturers would come up with a new cheat-proof slot machine to foil the hustlers and they in turn would buy or steal the new machine or schematic to figure out how to beat it. When some new machines came on-line at the Sahara-Tahoe, two slot hustlers dressed as repairmen, loaded one of the new machines onto a dolly, and were seen wheeling it into a van and driving away.

Slot hustlers weren't the only innovators. The Las Vegas *Sun* reported in May 1974, that a daring thief grabbed $10,000 in $100 bills from a baccarat game at the Aladdin Hotel-Casino. He made a spectacular escape as he dove through a renovation construction chute in the casino and slid into an outdoor dumpster and drove away. Eventually, casinos did away with cash and used chips for bacarrat.

At Amarillo Slim's "Super Bowl of Poker" at the Sahara-Tahoe, a thief watched a cash player leave his chips on the table as he left for dinner. The thief asked a poker room employee to move "his" chips to another game. He sat down, played two hands, and left with the chips.

Henry had quit dealing 21 at the Carson City Nugget and was working with a crew of hustlers who were daubing cards, and beating roulette and craps games. He said his crew would set up on a roulette table to make winning bets and he would quickly move the ball to their winning number when it stopped as the dealer turns away to pick up losing bets. The hustlers stop him, telling him he's picking up their winning bets. The dealer then corrects his "'mistake" and apologizes to the hustlers." Eventually the casinos caught on and put a clear plastic shield around the wheel.

Another move his crew was using was a craps move called "The jockey move." He said, "One of us would intentionally throw a die off the table and one of our crew would step on the die then steal it. We return with it later to use for our move. A crewmember pretends he's drunk and makes a field bet using cash to cover his move. As he bets, he spreads the bills out and sets the previously stolen die down with a six up as he pulls his hand away ostensibly to avoid the dice thrown by another crewmember. But the shooter throws just one die and holds out the other one. I stand behind the shooter, and as he reaches under the table for his drink he drops me the die he held out and I 'jockey' it to the field better and slip it to him to repeat the move if it looks safe. It is all timing and we had practiced it several hours each day for a week before we got down with it. We beat every joint on the Strip and are giving it a rest for now."

Bill Price told Wesley he had a fix for the new slot machine alarm at Fitzgerald's Casino. Wesley told me, "You open the slot machine door and jam a steel guitar string and the chrome button into the sleeve using miniature pliers. The machine will black out until you put a quarter in to restart it. When you restart it and open the door to put up a jackpot the jammed button prevents the machine from blacking-out. After you put up the pot and close the door, you yank hard on the guitar string and it comes out of the machine and releases the button to its normal position."

I told Cap and he said, "Bobby, beating the slots is like a burglary move, and the key is material evidence. With our 21 move, we'd use the tools we were born with, our hands and wits and it's more honest to challenge the casinos face-to-face." I agreed with Cap as always and Jesse seemed like the right partner so we decided to give up the slots. I told George and Wesley, and gave George the key Price had made. I set up a meet with Cap and Jesse at my house.

I told Karen I had some friends coming over for a couple of hours and she took Sierra to Virginia Lake to feed the ducks and do some antique shopping. Karen knew I hustled casinos but never asked me why or how and I never told her—it was for her protection, if I were to have police trouble and she was questioned, she wouldn't have to lie.

Jesse watched as Cap dealt out seven hands around our 21 table: two cards to me, sitting in the first seat, and two cards to six imaginary players. I scratched my two cards for two hit cards and said to Cap, "I'm good," as I appeared to put both of my cards under my chips. I turned my hand over to show Jesse the ten I had palmed and pointed to the one card under my bet. I put the held out ten behind my right knee as Cap continued to deal to the imaginary players. I said, "I'm going to turn up the one card under my bet and mix it with my two hit cards when the hand is over as Cap turns up the last player's cards to compute the hand. I'll pick up two of my cards and put them under my bet where they belong. Dealers are robotic and don't remember how many hit cards they give a player. And palming out the one card is so subtle and effective because the dealer sees you have two cards in your hand as you're scratching for a hit or putting them under your bet. She doesn't see you palm the bottom card because it's behind the card you're sliding under your bet, and she's already looking away to act on the next players hand. It's a magician's move and to a dealer, who watches players put two cards under their bets all day, every day, one tucked card looks like two. And if a dealer reaches to check the cards you could replace the palmed card before she reaches it."

Cap dealt me a ten and a four. I palmed the four, as I appeared to put both my cards under my bet. I showed Jesse the four and said, "I'll trade this for the ten behind my knee to make twenty. Cap dealt me a ten and a six on the next hand and I scratched for a hit card. My hit card was a nine so I palmed the ten and exchanged it for the four behind my knee and finished with nineteen. On the next hand, Cap reached for the one card under my bet to test me. I quickly slid the palmed card I held under the one card and picked both cards up saying to Cap, "I didn't bust my hand—look." I showed Cap my two cards and said to Jesse, "You always want to be ready to beat the dealer to the one card. You look the dealer in the eye when you put the one card under your bet. Her eyes will give her away before she reaches for the card and you'll have time to return the held out card." After another hand, Cap called for a break.

I told Jesse I didn't have anything against dealers or bosses personally, but I was at total war with the casinos and I explained how some casinos had been caught cheating the public and closed down.

He related a story about gambling at the Stardust in Vegas, where he had competed in a pool tournament and the casino people knew he was underage. They let him play craps until he was broke then barred him.

I gave Jesse two cards and taught him the mechanics of the one-handed palm move. I held two cards lengthwise in my hand with the corner of the bottom card pinched in the niche of my thumb. In slow motion, I folded my four fingers back into a semi-fist on the middle back of the top card as my thumb pressed on the center face of the bottom card to keep both cards together. When I extended my four fingers and moved my hand forward, the top card moved forward and slid under my chips, the bottom card remained secure in the niche of my thumb concealed under my extended fingers as I pulled away.. I turned my hand over to show the position of the palmed card. Jesse had thick fingers, big hands, and good eye-hand coordination. He did the move after several attempts and improved with practice.

Cap explained the method of play we would use. "Jesse, you'll sit on Bobby's left side and when you palm a card you'll put it behind your right knee where Bobby will take it. It doesn't matter what your hand is because you'll be betting small. After Bobby plays several hands, he'll put the held out card behind his left knee and you'll take it and mix it in with your hit cards." I said, "I'll distract the dealer when you make your moves, and opportunities come up to return the extra card early instead of waiting for the dealer to turn over the last player's cards. You could return it when a player distracts the dealer asking for change, a *double down*, or a *split* hand."

We practiced to simulate a live game. Jesse scratched his cards for a hit card. I asked Cap, "Do you ever gamble?" He answered, "Sometimes." Jesse scratched for another hit card and I asked, "Do you ever win?" Cap answered, "Not often, that's why I'm dealing to you guys." Jesse tucked one card and palmed the other as Cap continued to deal to the imaginary players. After he acted on his own hand, Cap turned over the last player's cards as Jesse picked up his one card, mixed it in with the two hit cards, and put two under his bet. Cap said, "Good work, fellas. Let's do it again." On the next hand when Jesse put his one card under his bet, Cap reached for it but Jesse was ready and beat him to it, saying, "I think I do want a hit card."

Cap had been a 21 dealer and he watched us with a critical eye and shared his honest opinions. He pointed out when we moved too fast, and when he saw a palmed card exposed. We called it a *leak* and we would stop and practice in front of a mirror until we fixed it. Our goal was to palm a card when a boss or dealer watched us make our moves.

We practiced for several more hands before a break. During the break, we went over the signals we would use. Touching our forehead or chin meant good or safe—*George* was the verbal expression; touching our nose or saying Tom meant heat; touching our mouth or saying easy meant standby or be cautious. If anyone felt like ending a play, he'd say: I'm getting *tired*—real tired if there was heat. Brushing a sleeve meant to leave the casino and the quicker the brush, the quicker the exit, touching our eye meant I want to see you in private. Izzy meant eye-in-the-sky, Clara for dealer, Bessy for boss, and Al for *outside man*. Jesse and I invented leg signals using knee taps: one tap meant yes, two meant no, a press meant freeze, and a long press meant leave.

After dealing several more hands to us, Cap suggested we quit for the day. He said we were yawning, a sign we were learning. He suggested we have two-a-day practices starting the next day and we left to grab a bite to eat and a few beers.

Jesse grew up in Oakland, California, where he played pool in the local poolrooms. He'd beaten all comers in the San Francisco Bay Area and decided to go on the road. He said the biggest pool action in the country took place annually in Johnson City, Illinois, and lasted two weeks. It attracted the country's top pool hustlers, golf hustlers, and gamblers. He said he'd won a lot of money there playing pool, but lost it all playing poker, tonk, and gin. After he had been cold decked in a poker game, a guy who was in on the play tipped him off that all the gambling there was crooked. Jesse said he had played poker with the top players in Vegas, some of whom were great pool players, but he couldn't get ahead and had planned to take his first ever job, dealing poker in Reno, before he met us.

At our next practice, we practiced our moves in front of a mirror to help our rhythm and timing. And we practiced a two-second-drill to clean up a held out card in case a boss opened a new deck of cards for our game. Cap would warn us by saying *Bessy*, meaning the boss was suspicious or changing decks and we would add the held out card to our cards. I said, "If the dealer is shuffling, we could ask to cut the cards and clean up the card on the cut." I demonstrated the move I had discovered the previous night practicing on my own. I showed Jesse a palmed card in my hand and placed it on top of the deck as I cut the cards. If a boss opened a new deck, Cap would try to stall him to give us extra time. He could ask for directions or a Kleenex. Cap said if we couldn't clean up the card to let it drop on the floor and leave.

Cap would stand behind us to prevent anyone from seeing or grabbing our hand with a card in it. He would evaluate a boss's mood to determine when it was time to leave. How much money a player is winning affects a boss's mood; some take it personally like it's their money. Cap would look for outside men and if he spotted security guards closing in on our game he'd point us in a direction away from them.

Everything Jesse did was natural, smooth, and effortless whether he was talking, palming a card, lighting a cigarette, pushing his full-head of blond hair back, or anything, and we worked well as a team. After another week of practice sessions, Cap suggested we take our maiden voyage to South Lake Tahoe on the weekend.

I parked on the California side of the state line, and we walked to Harvey's to check Wesley's favorite pit. Cap said, "Let's go slowly and do everything like we do at practice, and play scared like the champion Boston Celtic's coach told his players before a game."

Our plan was to check all the exits and meet in the entertainment pit. If we made a normal play, we'd meet at the Stateline Bar across the street from Harvey's, in California—if we had heat, we'd meet at the car or at the first restaurant on the right side of Highway 50 heading into California.

Cap pointed to his eye and we met him in the slots. He whispered that Wesley and his crew were playing 21. Wesley sat beside Fat Charlie, and Freddie-the-Cat was guarding their backs. Kevin stood nearby checking the eye-in-the-sky that Wesley had told us about.

It was a real treat for us rookies to watch old pros at work. Charley was an experienced crossroader and he had the boss laughing as he brought a fill of chips to the game. We couldn't actually see him muck a card out from where we watched but we guessed it by his actions and by seeing Freddy move in close to block. Instead of reaching down for the card behind his knee, Charley would lift his leg up to his hand to palm it. After watching several hands, we left and met at the bar to give Wesley's crew a chance to leave. Cap said he saw the light bulb behind the thick tinted plate glass meaning no one was in the eye, and he would lead us to it when we went back in to make our first play which had an unlikely bizarre ending.

Wesley's crew had gone and I could see the light bulb so I found a friendly talkative dealer nearby and sat down. The boss was more interested in the show on stage than his 21 games. I conversed with the dealer to make Jesse's job easier. He palmed a card after he scratched for three small hit cards. He looked at the dealer's eyes when he put his one card under his chips and palmed the other card as we had drilled at practice. When the dealer turned up the last player's hand, Jesse turned up his down card, mixed it in with the three hit cards as if to figure what he had and put two under his bet.

I took the borrowed card from behind Jesse's knee and put it behind my knee; it was a five. I was dealt a ten and a four and scratched for a hit card and was given a ten. I looked at the dealer and said, "I'm good" as I buried the four under my bet and palmed the ten. The dealer's eyes moved to Jesse who scratched for a hit. I finished the hand with nineteen by adding the five to my hand. I had a ten held out and increased my bet. My first card was an ace. I reached down to get the ten and *chopped* in a blackjack as I palmed the random card. It was the same move I had watched Anrino do a few years earlier at Harrah's, just across the highway.

The boss stood beside the dealer to watch the action. He surprised us as he opened a small drawer at our table and took out a deck of new cards—no time for our two-second drill. Cap whispered, "Let the card drop on the floor." I pressed Jesse's leg to leave as I waited to be paid. The card dropped as I stood up and Cap stepped on it. Jesse and I met at my car.

Cap arrived laughing and said, "It's Jake; let's have a beer." He said he stayed at the game with his foot on the card while the boss sorted the shorted deck. He counted it down and never realized it was short one card. He put the cards into a card box that he initialed and put into a drawer with the other used cards. Cap showed us the Jack of spades that he picked up from the floor and we had a good laugh. It was a comfort to me when Cap said to leave the card on the floor. Since I've known him, he's always made quick, and correct decisions. We would find out that Harvey's was the only casino that kept new decks of cards at the 21 table.

Our next play was at the Sahara-Tahoe Hotel-Casino. It was a casino factory with over one-hundred 21 tables in several separate pits. They didn't have a *catwalk,* but several surveillance cameras dotted the ceiling concealed in lightly tinted domes. We could easily see the camera through the domes by looking at the ceiling lights behind it. I'd sit on a game with no camera on it and if one moved to our game, Cap would warn us and we'd move to another game. At the time, only a few casinos used cameras. Cap said that someday all casinos would have them.

Jesse and I would approach a game from opposite directions and would leave in opposite directions. I'd signal him a dealer I liked, and he would play a hand before I sat down.

I found a game with two empty chairs, side-by-side and we staggered sitting down. The boss was responsible for five other games besides ours and he seemed interested in one particular game two tables away from us. I won several hands and he never knew I was there. After another successful play, Cap suggested we quit on a good note and have a few beers.

The Captain was four years older than I was, and I was five years older than Jesse. Cap was a fifties' generation southerner, Jesse was a sixties' Californian, and I was an east-coaster with a blend of both generations. Our age differences and personalities complimented our friendship and disguised it while we played. We had a good work ethic with an emphasis on safety, efficiency, and longevity. After critiquing our plays, we split our winnings and made future plans.

During the week, we had several practice sessions to get ready for our return to South Lake Tahoe for the weekend.

Saturday night at the South Shore casinos was like New Year's Eve. The many games and crowded aisles at the Sahara suited our hit-and-run style. Going from *pit* to *pit* was like going into different casinos. The outside men spent most of their time watching for slot cheaters and they were easy for us to spot. When they weren't in the slots or prowling table games, they'd hang out at the cashier's cage talking to the shift boss. Eventually, they'd head for the slots not knowing they tipped themselves off to us. If one approached our game, we would play on the square until he left.

After we played a few hands, Jesse and I would get lost in the crowd to find another game to play on while Cap hovered around the game we left to make sure nobody knocked our play. He would find us setting up on another game.

Cap had a demanding job: besides guarding our backs, he had to look for outside men and check that a camera didn't move to our game. He would watch that a boss didn't reach for a new deck of cards for our game, and if a boss picked up a phone, he had to determine if it was for a fill, or a call for help. And he didn't get to sit down until we took a break.

Like other casinos, the Sahara-Tahoe had standard operating rules that we knew and took advantage of. How much to win and how long to play dictated itself. I changed my appearance from play to play by taking off my jacket, my sweater, and eventually I'd roll up my long-sleeved shirtsleeves. I combed my hair back, forward, or parted differently—I didn't want the shift boss to hear the same description of a constant winner. Speed was our friend, and our plan was to hit-and-run the casinos and not win too much money to hurt a boss or dealer who might remember me. If a boss camped on our game, we'd "Quit to fight another day." Our morale was good and our motto was, "One for all, and all for one," like The Three Musketeers of old.

Cap recognized a boss who was a pit boss at the Lucky Casino when we worked there. He was now the casino manager at the Sahara-Tahoe. He'd stand near the cashier's cage with a drink in his hand talking with another boss or outside-man. Cap would check on him between plays. He said that as long as he was drinking and laughing we didn't have any heat because he'd be the first one to know.

On one play, I chopped in a blackjack and forgot to straighten out the ace. It had curled up in my moist hand and looked like a potato chip as it lay face up in front of the world. A boss looked at it and wheeled around to the podium. We knew he left for a new deck of cards and we went into our two-second-drill and cleaned up the held out card. The boss walked to the podium with the old deck and I left while he had his back to me.

At our meeting place, Cap said the boss checked the sides of the deck for bent cards. He counted them, placed them into a box, initialed it, and put them in the podium drawer with the other used decks. He went back to pacing the pit and his mind slipped back into neutral. We named him *Tom*, and would duck him on future visits to the casino.

We decided to check out Harrah's. We were aware that it had an active eye but we had to play there. Unlike other casinos, Harrah's dealers didn't call a boss when a customer broke a $100 bill or made a big bet. Bill Harrah's policy was to treat every customer alike whether they bet $2 or $1,000.

I found a rookie dealer and won a few bets. Jesse and I left the casino and stepped across the state line into California. We would watch for Cap to step outside the casino to give us the *George* sign and we'd go back in and make another play. After a few plays we'd take a break.

The Captain and Jessie were entertaining and the breaks were as much fun for me as working with them. Jesse had a unique vocabulary and conversation that fit him and he was mischievous like me and we needed Cap to rein us in.

Back at Harrah's I had a card palmed when a young boss surprised us by opening a new deck of cards. He was routinely changing all the decks in his pit for the change of shifts. We couldn't use our two-second drill and I didn't want to leave a card on the floor again. I stared at the old deck in the dealer's hand. Surprising the dealer, my partners, and myself, I grabbed it from her and capped my palmed card on top of it. I said, "Let me keep this deck for a souvenir." The dealer nervously smiled in space as the boss glared at me and said, "What're you doing?" I acted surprised and set the deck down saying, "I was only kidding." He had no idea what I'd done and thought I was a fool, but he was angry and said, "If you did that at the Sahara they'd break your hands." I feigned bewilderment and said I was sorry. He arrogantly walked away to change decks on his other games. I gave the dealer a tip, apologized again, and left. Cap hung around and met us at the car.

Cap said, "Good clean-up Bobby. The boss didn't call anyone and he slipped into his normal routine.

At Harvey's a middle-aged mechanic arrived at our game. We spotted her peeking and Jesse cleaned up the held out card. We left separately and met at the car. Cap said, the mechanic didn't have a clue that Jesse cleaned up the held out card, and that it was good we nailed her move, and a wake-up call that there are mechanics out there. We quit for the night, and celebrated with a couple of beers.

The results of our practice and strategy sessions had paid off. I didn't lose a hand and we each made over $1,000 in 1977 dollars. The money was big for the time and our place in the world. We were young and our morale was high.

Wesley phoned me to ask if we could be in Vegas on Saturday to do some business. Cap said we should definitely go to get some experience and to check the casinos there. We had several practice sessions and had a good laugh when Cap said, "Most bosses are struggling to get through their boring day having no idea that three young guys are home practicing a move to beat them."

We drove to Vegas and met Wesley at a Denny's restaurant where Wesley explained the play. A friend of his was a boss at the Sands who wanted to do some business. Wesley would bring us to his pit and the boss would indicate a game to play on as he stood at the table and touched his chin. When he wanted us to leave, he'd reach for a Kleenex at the podium. We'd keep half of the money we won.

The boss signaled us in and he whispered to the dealer, "Take care of my friends." We didn't know the dealer would be in but it made our job seem easier. I moved several times winning several $500 bets. The boss reached for a Kleenex and we left to meet Wesley. He told us that was all for the weekend. It had been a good experience and we found most of the casinos in Vegas fit our style and we looked forward to returning.

We made plans to play in Reno the next weekend. Harrah's was the most popular casino and like its sister casino at Tahoe, its hotel had a AAA Five-Diamond rating, top-flight entertainment, big action, and the casino standard operating rules were the same.

We played on Friday night to warm up for the weekend. Saturday was a big day in Reno and Saturday night was special. People from Sacramento and the Bay Area would make the scenic drive over the Sierras for dinner, a show, and some gambling in the packed casinos.

I found an end game where two bosses chatted at the podium. I bet the $200 limit and won four straight hands. The bosses didn't know I was there. Cap whispered, "I'm getting tired," and I left for the Nevada Club snack bar, our regular meeting place. It had a front and rear entrance and a maze of slot machines with several turns. When we left a game, we usually left through the slots to give a possible pursuer as many choices as possible to guess the wrong way we went.

After a ten minute wait, Cap arrived and said a boss eventually noticed the $800 in chips missing and called the cashier for a fill of chips. When the dealer signed the fill slip, the boss remarked how busy the casino was and didn't ask her who won the missing chips. We laughed shaking our heads and headed back to Harrah's.

A boss parked himself at my side and introduced himself. I always had a bogus name and address ready to offer a boss. I shook his hand and said I was Bob Johnson from Sacramento. I had memorized a street address there several weeks earlier when I visited the Sacramento Zoo with Karen and Sierra. He walked away confident I'd lose like most players, but when he returned I was gone and the chip rack was short $1,000.

Bosses weren't suspicious of me because of the sucker persona I projected. Through the years, I had watched and listened to many square players as a dealer, a shill, and a crossroader and I mimicked them. And I would sit at a casino bar to watch how people walked through a casino and how they acted when they approached a game and sat down. Tourists walked slowly through casinos curiously observing sights and sounds, while employees and rounders hastened through.

After two plays at the Eldorado, we quit for the night and had a couple of beers at an out-of-the-way bar. Cap overheard a guy on the phone say: "It's a $500 jackpot and we'll split it." When his partner showed up, I followed them to the Riverside Casino and watched the mechanic. He didn't swing open the slot door, but pulled the handle a few times and somehow put up a $500 jackpot. His collector stood in front of the machine to claim it and the hustler left the casino. I scurried up an alley and beat him back to the bar. When he had left the bar, I was playing pool with Jesse and when he came back, I was at the pool table. He had no idea I had followed him and watched him put the jackpot up—it reminded us to check our backs. We talked about warning him but Cap said Reno was a small town and we decided not to give up our identities.

Harrah's was our first stop on Saturday. After a few plays there, we hit several other casinos and had another good weekend. Cap suggested we go to Vegas the following weekend.

My first job in Vegas was at the Stardust and that would be our first stop. They dealt single and double-deck 21 games *face down*, with over one hundred tables in six separate pits. The ceiling was low and there was no catwalk. Several surveillance cameras dotted the ceiling concealed in large, lightly tinted domes that were easy to see through. It was a mob-owned joint, reflected by the attitude of the bosses. Most strutted back and forth acting tough, but they were more image than substance like most things in Vegas and were easy for us to beat.

I used a similar style on each play. On the first hand, I wouldn't pick up my cards but would scratch my finger on the table for a hit card like a first-time player. I'd bet a few $5 chips on top of a $25 chip and the dealer would call to the boss, "Green plays." The boss would take a cursory look at me and walk away. I would increase my bets according to how much *air* a boss gave me. I would palm a card in some bosses faces—they would watch me put one card under my bet never realizing it was one card. It was a bold move, but like shooting tees it was unexpected, and if something is not known, it doesn't exist.

After the Stardust, we hit the Riviera, the Circus, the Sahara, and the MGM Grand casino. We played in all the downtown casinos except the Horseshoe out of respect for Wesley who was a friend of the owner, Benny Binion.

We played at the busiest times in the busiest casinos especially on holiday weekends and during special events and conventions. We played against most bosses and dealers, and felt safe since no one knew whom we were or when or where we'd play. After three straight weeks, we would take a weekend off.

When we returned to work, it was business as usual. We worked Friday night, all of Saturday, and early afternoons on Sunday. We averaged $2,000 each for a weekend and hadn't taken any heat. We remembered the dealers and bosses we played on and the particulars of each play.

Two weeks before Christmas, 1977, Cap drove back east to stay a while. Jesse went home to Oakland and would return after the holidays.

CHAPTER 8

THE TRANSFER: THE REAL MILLION-DOLLAR MOVE

"There is a tide in the affairs of men, which,
taken at the flood, leads on to fortune...."
—SHAKESPEARE *(Julius Caesar)*

When Jesse returned, we met at the Peppermill lounge to talk over old times and the future. Cap hadn't phoned and we had no idea when he'd be back. I told Jesse, "Cap would go somewhere to philosophize about life, and no one, including himself, knew when he would return."

Jesse thought we could do our move if we checked each other's back. We left for Harrah's to see how it looked. We sat on an end game with no foot traffic. I thought we were too drunk to play but an idea came to me. I envisioned each of us palming a card and switching it with each other under the table. I needed his ten and whispered, "Take out the ten." He knew what I meant and when the dealer passed us, I reached under the table with the seven I had palmed and put it behind Jesse's knee. He put his ten behind my knee as we observed the dealer, the players, and our backs. I slid the ten under my bet and he put my seven under his bet. I bumped his knee with a friendly tap. The dealer paid me and we left. I laid my arm around Jesse's shoulders and said, "Partner, we just invented the greatest move of all time."

On the drive to Jesse's apartment, we talked about the virtues of our new move. We didn't need to risk stealing a card, holding it out, and cleaning it up. I'd have four cards to make my best hand against the dealer's two, and it was over and done quickly; it was the perfect hit-and-run move. We'd need to find an efficient way to switch our cards, and someone to guard our backs. No one could replace Cap as a partner and friend, but he was gone indefinitely. I explained to Jesse that Cap and I had been partners for a long time and I wanted to save his place if he returned. He felt the same way.

Jesse wanted to learn to ski and we both wanted to quit smoking and figure a way to switch our cards. We made a plan to ski at Squaw Valley to invent a card switch.

Driving to the resort, we decided that I would *bet the money* as I had with the old move. I would sit in the first seat and Jesse would sit next to me. Jesse said we needed to invent a hand-to-hand exchange. I handed him a deck of cards and we experimented on the drive to the ski resort.

I spent an hour teaching Jesse the basic ski lessons I had learned in Austria. He was a natural intelligent athlete and caught on quickly and we headed to the chair lift where we removed our gloves and explored ways to trade our cards. Jesse sat on my left and used his left hand and I used my right hand as we fumbled for the simplest give-and-take transfer. Eventually we found it. When our fingertips met, we curled our fingers into a semi-fist. Jesse slid his card over my card and into the niche in my thumb. I pushed my card underneath his card and into his thumb's niche. We pulled away with our cards locked in place and our fingers extended concealing them. Our hands remained parallel to the ground. We exchanged our cards in slow motion, speeded up, and studied each facet of the switch. We exchanged cards behind our biceps, as we would do on a 21 game. Our shoulders pressed together with our arms crossed across our chests. After switching cards and skiing a few runs, we left for my house to practice our discovery on my 21 table.

We approximated game-like conditions in front of a mirror as we sat side-by-side in the first two seats. We each picked up two cards and talked about the possibilities to make me the best hand—Jesse's hand didn't matter since he would bet small like with our old move.

If one of us had an ace, and one of us had a ten, we'd quickly switch cards to make a blackjack. The next best hands were twenty and nineteen. If those hands weren't possible, I'd scratch for a hit card. The best hands to hit were eleven, ten, and nine. Beyond that strategy, I'd take hit-cards randomly to improve my hand. If I took two hit cards, I'd have six cards to make my best hand: Jesse's two cards, my two, and the two hit cards—I'd likely make twenty or twenty-one on most hands I played.

We realized that playing in the first two seats facilitated our move. We'd have extra time to switch our palmed cards, and dealers thought that cheating occurred in the end seats so that's where they focused their attention.

We lifted up our cards so only we could see them. We wouldn't want another player to see them, or worse, the eye-in-the-sky if he happened to look at us. We soon realized that if we made all the right moves, we could play indefinitely. We did speed drills palming and switching our cards and experimented tossing them to each other like two acrobats exchanging places in mid-air. And we practiced on our own. I held a card in each palm and switched them as I jogged each day, and Jesse practiced while he watched TV.

After one week of drills, we were ready to try our new move that Jesse named the *transfer*. We needed someone to block our backs like Cap had done with our old move. Jesse suggested Mack who he had hustled pool with, and who I had worked with at South Lake Tahoe doing the mini-baccarat play with Rabbit and Mack's dealer friend Joe D.

Mack grew up in South Philly and wasted his youth playing poker and pool. After a hitch in the army, he and a friend drove to Vegas and decided to stay as so many others had. He was doing business as a 21 dealer at the Golden Nugget, and ironically, was promoted to a floorman position. He and other bosses, dealers, and their agents were going gangbusters until Steve Wynn, the new owner, fired them in the middle of the shift.

Jesse and I taught Mack what Cap would do and not do. His most important job was not to let anyone grab or see our cards as we switched them. After we looked at our cards, we palmed and switched them in an instant so Mack didn't have to stand behind us long, and would move to look at the game next to us or a slot machine player acting like a curious gawker before returning for our next switch.

We would use the hit-and-run strategy that we used with our old move. We made our first play at Harrah's in Reno on an end game with three players where the boss was talking to a customer at the opposite end of the pit. We lifted our cards to show each other; I had a ten and an eight, Jesse had two tens. I palmed my eight and he palmed a ten. We traded cards and I won the hand by turning my original eighteen into a twenty. Next, I was dealt a five and a seven and Jesse had a ten and a nine. My hit card was a five so I palmed my seven to switch with Jesse for his ten to make twenty. I gave the dealer a $5 tip and left.

We waited for Mack at the Nevada Club snack bar. He arrived rubbing his chin and smiling. He said the boss was still talking to the customer when he left. We were happy to break the ice and hit the Eldorado Casino. We switched cards twice there then left for Fitzgerald's and made two more switches. I suggested we pack it in and we had a few beers to celebrate our success. The next day, we'd have a practice session before driving to South Lake Tahoe.

A dealer at the Sahara-Tahoe noticed Jesse re-check his cards as he tucked the card I switched with him. Most dealers didn't mind if a player re-checked his cards because it wasn't a hard rule. However, some dealers were concerned that a player would add or take money from their original bet—their ideas about cheating came from hearsay and their own imagination. Because of their ignorance, they expressed themselves in the strongest terms often embarrassing honest players. A little old lady would unknowingly use both hands instead of one to pick up her cards and the dealer would stop the game to berate her in front of the world. It was the same when a craps player used two hands handling the dice, the stickman would stop the game and embarrass the player.

We knew Harrah's had an active eye, but no one knew about our new move. If we kept our cards down and our arms pressed together while we switched them, we could beat the eye. After making a play, Jesse and I waited across the state line for Mack to leave the casino to give us a signal as Cap did with our old move. After several plays at Harrah's we hit the Sahara and Harvey's before we quit. We celebrated with a couple of beers, and split over $3,000 each. We would have a practice session on Tuesday, Wednesday, and Thursday and play the weekend in Reno.

On Friday night, we hit several casinos. At the Ponderosa, Mack spotted a hand mucking crew at a 21 game across the pit from us. I watched the mechanic use the *chop* move to steal a card and move it to his knee. He was in his early thirties, like me, and had three helpers who didn't look twenty-one. They were animated and do-ing a lot of talking in stark contrast to the mechanic who sat still in the middle of the table concentrating on his work. I enjoyed see-ing them work and glad they weren't aware of us. A boss who had watched them, hiked to the podium for a new deck of cards and the young crew didn't see him. As the boss neared their game, I called to him for a Kleenex. When the boss turned, the mechanic cleaned up his card unaware that I had distracted the boss for him. We left the casino and appreciated how safe our new move was.

Most dealers didn't like to lose because they felt pressure from their boss who felt pressure from his boss. To lessen that pres-sure, when I left a game I would say to the dealer or boss, "Wow, I can't believe I got even from an earlier play." I would leave toward the cashier, but would turn back in the opposite direction, usu-ally through the slots, to shake off a possible follower. Mack would cash in my chips. After our successful fun-filled weekend, we made plans to go to Vegas the following weekend.

We would make our first play at the Stardust, as usual. Mack said the word on the street was that no crossroaders played there because they could wind up in a hospital or worse. I said, "Mack, we call the Stardust 'the old whore' because she never turns us away. It's a soft spot and we always play there first to get off the *nut*. Those backroom beatings and one-way ride stories are outdated. I was in the backroom of Meyer Lansky's joint in the Bahamas for shooting tees and turned loose, unharmed. No one knows our move exists and it would be hard for anyone to set a trap for us since no one knows who we are, or where or when we'll play—I don't always know where we'll play next until we get into our car. And the only way they could prove we switched cards would be to grab our cards while we're switching them." After three plays at the Stardust, we played at the Riviera and Frontier, and then quit for the night.

On Saturday, we started downtown at the Union Plaza and ended at the El Cortez before heading to the Strip and outlying casinos. The downtown casinos didn't get the big action the Strip casinos did but we'd tax them for one good play. We occasionally played on games near the *pit podium* where bosses did their paperwork. Besides being busy, they thought no one would try a move under their noses.

My first bet would be at least $50, to announce myself to a boss as the dealer calls out, "Money plays." The boss would say OK, or cruise by the game to look at my bet and me. He might introduce himself, hand me his business card, and ask if I wanted to be rated, meaning to qualify for *comps* and be put on their mailing list. A boss offered big bettors comps to induce them to return to impress casino manager. I'd try to win a boss over right away saying, "No thanks, I get enough junk mail at home, and I don't want my wife or business partners to know I'm in Vegas."

A boss' job is to watch that the rules are followed, to act as a referee in a disagreement between the players and dealers, and to keep track of how much money his assigned tables are winning or losing. Many bosses lose their heads when a player is winning, and conversely, they pay attention and play defense when a player is losing. The bosses with big egos were the easiest to beat, and there were plenty of them, especially in the mob-run casinos. They dressed and acted like gangsters and thought no one would dare to try any moves on them, especially in a mob joint—we'd win an extra bet or two from them. We respected the bosses that were nice guys and we quit their game early. We considered the dealers and never intentionally hurt anyone. At the end of a month, we may have cost a few pennies to the casino shareholders and mob owner's bottom line.

I had learned from experience, how much to bet on each hand

and how much to win on each play. I knew the bosses' and dealers' mindset from working in casinos. In addition, I had learned about casinos from old-time crossroaders and had formed a living foundation on which I built my own style. When Cap told me I was born to do what I do, it set me free to push my creativity and boldness to their limits. I was never at a loss for words, finding solutions, and making quick decisions while playing.

The transfer was so subtle, quick, and unexpected that we did it in plain sight—a boss and dealer would watch us make our moves and not have a clue. Occasionally, I would hit my small hands like fourteen and fifteen against the dealer's small up card to win the hand like a sucker would play. During one play at the Stardust, Mack overheard the floorman telling the pit boss that I was a sucker and couldn't win. After I left winner, the surprised pit boss asked the floorman, "What happened? The floorman sadly said, "He got lucky."

After one month, we realized we could play anywhere, anytime. We were confident, daring, aggressive and determined and outwitted every boss and dealer we played against. If an alert boss watched us, we would tap each other's knees to communicate our cards' values, and as I talked to the boss, we'd switch our cards in his face.

Some bosses knew about flashing, coolers, dealing seconds, and other moves, but it was unlikely anyone knew about the one-handed palm, and no one knew about the transfer.

We'd play one weekend in Reno, one at Lake Tahoe, one in Laughlin, and one in Vegas before we'd take a weekend off—it would be at least five weeks before we played in the same town twice and wouldn't play on the same boss for several months. I kept coded notes to describe the details of each play including my clothes, jewelry, and personal grooming.

We averaged winning $5,000 each weekend and called it "the quota." I kept a mental running count of our winnings after each play and never felt any pressure to make the quota, it happened on its own, it was magical.

We realized the possibility of a heist and we checked our backs for would-be robbers as well as Griffin and gaming agents. Mack would cash in most of the chips I won and would keep our cash pressed against his shins in long socks, sealed at the tops by thick rubber bands as Cap had done.

After a play at the Hyatt Hotel-Casino at Lake Tahoe's North Shore, I coaxed the owner of the Cal-Neva to deal to me. Ron Cloud was an anomaly for a casino owner: he would sit the box on a craps table, walk the pit like an ordinary floorman, and I had seen him deal 21 and show his hole card to the customers to promote good public relations.

I had been betting the $500 limit when Cloud arrived at our game to watch me play. We played on an end game under an over-hang that blocked a possible eye. I asked him to stay at our game to bring me luck and eventually I asked him to deal to us. He said, "Sure." I surprised Jesse and Mack but I knew we were all adrenalin junkies and it seemed like the right thing to do. After two hands, I asked Cloud if I could bet $1,000 and he nodded with a smile. I won the hand and bet $2,000 on subsequent hands without asking if it was OK.

A crowd gathered to watch the spectacle so Jesse and I communicated our cards values with leg signals. During a shuffle, a reporter for the *Sports Form* newspaper cut into me to ask my permission to write a story about the unique drama of a casino owner dealing to me. I said sure and gave him an alias. When the spectators grew, I left for the cashier's cage.

Cloud met me at the cage to chat. I cashed-in over $18,000 and my adrenalin was high. I joked with him saying, "Next time I stop in Ron, I'm gonna win your casino." Jesse, Mack, and I were flying-high as we headed to the South Shore.

Before I saw Cloud again, the Nevada Gaming Commission revoked his license. The charges against him had nothing to do with him cheating. They said he used inappropriate dealing rules by occasionally showing a dealer's hole cards to customers and other frivolous accusations. The gaming commission brought up a prior settled cheating case to use against him. In that case, gaming agents found forty-six slot machines tampered with, probably by slot employees and their agents. The gaming commission exonerated Cloud for cheating then but fined him $325,000 for not monitoring his casino employees properly.

At the South Shore, we stopped at the Sahara-Tahoe, where something special was happening. There was $100 chip action on most games, and the bosses were busy giving out credit and making fills. The casino was hosting a golf charity event that ended the next day. I found a golf hospitality table that had a list of all the entrants and the current leader board. I memorized three player's names and we found two empty seats. A boss looked at my limit bet and asked if I was with the golf tournament. I nodded yes and he told the dealer I could bet up to $1,000; the sign on the table said "Maximum Bet $500." The boss was busy with a fill and never saw me win three $1,000 bets. On the next play, I bet $500 and the dealer called out, "Green plays." A boss assumed I was a golfer and said, "OK," and nodded at me. He told the dealer I could bet up to $1,000. After making several similar plays, we quit and had won over $30,000 for the unexpected special weekend at the three casinos.

We worked three weeks on and one week off over the next several months, playing in Vegas, Reno, Tahoe, and Laughlin on the Colorado River.

In December, I was in Hawaii with Karen and Sierra and remembered that the MGM Grand in Vegas was celebrating their yearly anniversary party. The original MGM Grand opened as the biggest casino in Vegas. Three mob factions from three casinos had gotten together to combine their sucker lists of hi-rollers to play under one roof and built the MGM. Each year in early December, they celebrated their anniversary and invited their best players. They comped everyone and gave them personal gifts. Special food was prepared, and a special superstar appeared in their showroom.

I phoned Jesse and Mack and they'd meet me in Vegas. Karen and Sierra stayed in Waikiki, and I'd be back on Sunday to spend an extra week with them.

I left Honolulu for Las Vegas via Los Angeles. Jesse and Mack met me at the airport and we headed to the MGM. The show had just let out and the bosses were overwhelmed as they gave out credit and made fills. We moved from pit to pit and banged out scores of $2,000 to $3,000. There was so much $100 chip action that some dealers quit calling out, "Money plays." When a boss watched me play, he assumed I was an invited guest since I bet so high. No one asked me my name, and one boss complimented the "diamond" ring I wore that I bought at the LA airport gift shop for $12.

I was back in Waikiki on Sunday afternoon. In less than forty-eight hours, I'd flown round-trip to Vegas and made over $14,000.

After my vacation, it was business as usual except for a close call at the Stardust, where Mack screwed up and let someone get behind us. Luckily, I turned around and saw a middle-aged man just before a new hand was dealt. I felt uneasy and wondered if he'd seen anything. I won the next two hands on the square, turned around to the guy and said, "Hi, would you like to play? He nodded, no. I said, "I'll make a bet for you because you're lucky for me." He said, "I can't gamble, I'm a gaming agent." I said, "That's interesting. What do you do, watch that dealers don't cheat?" He said, "Yea, and watch that players don't cheat using mirrors and don't hand muck." I said, "Uh huh" with a look like I didn't know what he meant. I won another hand on the square, cheered loudly for myself, and asked for another drink. I told the gaming agent that I'd been on a hot streak all night long. He said, "I know, I saw you play at the Hilton and you won there too. Let's see, I think you played on table 23." I smiled and said, "You're right, I did win at the Hilton."

He left and sat on an empty 21 game three tables away and conversed with a boss. They didn't look back at me so I quickly left and headed toward the cashier. I slipped into an employee's only door, and made my way through a kitchen and exited a door to the parking lot.

Jesse said the gaming agent and boss never looked back at where we played so apparently he didn't see anything suspicious. We made a beeline to the Hilton to check the table we played on earlier—it was table 23. We were amazed at what seemed to be an otherworldly coincidence. The gaming agent possibly hadn't noticed Mack and Jesse at the Hilton, or maybe he did and thought we were a 21 card counting team and he didn't care. And maybe he watched the whole Hilton play head-on from across the pit but Jesse and my moves look so normal and the *transfer* is so subtle that our play fooled him like it did so many bosses, dealers, and surveillance employees. Whatever it was, it was weird. Mack knew he screwed up and there was no need to remind him.

Jesse suggested that he bet the money to give my face a rest. It was a sound idea and we switched positions at a practice session.

He said, "Bobby, we should bet more money since the penalty for getting caught was the same." I said, "It's OK in Harrah's, and at special occasions elsewhere, but if we wanted to last long, we had to play under the radar and can't be the biggest bettors in the casino." He suggested we use an extra man to distract the dealer and I phoned Wesley.

We had a practice session at my house where I stacked up some wooden crates to set up a mock eye-in-the-sky to see how good our moves looked. From atop the eye, Sierra, five at the time, took some instant Polaroid pictures of us transferring cards. We were amazed how far apart our hands "appeared" to be—you could see my right wrist at the inside crock of my left elbow, and Jesse's wrist was in the same position—it looked impossible to switch cards.

We started our weekend at the new Reno MGM Grand. It was the largest casino in the world and great for our style of play with seven separate 21 *pits.* We would make a play in one pit and move to another never leaving the casino like at the Stardust and Sahara-Tahoe. We played in the other Reno casinos including the newly opened Sahara-Reno, Circus, Money Tree, and Onslow casinos.

Jesse had witty conversational skills and relaxed every boss and dealer we played with. Wesley paid his own way by the extra blackjacks we were able to make because of his stalls. When Jesse and I saw we could switch to make a blackjack, Jesse would say, "Lovely!" and Wesley would hold up the dealer to give us time to switch for the blackjack. Also, if a boss was "out-of-town," and we needed a stall, we would double-switch our cards— Jesse would have two small cards, say a six and seven, and I would have two tens—Jesse would palm his seven and switch it for one of my tens. He would lay my ten on his six, pick his cards up as if to re-check his hand's value, and palm out the six to switch for my other ten to make twenty as

I slid his six under my seven. Our moves were unhurried, precise, and we used different moves to re-check and replace our switched cards. Jesse would return a palmed card to his bet by laying it on "top" of his other card as he picked it up to re-check and I would slide my card "under" my other card and lift it up to re-check. We made the quota for several weeks, and took a break for three weeks.

During our time off, we played poker at the new Reno MGM Grand. It attracted all the top poker players and hustlers from around the country, some of whom Jesse knew. I knew inside information on some of them from gossip I picked up from Clint, Bentress, and others. It was challenging playing with them and looking for their signals and *moves*.

Gabe Kaplan from the "Welcome Back Kotter" TV series, was appearing at the newly-opened Sahara-Reno and would beeline to the MGM poker room after his midnight show to play in the high-limit Razz game. Joe D and some other local rounders started the Razz game every night to wait for him to arrive. Gabe was a good all-around poker player but didn't play Razz well. A hustling crew from Vegas soon arrived and ruined the game. They used a system of strategic raises that no one could overcome. It was the same system that Ken Lundy had explained to me on our trip from Lake Tahoe to Vegas with Anrino and Clint. Joe D and some local rounders finally hired some muscle and chased Sapiro and his gang back to Vegas.

Mack lost his bankroll playing craps and poker at the Grand and he crewed up with his old partner Joe D and a poker rounder, to use the transfer. It was a disappointment that he taught someone our move, but they didn't last long or affect us and wound up the three stooges. A friend of theirs told them they could play on a 21 dealer he knew named Jim at the Lake Tahoe North Shore Club.

They found Jim but it was the wrong Jim. The dealer saw a *leak* and called to a boss. Mack's crew left and a security guard chased them outside. Mack threw his chips in the air, slid down an embankment, crossed the highway, and hid in a stand of trees. His partners eventually found him and drove him to the VA hospital in Reno for injuries he suffered in his escape. He sprained an ankle, cracked a rib, and had a concussion.

Mack got the idea to use the transfer to beat poker games. He and his crew played mostly *Omaha* because each player was dealt four hole cards that they checked and re-checked often, given Mack and Joe ample opportunities to switch their cards. They would start up a new cash game so they could sit next to each other. Before the *flop*, they would use leg signals to communicate their cards values. After the flop, they had eleven cards to use to make a powerful hand, and thirteen cards after the *turn* and *river card:* their eight cards and the five community cards. Instead of putting their four cards under their card protector, they would put three under it using the one-handed palm then switch their fourth card with each other to improve their hands. Playing *Holdem* gave them four cards before the flop to make their best hand compared to two cards for the other players. If Mack and Joe each had an ace or king, they could raise before the flop to end the hand and not have to switch. If the hand continued to the river card, they'd have nine cards to make a solid hand. They made a lot of big flushes, straights, and sets, all-powerful hands. They would find games with no cameras on it where they would sit with their backs to a wall. And they found games with high-back chairs that they draped their goose-down coats over to cover their switch. Mack and Joe switched their cards when their poker-playing partner signaled them no one was behind them, as he distracted and stalled the players and dealer.

Mack said they played against *mechanics, daubers,* and *hand muckers,* but the *transfer* destroyed everybody.

In December 1978, my older brother Johnny came out for a visit on my birthday. I mentioned to Jesse and Wesley that he could take Mack's place. It was OK with them and we had a practice session and headed to Lake Tahoe. After a successful weekend, Johnny left for Jersey with an invitation to work with us in the future.

We played three-handed and it was business as usual. After several months, Cap came back to town and I filled him in on our new move. Wesley hadn't seen him since we took off the slot machines in Reno, and Jesse and I hadn't seen him for over two years. We invited him to go out with us and he picked up where he left off. Wesley moved to the end seat and I changed places with Jesse to give his face a rest.

Most of the casinos had installed surveillance cameras but we were able to play around them. The new cameras were attached to the ceiling, inside opaque reflective semi-globes. Each globe had a three-inch wide transparent strip that the camera peered through and revealed to us the game it pointed to. We set up on games that no cameras pointed to, and Cap would check them to see if they moved to our game when the dealer shuffled, and between hands. We knew surveillance people weren't actively monitoring cameras in some casinos where the cameras stayed on lo-limit games over long stretches of time. A camera at the Stardust pointed to the same lo-limit 21 game for over a year.

We made the quota every weekend and hadn't taken any heat. Hit-and-run was our standard tactic and I rarely played more than several hands.

If a boss stood beside me, I'd ask him to stay there to bring me luck. It was a ruse to influence him and the dealer to think

I wouldn't do that if I was *doing business*. He would usually walk away and if not we would move under his nose—it was like handing the boss the tees to shoot for me in Henderson.

After Labor Day Weekend, Wesley unexpectedly quit the crew and the original Three Musketeers were back in action. We all liked Wesley and no one asked his reason for quitting. Tactically, it was better to work three-handed because we could travel quicker and we didn't need to play as much to make the quota.

At the Sahara Tahoe, A mechanic was sent to our game by a pit boss that Wesley had previously told us had done business with him. We were already ahead when the mechanic arrived so I signaled Jesse to leave and I played on the square. The mechanic was talkative and overly friendly like other mechanics we had seen. When he turned his deck hand over to check if he had a blackjack, he bubble peeked at the front of the top card. The back end of the card bubbled too and I got a glimpse of it by looking under the dealers hand from first base. He proceeded to deal seconds to the players and finished dealing the top card to himself for a winning hand of twenty. I asked him where the rest room was as an excuse to leave. When Cap arrived, he said the mechanic was relieved and said a few words to the pit boss then left the pit. We had come across other mechanics and felt the transfer could overcome them but there were tons of straight dealers to beat.

In early December, we played at MGM Grand's anniversary party and made a double-quota. Afterwards, we went home for Christmas. We returned to Vegas for New Year's Week, which lasted five days, and it was business as usual for several months. After one long play, Cap told me I was the biggest bettor in the joint and I stayed too long on the game. I always deferred to him so I decreased my bets. Jesse was unhappy and told Cap he turned a lion into a lamb. On a play at the Golden Nugget, a boss stood outside of the pit near our game. Cap whispered not to move, but Jesse turned around to look at the boss and moved anyway. I didn't move and Jesse stormed off the game. Back at the car, he said he quit the crew and asked me for a ride to the Stardust to play poker. Cap and I decided to take off for the summer.

CHAPTER 9

THE ICBM CREW

F all, 1981, approached and it seemed like a good time to get back to work. Mack joined Cap and me at South Lake Tahoe for a meeting. He had been humbled again after losing his bankroll gambling on the square, and he was serious about working. We had several practice sessions and Cap suggested some new safety tactics. We would meet at the craps pit in a triangular pattern. We'd start cruising for a game in the same pattern, keeping each other in sight. If we couldn't find two empty seats side-by-side in one casino, we'd keep moving to the next one. We would make three or more plays before we met to lessen the chance of being seen together by gaming agents, outside men, or anybody. Between plays, I would pass Cap the chips I won as we walked through a crowd of tourists.

When we'd meet, Cap would tell us what a boss or dealer had said about me when I left a game. Most dealers said I was a nice guy. A boss at the Golden Nugget teased another boss that I had cheated him. He responded, "That guy—no f,,,,,, way!" We had a good laugh on that one.

I always bet a few hands for the dealer, usually two or three $5 chips. One night, I accidently bet a $100 chip with two $5 chips on top of it. I won as usual and the dealer was elated to pick up his $220 tip and overly thanked me. It was a happy accident for us because I'd make the same bet in the future in special situations. A dealer's tip didn't cost us anything because it was the casino's money and I rarely lost a hand. A few times, we played through an entire weekend (about 200+ hands) without me losing a single hand.

The triangulating was easier, safer, and more efficient. After a play at the Stardust, Mack and I would get lost in the huge crowded sports betting parlor and wait there until Cap found us. I'd furtively pass him my chips to cash in and we'd triangulate to another 21 pit to make another play.

After several plays at the Stardust, we'd make a play at the Riviera, the Circus-Circus, and the Sahara. Next, we'd hit the MGM Grand when the shows let out. After a play there, I'd leave the casino and cross Flamingo Road to conceal myself in the multitude of tourists that waited at the crosswalk for the light to change. Mack would wait nearby behind a small tree. We would face the MGM front entrance to wait for Cap to signal us if it was George. We'd go back in and repeat the procedure a few more times. We'd hit the rest of the Strip casinos, and the Rio before driving downtown to Fremont Street, and the outlying casinos.

The Union Plaza would be our first stop downtown. They had decent action, and the cameras were easy to see. The new Golden Nugget was the most lucrative casino downtown. They had big action, with several 21 pits, and we could always find games with no cameras on them.

When the new Golden Nugget was under construction, I had checked-out the eye-in-the-sky and discovered a dummy-eye and it was now paying dividends. When a casino was renovated, or a new one was under construction, I would check out their eye-in-the-sky. I'd wear a white shirt and tie, and carry a clipboard to look like an engineer or supervisor. I also queried maintenance personnel for information. When Harrah's in Reno bought the old bank building on Virginia Street and converted it to a casino, the high mirrored ceiling stymied me. I had noticed a cracked mirror, pointed it out to a maintenance man, and said it will fall on a customer. He said they were plastic tiles and he planned to replace it—it was a dummy eye and we put the bank on our list.

After the Golden Nugget, we played at the Four Queens, Fitzgerald's, the Fremont, the Mint, and the California Casino. Next, we'd drive to Sam's Town, the Rio, the Hilton, then replay the Strip casinos after a food or beer break. I had to duck two bosses at the Hilton who were in on plays at the Carson City Nugget when I was doing business there with Henry.

We were serious about our work and always tried to improve. We worked the downtown Vegas casinos on foot in sub-freezing windy weather in winter, and 115-degree temperatures in Laughlin in the summer.

After a six-month run, we all moved from South Lake Tahoe. Mack moved his family to Texas, I moved mine to Florida, and Cap moved to Southern Maryland. We would meet in Nevada to work two weekends and then return home for twelve days. Cap said we were like inter-continental ballistic missiles, attacking Nevada from different parts of the country so he christened us the ICBM crew.

We had our beer and dinner breaks at places where we were less likely to run into off-duty dealers and bosses. I always faced a wall since I was the hi-roller and the most likely to be recognized. We enjoyed our breaks, especially Cap, because he never sat down while we worked. We liked his stories and his philosophy about life and History; he was interesting, entertaining, and enlightening. He pointed out that all good things end, and that we should invest our money and then we could fly to Vegas two or three weekends a year for a reunion, to 'keep our hands in it,' and to make some extra dough. None of us including him followed his advice.

I obtained from the Las Vegas Convention Authority their schedule for conventions planned for ten years. Through the years, we had learned that some events and conventions were better than others were. The COMDEX computer show in November brought 75,000 conventioneers to town, but they didn't bet a lot of money. The Winter Consumer Electronics Show was decent, and it followed the busy Christmas-New Year's Week so we stayed in Vegas for both occasions. Christmas Week in Nevada casinos was like the Mardi Gras and July 4th Week combined. The casinos added extra gaming tables and raised their limits for the overflow of gamblers. And we worked every three-day holiday weekend with Sunday being the busiest day and night.

Other big events were golf tournaments, national rodeo finals, Grand Prix races, and boxing championships. Big sporting events like the Super Bowl, NCAA basketball playoffs, and major league baseball playoffs attracted many out of state sports bettors. I knew enough about each event to pose as a conventioneer, or enthusiast.

When Thomas Hearns fought Marvin Hagler in Vegas, in 1985, it was the biggest grossing money fight of all time. The Nevada sports betting books took in a record $50,000,000 in bets on the fight. Caesar's Palace hosted the fight and had the biggest action in town, but we couldn't play there because they dealt face up out of a shoe. They had one high-limit, heavily surveilled face down single-deck game for celebrities who performed there, like Diana Ross and Frank Sinatra.

The Golden Nugget had a connection to get numerous ringside seats to the fight and comped their best players to the fight. They had big action and the casino had a winning weekend. A dealer told me one player lost over $200,000 playing 21. We only played at the Nugget for the three-day weekend and made a double quota before Monday, the day of the fight.

We felt like we owned Las Vegas. Cap said, "When we enter a casino we're like a pack of jackals sniffing out weak game to prey on." For fun, we made jackal sounds as we passed each other in the aisles. We knew the procedures and personality of each casino, and when we walked into a joint, we knew we could play on any dealer and boss. We played so much in the MGM Grand in Vegas that some bosses there knew my face and nodded at me when I sat down. The pit bosses who saw me assumed the floorman whose pit I played in had my name and playing information recorded in the pit computer. In fact, no one knew who I was. I'd bet just enough to keep a boss away from the game until he was busy then I increased my bets and left before he realized I was gone.

State gaming agents and surveillance personnel didn't know we existed and they stayed busy looking for crooked employees and tracking the MIT team and other 21 card counting teams that were active at that time as portrayed in the movie "21" with Kevin Spacey. And they looked for other crossroaders, and crooked poker games.

Poker was becoming popular and mechanics were using a new, hard-to-detect move in Texas Holdem games called "controlling the flop". The mechanic kept his *agent's* two discards on the bottom of the deck with the two winning cards from the current hand. After a false shuffle to preserve the bottom slug, he'd cut exactly thirty cards, or however many were needed, depending on the number of players. The *slug* he made would then appear on the new *flop*. With two *agents* in the game, the dealer controls all five community cards and the agents play their hands accordingly.

At the Reno MGM Grand, gaming agents busted several employees and their agents in a 21 cooler scam. A couple of dealers there had been catching six-deck coolers winning over $50,000 per play. The cold decker would take the six-deck cooler from his wife's purse to switch into the game. The gaming commission got wind of it and phoned the FBI because of the amount of money stolen. When they sprung a trap, the cold decker's wife escaped to the parking lot and threw the casino cards under a car. While two FBI agents questioned her, a rookie gaming agent retrieved the cards, dropped them into her purse, and said, "These belong to you." She responded, "You just lost your case for planting evidence." Her husband went to prison and the others got probation; her charges were dismissed.

The Las Vegas *Sun* reported that two men were arrested at the Riviera Casino for using marked cards. Gaming agents had tried to catch the marked card expert for over a year. He invented a new substance to mark cards that only he could read. He had made several other plays in Vegas that gaming authorities knew about but couldn't prosecute for lack of evidence. They eventually placed an undercover agent in the Riviera to trap him. He was a gaming agent, posing as a pit boss, who met the card reader through another crossroader who was an informant. The phony boss agreed to get the reader the cards he needed to mark, and insert them onto a high limit 21 game. When the card reader and his partner played and were ahead, gaming agents busted them. The reader made a deal with authorities to surrender his card marking knowledge and ink in exchange for probation for him and his partner.

Electronic technology provided crossroaders with new ways to beat the casinos. The *Sun* reported that three men were arrested at the Marina casino for cheating at 21. One of the men had a mini-television camera in his belt buckle to spy the dealer's hole card as he stood at the game. The card's image was transmitted to a monitor in a van in the parking lot where an accomplice electronically signaled the value of the card to his betting partners on the game.

And gaming authorities had their own internal problems. According to local newspapers, one of their agents was arrested using $1 slot machine slugs at Caesar's Palace that he'd stolen from a gaming control evidence locker. Another gaming agent tried to rob a guest at gunpoint, at Caesars. Their biggest "reported" scandal involved the gaming control board's chief computer programmer whose job was to find flaws and meddling in software that ran computerized slot machines. In an elaborate scheme, he swapped software in Keno slot machines that guaranteed huge payouts. According to Wikipedia, Ronald Dale Harris had fixed over twenty faked slot machine jackpots in Nevada, and had set up a $100,000 jackpot in Atlantic City, where he was caught. The Atlantic City *Press* reported that Harris's partner, who collected the jackpot, turned on him when questioned by police. Harris received a seven-year prison sentence

We had our cruising down to where we were like robots and felt like we were on a treadmill. Cap remarked that making money was boring—it was funny and true.

During the week, we went to casinos where we didn't work to try a dice shot I had been practicing at home. It was a controlled shot to *kill* one die that I called the *air ball*. The die I tried to kill stayed airborne instead of sliding like a sail shot. When it worked, it landed and glided six inches or less from the end of the table while the random die bounced alongside of it and hit the end of the table.

On our next trip to Vegas, we were disappointed to find the Golden Nugget was dealing 21 face up, precluding us from playing there.

I bought in on a game to find out why. I said to a boss, "I played here several weeks ago and the cards were dealt face down, why are they face up now?" He answered in a serious tone: "For a very good reason." We wondered if we were the reason—perhaps a camera or someone had picked up a leak—was it a sign of the future. Cap had said early on that we would make a lot of money if we could last eighteen months and that time had passed.

After we worked the following weekend in Reno, we agreed to disband. It wasn't anyone's fault—we all sincerely liked each other but something was not as it should be. Maybe it was a combination of making too much money and too long on a treadmill.

I set up a mock craps game with a piece of felt on a long workbench in my garage to improve my air ball. Jesse phoned and asked me to work with him. He had taught a slot machine hustler name Jacky and a poker rounder named Terry our move. He said they made big scores but he didn't get along with them. I agree to meet with him in Reno.

Our first play was at the Club Cal-Neva. Jacky *bet the money* and I could see he had a killer instinct. He chatted with two shocked bosses who watched him bet the maximum limit as he and Jesse palmed and switched cards; they had no idea what they were looking at. Jacky won several hands and left as I watched the bosses cook up their story before they phoned the shift boss. When he arrived, they described Jacky and said he was a drunk, won five hands in a row, and cashed-in. We made several similar plays over the weekend and made plans to meet in Vegas the next weekend.

A young boss at the Tropicana looked startled as he watched Jacky make a sloppy move. I called to the boss to distract his attention but he ignored me. He said to Jacky, "What are you doing?" Jacky said to the other boss, "I don't know what he means." Jesse left unnoticed and the two bosses watched Jacky win several big bets on the square. When Jacky lost a hand, he cashed-in and no one followed him. The suspicious boss remained silent and no one came down from the eye. We speculated that the boss saw a leak but he wasn't certain and Jacky's square play and conversation cooled him out.

Jesse complained to me about Jacky and Terry's ragged work. I told him I'd join him if he wanted to quit; if not, I would bet the money. In spite of the bad plays and bickering, we each made over $20,000 in my two weekends with them, and it didn't feel like being on a treadmill.

I didn't want to let them down by cutting their pay so I continued to bet big. It was a new world to me watching the bosses going into shock as they watched me start out making maximum limit bets. They must have wondered who I was, and if it was a marked card play, a cooler, or what? Before they had a chance to introduce themselves, I'd leave. Over the long run, the new betting style would be a disaster.

If a concerned boss stood beside me, Jesse and I moved in front of him, or I would play my hand on the square. When I lost, it relaxed him, when I won, it crushed him; either way he usually walked away to get help and we'd transfer a few hands and leave.

I could sense my partners didn't like me to play a hand on the square so I explained to them that the odds against me were about 2 percent, so the $2,000 I bet on the square cost us $40, or $10 each. It was cheap, considering the air that it bought, especially when we come right back and move for $2,000 where the odds are 90 percent in our favor.

At Caesar's Tahoe, a boss called for help when I made a limit bet. When he hung up the phone, I was ahead $9.000. Two other bosses huddled-up at the podium to watch me play. I won two hands on the square and we switched on the last hand for another winner. I won $15,000 in six hands.

Super Bowl Weekend 1987, was a busy time in Vegas and we were there. A game at the Flamingo-Hilton had a $3,000 limit and that was my first bet. We switched cards for a blackjack as a boss phoned for help. I won three more bets before a second boss arrived. On the last hand, I got a blackjack on the square, and walked away with $18,000 in just five hands as the bosses stared into space.

The betting style increased everyone's adrenaline, and mixed with alcohol we played non-stop through the weekend. When the action was slow, we'd eat and hang out at the topless joints. I had read that nothing stimulates a man more than the sight of a naked woman and it seemed to be the case with us. At the Palomino club, Jacky said he'd like to bet the money. We all agreed and headed to the Tropicana at six a.m. on Super Bowl Sunday.

Several games were open, with a few big bettors. Jacky picked a game with a tired dealer and boss and no camera on the game. He made several $2,000 winning bets and won $14,000. For the weekend we cut up over $15,000 each before the Super Bowl started. We planned to meet the following Friday in Reno for Saint Valentine's Weekend.

In Reno, we met at the Nevada Club bar and headed to the Hilton. A full moon was out, and it was Friday the 13th. We set up on a $2,000 limit game and that was my first bet. The pit boss phoned the main casino and the shift boss and his assistant came over to watch the play. We moved in front of the four bosses and they didn't have a clue. After I lost a hand, I sent Jesse and Jacky packing as I left to cash in. The shift boss followed me to the cashier and chatted with me as I cashed out the $8,700 I won. He handed me his card and said if he could do anything for me to let him know. It was all recorded on a surveillance video tape and given to us prior to a future trial, as well as videotapes of the Tropicana and Caesar's plays—Terry hadn't been watching the cameras.

Fortunately, the MGM Grand casino didn't produce a videotape of our plays there. They had hosted the Holyfield-Tillman fight and had comped their biggest bettors to the fight. The action was huge and we spent most of the weekend there. In thirty hours, we set a new winning record. We quit and wound up at the topless bar across from the MGM Grand. After a few drinks, Jacky suggested we check the Hilton again. Jesse said OK and Terry looked at me for my response and we headed out.

When I sat down, I bet $2,000 and the boss picked up the phone to call for help, I thought. I lost the hand and placed another $2,000 in the betting circle. We moved on the hand but the dealer made twenty-one again to beat me. On the next hand, we moved for a blackjack. Two bosses and several security guards appeared and trapped us—they had been waiting for us to return. They took Jesse and me to the security office as Jacky and Terry left, unnoticed. A gaming agent and cop arrived and arrested Jesse and me for cheating at gaming. Marty, a friend of ours from LA who was in town for the fight, bailed us out of jail and we met at Jacky's house to split our winnings.

A friend of Jesse had recommended a lawyer who was a law partner in a prestigious Nevada law firm. He suggested we hire an expert witness he knew who had been a dealer, a casino manager, and a gaming agent. We paid the witness $1,000 and his expenses from Las Vegas.

The gaming agent assigned to our case knew Terry and Jacky from a previous rigged slot machine case and recognized them on the casino surveillance videotape. A warrant was issued for their arrest. Terry hired a local lawyer and Jacky fled the state.

The gaming agent and a Hilton boss testified at our preliminary hearing, and the judge bound us over for trial on suppositions by the gaming agent.

Jesse's friend, Jimmy, who recommended our lawyer, told us he'd been on a double date with his girlfriend and her best friend. Her date was the dealer we moved on at the Hilton. He was from Iran and had lived and worked in the U.S. on a temporary work permit. His shift boss asked him to testify that he saw us switch cards but he refused in spite of a threat of losing his job. We asked our lawyer to subpoena the dealer. He said the judge wouldn't allow it—it was a sign of things to come.

At the trial, the videotapes contradicted the eyewitness who testified that he worked in surveillance, videotaped our play, actually saw us switch cards live, and identified their values. Whether he saw the event live, or what he thought he saw on the surveillance videotape didn't matter because the videotape exposed his false testimony. It showed the cards that he said he saw us switch were actually in the player's hand next to me. Because of the camera angle, it did indeed look like the player's cards were in my hand. The truth was revealed at the end of the hand when the dealer turned everyone's cards over. The cards identified by the so-called eyewitness were seen in the player's hand next to me and neither in Jesse's hand nor mine. The trial was recessed for the day and I asked our lawyer to ask the judge to recall the witness but he said the judge wouldn't allow it because it would delay the trial, and the judge had a vacation planned to begin on Monday. Jesse and I looked at each other and touched our noses knowing we were hung. We didn't have any court savvy and remained quiet. Our expert witness testified that he couldn't see any cards being exchanged but it didn't matter.

We had no chance to win because of the amount of money we won and the ease that we won it as shown on the casino's surveillance tapes. The videotapes didn't show anything illegal, and the evidence used against us was conjecture and some of it was inadmissible and spoon-fed to the jury who found us guilty in the kangaroo court setting.

The state had *cold decked* us but they were justified and had to do something to stop us since the casinos couldn't. We were sentenced to five-year's probation that we deserved. If the judge knew we had been out there working steady for the past ten years, he might have given us a life sentence.

We all returned to our natural element: Jesse had his probation transferred to Montana and soon went on the road to hustle pool and poker with an expert card hustler named Jimmy Tehadi. Jacky got busted beating the slots again, went to prison again, and placed in the *Nevada Black Book.* Terry was back hustling poker and I had my probation transferred to Florida, where I bought a limousine and opened a service to satisfy my probation requirements.

Karen and Sierra wanted to move back to Lake Tahoe where Sierra would begin high school. I decided to stay in Florida, but returned to Tahoe with them to find a place to live. We rented a house and I returned to Florida to arrange to have our furniture and Karen's car sent to them. I would get a pass from my probation officer to visit them periodically. We were divorced eventually, but remain faithful friends and parents.

The expert witness we hired told us that Nevada Gaming Control would use the Hilton surveillance tapes as a training aide for their enforcement agents. It appeared my career of switching cards might be over. I hadn't learned a trade and making a fresh start in life didn't appeal to me. I wondered if my *air ball* might work.

I put together a craps table in a spare bedroom to try to master the air shot. I didn't know if it was possible but I had plenty of time to find out and it was a legal shot according to Nevada rules. It was an unknown move and my best future option. I could take advantage of the multitude of ways to bet on the many craps games throughout the world. Before I had left Reno, I stopped at a casino supply store and bought ten pair of new razor-edged dice, ten pairs of used dice, and a new felt layout that Harrah's had ordered and canceled due to a design change.

I fashioned my practice sessions as realistically as possible, and fired my shots from different positions. I used my left hand to toss the dice in one direction and my right hand to toss them back. My thumbs and middle fingers formed blisters from the sharp edges of the dice and I could only practice a few hours each day. After two weeks, I developed calluses and would practice eight to twelve hours a day.

As in other moves, I designed my shot to do in front of anyone. The ideal shot was when both dice were airborne and the air ball landed flat and spun the final six inches to the end of the table. The random die would rumble along a little ahead of it and bounce hard off the table end creating the illusion that both dice hit the end of the table. When it held up it was a thing of beauty and encouraged me to go on. I took notes of what worked and what didn't.

The practice sessions became tedious but the charm of creating a new move made it bearable and I took up golf for relief and exercise. I listened to the music of Mozart and Beethoven for inspiration, and I taped a quote of Beethoven's on the wall of my practice room that moved me. It read, *"Strength is the morality of those who distinguish themselves from the rest, and it is mine too."*

I phoned Cap every few days to talk about my progress. He

suggested I keep track of how many shots worked. I was disappointed with the statistics, but they proved the difference between reality and my idea of what was happening so I kept practicing to improve.

Half-way into my probation I requested an early release. Cap helped me draft a letter to the judge who sentenced me. I figured he owed me one since I didn't appeal the outcome of my trial. In April 1991, two weeks after I mailed my request, I was notified I was free. I phoned the newspaper to put my limousine up for sale and called Cap to make plans to drive to good old Nevada. In one week, we left Florida in Cap's car for Wendover, Nevada, to start our new adventure.

At the main Wendover casino, we set up on a craps game on opposite sides of the stickman. Cap would distract the employees just as I let go of the dice. Together, we were a favorite to control anyone on any game—we had over fifty years of combined casino experience between us.

I was able to kill one die in several attempts and no one knew it but us. Cap brushed me out and we drove to Reno. We had some success in Reno and found that the shot worked better on some tables than others. One constant was that the employees were easy to distract. After one day at Lake Tahoe, we drove to Vegas. When we saw the lights of Vegas reflected off the night sky, Cap came up with a great idea as usual. He said, "If the air ball works we could own the town again. We could use bicycles to hit-and-run each Strip casino to avoid fighting traffic and parking, and eventually we'd get in shape and could ride to the downtown casinos."

Vegas had grown since we were there in 1986, and we were excited about the new places to play. Our first stop was the Stardust as usual, where we noticed that half of the craps tables were gone from four years earlier; the same had been true in Reno and Tahoe. Craps was popular among World War II veterans, but as they died out the popularity of craps died too, and the casinos were glad to replace the floor space with slot machines that worked non-stop without pay.

We worked eight to twelve hours every day except when we were on the road. The air ball was pretty when it held up as bosses and others looked at it and didn't have a clue it was a controlled shot. But the shot would come and go and after eight weeks our bankroll was even. Our nut averaged over $100 daily so we figured the shot worked, but not strong enough to do full-time. We decided to take a break and headed home.

CHAPTER 10

ROAD HUSTLING

C arlo phoned me and said an old friend of his needed an agent to take off some money from a new casino on an Indian reservation in Morton, Minnesota. I left home that night for the fifteen-hundred mile drive.

Jackpot Junction Casino was about an hour-and-a-half drive from Minneapolis. The customers were mostly working-class people and professionals from The Twin Cities. I saw two crossroaders there that I knew, Florida John and Fat Charley, who Wesley and I had shilled for on a hand mucking play in Reno. They were working with two dealers whom they had recruited in Nevada, and were putting in coolers with marked cards. John told me the camera system was out and that's why they and other crossroaders and mechanics were there. I also spotted an outside man in the casino.

Carlo's friend, Tony Paxon, was eighty-years-old and had been a crossroader most of his adult life. He had done business with Carlo and other crossroaders that I knew. He and his dealer were using the *coffee cup move*, an old move that was burned up (overused) in Vegas years earlier. Tony was using a new version of it that was as simple and effective.

I watched Tony set his coffee cup on the felt covered 21 tabletop. His dealer lightly scolded him saying, "Sir, please keep your drink in the drink holder." The dealer had dropped several palmed $100 chips into the cup as he laid his hand on top of it and moved it into the drink holder. Tony removed the chips under the table and several minutes later, he set the cup back on the table. The dealer dropped more chips into it and again set it in the drink holder. They had been taking-off about $1,000 daily.

The bosses were weak and didn't even keep track of the $100 chips. How different compared to the bosses I had worked for at the Lucky Casino who kept track of the fifty-cent pieces in the rack!

Tony's face needed a rest and that's why he had phoned Carlo. I took over for him and after I made several plays, the casino fixed their camera system and the game was over.

I phoned Cap and we made plans to meet with Mack in Reno. Mack had been practicing a dice shot and we were curious to see it.

In Reno, the old ICBM crew talked over old times and we set out for Harrah's to try our dice shots. Mack set and spun both dice and they'd bounce off the end of the table. He tried to kill two sixes, but we couldn't tell if he was succeeding. My shot hadn't improved and we decided to build a craps table to practice on and to videotape our shots.

We rented a three-bedroom house to live in and to use for our practice sessions. Mack rented a camcorder and monitor and we watched our shots in slow motion. We couldn't tell if Mack's shot held up, but the numbers to overturn the odds weren't there. Cap wrote down the result of each shot and after one thousand shots, the percentages were the same as if Mack shot on the square. We talked about the *transfer* and after a practice session we all agreed that the "over the hill gang would ride again." We made plans to go to Vegas for Memorial Day Weekend.

When Cap and I became friends in 1963, we were young and

we joked about middle-aged crossroaders we knew who were still out there hustling. We had a good laugh on them never thinking it would be us some day.

It was 1991, and six years had passed since the ICBM crew had worked together. We found the bosses and dealers were still asleep to our move. The casinos surveillance cameras gave them a false sense of security, and we were able to play around the cameras as we had in the past.

I felt shaky on our first play, and told Mack and Cap that I wanted to play in the last two seats that I thought was a safer play and that I was gun-shy after my Reno conviction. We would have ample time to switch cards to make a blackjack, nineteen, twenty, or a double down play, but I would lose the opportunity to take hit cards as I could do in the first seat. We tried it, finished the weekend on a good note, and headed back to Reno.

We put the Boomtown and Peppermill casinos on our list of places to play in Reno. They were always busy and good for at least one decent play. We worked four weekends in a row alternating between Vegas, Laughlin, Tahoe, and Reno, before taking a twelve-day break.

In Laughlin, I saw a boss at the Ramada Casino point out Mack to another boss as he set up on a game. I gave Cap the brush sign and he and Mack left the casino. Mack said he didn't recognize any of the bosses there but we decided not to play there again.

Next day, we set up at the Gold River Casino in Laughlin. Mack had a card palmed as a boss cruised by our game. He suddenly reached for Mack's one card. Mack raced him to the card, but the boss grabbed his hand and turned it over exposing a palmed card. Two security guards and two bosses suddenly closed on our game—they were expecting us.

They brought us to the security office and told us we were under investigation for switching cards. Two gaming agents arrived and told us we were under arrest. The casino manager told the agents they had a videotape of our play. The gaming agents drove us to Metro jail in Vegas, where we used our credit cards to bail out through a bondsman.

Cap phoned Carlo who recommended a lawyer. The lawyer asked us what evidence the casino had and we explained what happened.

He said, "It wasn't illegal to take a card off a table if it's not switched for another card." He called our case an up-crime meaning it wasn't malicious and said, "People living in Vegas don't like casinos and it's hard to get a gaming conviction here." He said we should have an arraignment within thirty days and we didn't have to appear for it.

A few days before our preliminary hearing, we met at our lawyer's house to watch the casino's videotaped evidence and read the employee eyewitness statements. Our lawyer's nephew, who was also an attorney, said the videotape didn't show our cards' values or a card switch. We pointed out that the videotape contradicted the casino manager's written eyewitness statement that he'd seen us switching cards to make a blackjack. The videotape showed he had his back to us during the switch. Our lawyer said that he would try to get the casino manager to confirm his statement and show the judge the contradiction and ask for a dismissal.

At the hearing, the prosecutor put two witnesses on the stand: the surveillance camera operator who filmed the event and the casino manager, Jim King, who had exposed Mack's palmed card. The surveillance man testified he filmed the event and the judge dismissed him. Our lawyer asked King to look over his eyewitness statement and asked him if it was correct. He testified that it was. He asked him if he actually saw cards switched between Mack and me to make a blackjack, as written on his statement. He said he did. He asked him, "About how far were you from the game when you witnessed the card switch." He answered, "About ten feet."

King left the courtroom and our lawyer asked the judge if he could review the casino video surveillance tapes. The judge looked at the prosecutor and he had no objection. The surveillance tape didn't show any cards being switched, but it clearly showed that King had his back to us when I had a blackjack. Our lawyer asked the judge to dismiss the case based on King's false testimony. The judge said he could see Cap move in close to block a possible card switch, and that was enough for him to bind us over for trial.

On the drive back to Vegas, our lawyer told us that someone had sent the regular Laughlin judge fishing for the day and brought in the judge from Searchlight to bind us over for trial. He said he would put in a motion to District Court in Vegas to have the charges dismissed based on King's perjured testimony.

I was less hopeful than my partners were because of my Reno courtroom experience. And because of that conviction with a conviction for the present case, I would likely go to prison for at least one year.

Florida John phoned me at home and invited me to go hustle with him on a gambling ship near Fort Lauderdale. He had learned the transfer from Wesley and said we could use it on the Caribbean Stud game and shoot the sail on the craps game. A friend of his would come along to distract and to take off some money, and their girlfriends would go along as shills to help distract and earn a day's pay. I thought it was foolish to risk breaking the law with charges pending, but I felt safe playing in international waters and decided to throw caution to the wind.

The casino opened past the twelve-mile limit and we were the first ones in to get the seats we needed on the Caribbean Stud game. John would bet the money and I'd feed him my cards to improve his hand. His friend Tom and the girls would distract the dealer.

A boss parked himself at our table to watch the action. He wouldn't leave so John aborted the play. At the craps table, I stood beside the stickman to shoot my sail shot. I had mastered it at home when I practiced my air ball, but had never done it in a live game.

The stickman passed me the dice and I gave the signal I'd go on my first roll. I killed a six while the bettors bet the pass line, the field, and the eleven/twelve prop bet. John distracted the boxman and blocked-out the stickman as he bet. I caught a random five with my six for a winning eleven. The boxman reached for two stacks of $25 chips to give to each dealer to make their payoffs. After three winning field rolls, I brushed-out everyone and we met on deck and decided to quit.

I was elated with my new success. The sail shot is a winning play when done with good shills distracting the bosses and dealers. It's not as strong as shooting tees, but there's no material evidence. John said he and his crew had shot the sail in Atlantic City and the Caribbean Islands for years. They would get to the casinos early when the shift boss put new dice on the game and they would sprinkle fine beach sand on the craps table felt which wore off the sharp edges of the new dice so they would slide easier when they returned later.

He said several quasi-legal casinos operated in Maryland, and he had marked cards down in two places. He asked me if I was interested to take off some money there. I'd keep 10 percent of what I won plus expenses. He said he had several partners to share the remaining money. A friend of his had introduced two of the casino operators there to a friend of John's who had posed as a card supplier going out of business and had two gross of cards to sell at a discounted price. John's partner, Irwin, had taught and paid four Chinese immigrant women in Philadelphia $2 a deck to mark the cards. The marked cards were in action on every 21 and poker game in the two casinos. He said, "We're not worried about any heat because the casinos can't stand any bad publicity. They are operating as charitable organizations, and a local politician is trying to put them out of business. The dealers tell the customers they work as volunteers, but are paid $100 a day under the table and each casino has a mechanic busting-out." I told John to count me in.

I drove to Baltimore and John introduced me to his marked card reader, Irwin, whom I had seen with John at the casino in Minnesota. He was about sixty-years-old and John said he was an expert card counter who had played in casinos worldwide.

We had a practice session at John's motel room. Irwin signaled me with a *stinger* how to play my hands and said, "When I buzz you that the first card of a new hand is a ten or an ace, bet the maximum. An ace gives you a 56 percent chance to win and a ten gives you a 14 percent edge."

We played that night at the Elks Club in Riverdale. I was impressed there were so many games and so much action. I'd read about the daily poker tournaments there in *Card Player* magazine in Nevada, but I had no idea they dealt high-limit 21 and roulette with over 15 gaming tables. They used six-deck dealing shoes and I didn't see any surveillance cameras or outside men. The only security I saw was an armed, uniformed, off-duty Maryland state trooper who stood at the cashier's cage to discourage a heist.

Irwin led me to a $25 minimum bet game. I bought in for $500 and played slowly to appear to be a card counter. Some of the players moaned when I made unorthodox plays that were required for a marked card play. It was Irwin's play so I took the heat. I always responded with a reason that sometimes satisfied the players. When the play was over, I cashed-in over $8,000 in winnings.

The next night, I had a practice session with another road hustler named Jerry who was about my age, forty-six. We went to the Beltsville firehouse where I won over $12,000. A boss approached me at the cashier and told me not to return. I said, "Good, you're doing me a favor." I assumed he thought I was a card counter. Some bosses thought that counting cards was cheating.

John, Jerry, and Irwin were driving to Atlantic City and John invited me to go. John said, "We're picking up a kid who is the son of a former partner of mine. He had posed as the card wholesaler that had sold the two cases of marked cards to the casino operators in Maryland. Irwin had taught him how to mark cards and read them. He didn't have casino experience but he would do what was asked of him. We could make a sail play in A.C. if there's no heat. Every shot-shooter in the country had played there and the casinos woke up to their play. If they know someone lays a shot down, they won't pay if the shot is a winner; if it's a loser, the casino locks up the bets."

The casino employees there looked like everywhere else; they were robotic in their duties and half-asleep. They weren't paid enough money to be alert all the time and when they tried, they were easy to distract.

John's crew blocked and distracted for me, and all my shots held up and were paid. John's friend Gino blocked the stickman and bet eleven and twelve. Irwin made place bets while John and Jerry made field and prop bets and "cross bet" each other—John bet the pass line, and Jerry bet the don't pass line. It's a wash to create artificial action.

They had no liability because if a twelve rolled, we'd win in the field and on the prop bets. We played in four casinos and we each made over $1,800. I was again surprised how easy it was.

John told me that he and Jerry used to cross bet in the past for comps and credit scams. They'd cross bet the maximum limit on opposite ends of a craps table that had two boxmen. Each boxman would rate their play which went to the casino's marketing department. Their line of credit would increase and the casinos would invite them back with all their expenses paid. They played in all the major casinos in Vegas, Atlantic City, and the Bahamas. Eventually, they'd go on a "gambling spree" borrowing as much money as each casino would credit them. After making a few bets for show, they'd cash in their remaining chips and leave to beat another casino. Jerry had maxed out his credit for over $200,000 on one weekend spree, flying to Atlantic City, the Bahamas, and Nevada. After three years, the casinos caught up with him. At his bankruptcy hearing, he told the judge that over time the casinos had romanced him into becoming a degenerate gambler. He said the weekend he'd gambled away all his credit, he was unlucky and desperately tried to get even, and the judge discharged his debts. Jerry saved most of the money he had made hustling and he was thrifty like most crossroaders. He always got a phony travel agent rate at motels and never paid for his meals. He made free long distance calls using a rigged beeper containing a transistor mimicking the sound of coins dropping into a phone that fooled telephone operators, and he used slugs to do his laundry and to buy a newspaper.

On the trip back to Baltimore, John talked about past adventures. He was a sixty-year-old Korean War wounded veteran who after returning from Korea, decided he wouldn't work a regular job. He went to a library to study crime and discovered that gambling offenses were the least likely to result in jail time. He had met an old crossroader in Hollywood, California, who taught him how to switch dice and hand muck and he's been hustling ever since.

When he hooked up with a crew of crossroaders, they stayed on the road for months hustling throughout the U.S., Canada, and the Caribbean Islands. They hustled stag parties, the VFW, the American Legion, and other fraternal organizations that sponsored Las Vegas Nights. Some of the events were *flat,* but they'd use stronger medicine to win. In the summer, they worked union and company picnics, clambakes, or anywhere that had gambling.

John said, "There's always parties at the best hotels leading up to major sporting events where my crew start up craps and card games. We go to the Kentucky Derby, the Masters, the Indianapolis 500, the Daytona 500, the World Series, and the NBA Championship games. Super Bowl Week is the best single week of the year for hustling but there's always competition from other crews and sometimes we partner-up with them. After the Super Bowl, we go to the Caribbean resort hotels to hustle tourists at the swimming pools, and steer suckers to their rooms to gamble when the casinos close."

John was a good storyteller, and he passed on tricks-of-the-trade to younger crossroaders. He said, "The best way for air travel is to buy 'old man tickets.' Major airlines offer senior one-way, non-reserved tickets, to anywhere in the country for $100. You have to show ID to prove you are at least sixty-two years old to buy a booklet of six tickets, and they honor an international driver's license for ID." He said a partner of his had bought the cheap tickets since he was 45-years-old. He had obtained an international driver's license at an AAA office that showed him to be 62. He had falsified his date of birth on his application and the young clerk transcribed the information onto the driver's license.

He said, "Another trick is to call an airline the day before a flight and say a family member is in a hospital under a deathwatch. The reservation clerk asks for the name of the hospital and doctor. Before you make the call you go to a library and look in the regional Yellow Pages of the destination city for the false information. Once the reservation is in the computer, it's a done deal—nobody checks anything. Most airlines offer the special bereavement ticket at half the normal cost of a ticket and the return reservation is left open because of the circumstances."

He said, in the old days, crossroaders carried a dozen fake driver's licenses before credit cards were popular. He said, "A driver's license was your credit card and hustlers used them to check into a hotel for a while then check out without paying. Now they use travel agent ID cards for hotel rooms and rental cars for up to a 50 percent discount. You make up a name for a travel agency and use your own name, address, and phone number for your travel agent card. Any print shop will make the card. You call the rental car agency and hotel chain and ask for a travel agent rate to get the discount. It's another done deal when the reservation is in the system. When you check in at your destination, you show your travel agent ID card, if asked. When you call to make the reservation, some agents ask for an IATA number (International Air Transport Association) that identifies a member travel agency. You pirate a number by buying a bus, train, or plane ticket from a travel agency that shows their IATA number on the ticket. After you get the number, you return the ticket for a refund. You can use the same IATA number for all your future reservations."

John said he uses a fake press card to get into the annual gaming and electronics conventions in Las Vegas, to learn about the latest surveillance and camera equipment. And he uses it for free admission to sporting events, movie theaters, and amusement parks with his family. He asked me my full name and said he would make me one.

He said, "Most crossroaders 'rolled' their restaurant checks for free meals. After the server gives them their check, one of them rolls it up and pockets it on the way to the cashier. In case the server is watching them leave, one of them appears to pay the check as he makes change at the cashier, saying he needs it for a newspaper, the parking meter, or to make a phone call."

John said, "Kenny Smith was a good dice hustler and the 'king of the roll.' He never got caught rolling a check, and he bought a condominium on the beach in Fort Lauderdale with all the money he had saved and set aside through the years. During his first winter there, several relatives came down from up north to visit with him. He told them they could go out to eat with him free, or go out on their own. They said they were above that sort of thing, but it was the high season and after they paid high prices for two nights, they spent the rest of their vacation eating free with Uncle Kenny."

John said, "Jerry and I were hustling with Kenny in the Bahamas when he had a heart attack and died in his sleep. Jerry took Kenny's money to give to his wife and we packed our bags for the airport. When we passed the front desk, the clerk asked, 'Who's paying for the room?' I told him, 'the guy in the room.' I told Jerry, Kenny would have wanted it that way."

I liked the travel agent move, since I would be doing a lot of travelling. I would learn that most hotel and motel chains offered the rate based on room availability. If the hotel wasn't booked-up by a certain date, rooms were made available to travel agents rather than not rent them at all. Nobody gets hurt and it would save me a ton of money in the future.

After another big play at the Elks Club, John said they were pulling up. I told him a new casino was opening in Connecticut called Foxwoods and asked him if he and his crew would like to go to bet on my sail shot. He said he had to be in Minnesota, but Gino lived near the casino and would go. He asked me, "While you're there will you check the surveillance cameras, the type of cards they use, the different card games they play, and where they keep their cards." I called Gino and we made a plan to meet in Connecticut.

I arrived in Mystic, Connecticut, two days early to find that the casino would open to the public one day earlier than the official opening. It was so the employees could get some practice from the locals to prepare for the multitude of gamblers expected on opening day. Anyone could buy $1,000 in charity chips for $20 to play with.

I entered the casino with the crowd of mostly local residents. I counted more than one hundred gaming tables and more than fifty surveillance cameras. The poker room was one floor below the main floor with about ten or fifteen poker games and a few cameras. Like many casinos, security in the poker room wasn't a big concern since any cheating there would cost the poker players, not the casino.

I bought a $1,000 in charity chips and played 21. The dealers were mostly Connecticut residents who were trained at the casino's dealing school. Some bosses were local but most came from Atlantic City and Nevada. I recognized a few whom I had played against in Nevada.

The cards were paper made by the Paulson Company in Las Vegas, and they had the Foxwoods logo. I purposefully spilled a drink on some cards to see if the boss would change all six decks. The boss replaced the several wet cards with new ones from a podium drawer. The craps tables and dealing procedures were the same as craps games in Nevada and Atlantic City. Most craps dealers were green as well as some boxmen. I didn't spot any crossroaders or any casino outside men, but I assumed they were there. After a few hours, a warning voice came over the PA system saying, "The casino is closed. Turn in your chips and leave the casino immediately." I headed straight to the casino bar with my drink, sat down like I was an employee, and continued my surveillance as the warning voice blared out every few minutes. Employees filled up the bar area and it was a treat to listen to some bragging about their past casino experiences. One worked in surveillance and bragged to a cocktail waitress that he had worked in surveillance at the Horseshoe casino in Vegas where he would find all the hiding places where dealers hid their stolen chips.

I watched the 21 pit as the bosses closed the games. They removed the cards from the shoes and put them into a plastic bag with some paperwork. The bags were placed on a steel flatbed cart that a security guard rolled through the casino. I left the bar for a closer look and was challenged by a roving security guard. I told him I just finished my drink at the bar and was leaving as I walked toward the exit. I called Florida John to tell him the information I gathered.

Gino and I met at my room to make our plans. He would stand next to the stickman's left side to make his bets and block my shot like he did in Atlantic City. I would stand next to the stickman's right side.

Next day, we stood at the front of the cordoned-off line of players who anxiously waited for the casino to open. When the security guards unfastened the velvet ropes, everyone raced to a table game. Every game filled in seconds and we were lucky to get our places at one of the many craps tables. It took an hour for me to get the dice and it wasn't because the dice were hot; it was because the dealers were so slow and overwhelmed with the amount of chips and variety of bets made. I realized I would have to bear down on my shot to maneuver through the minefield of chips on the table. I signaled Gino I was ready and we made our bets. I killed a six but it quickly kicked off. Luckily, a field number rolled to win our field bets. I didn't see my shot hit a chip and there was no string across the middle of the table, so I was stymied. I gave Gino the George sign and we made our bets again. I bore down again with the same result. I hand-placed an eleven bet and discovered a taut wire or steel rod underneath the felt *layout* between the C and E prop bet that had tripped up my shot. I gave Gino the George sign again and bore down on my air ball to fly it over the concealed speed bump. My shot held up until it hit a chip in the come box. We lost our bets but were still ahead so I brushed Gino out. On the way to meet him, I checked another craps game. When the stickman slid the dice to the middle of the table, one die rolled over as it passed over a speed bump. I told Gino the bad news and we cut up our winnings and had lunch before Gino drove home to Rome, New York.

On my way home, I called Eddie Harrigan, my boyhood friend who had given me the idea to leave Jersey for Vegas, thirty years earlier. He had visited with me in Reno where he collected a big slot machine jackpot. He was living with his family near Atlantic City and I invited him to go with me to bet my sail shot in AC.

I gave Eddie money to bet with and explained to him the sail shot and how to block and bet it. We lit on a game at Trump Plaza where a hot hand was in progress. I had witnessed several hot hands as a dealer and when shooting tees and I recognized the seriousness that happens amongst the players and employees; everyone stops hollering and clapping to keep any new players from interrupting the flow of the game. The players quickly picked up their winning bets and solemnly watched the shooter. I scooted over to Eddie and told him to start making and pressing come bets. The hot hand ended after fifteen more minutes, everyone changed up their chips to a higher denomination and left the game like someone dropped a stink bomb. Eddie and I split up over $4,000 and passed on the sail shot play. After a celebration, I drove Eddie home and headed home to Florida.

Florida John phoned to ask me to agent for two 21 dealers at a new Indian Reservation near Hastings, Minnesota; I left that day.

News of a new casino opening spread quickly. Crossroaders and crooked dealers flock there from all over the country like a swarm of locusts.

In Hastings, I hooked up with John's partner Jerry who was leaving for Florida for a family visit. He had taught two 21 dealers a handoff move and said they each *pitched* about $3,000 weekly. The new casino didn't have a camera system, but one was being installed.

I had a practice session with the dealers before playing live on their game. We set up a mock 21 game in my room and the two dealers explained and demonstrated their move. They asked me to make a semi-fist and keep it close to my 21 cards. When the 21 hand was over and they picked up the losing players' chips, they would palm some of them and slide them under my curled-up fingers as they picked up my cards; it was subtle and effective.

After two successful weeks, Jerry came back with Florida John and Irwin. John had a laptop computer that was programmed by a computer engineer that John had recruited from MIT. He designed the program to play *mini-baccarat* or 21 perfectly when fed a known sequence of cards. He said he planned to use it with one of Jerry's dealers. It was an electronic version of the baccarat slug that Joe D had set up for Mack, Rabbit, and me at the Sahara-Tahoe Casino, fifteen years earlier. The move requires a dealer to false-shuffle a slug of about fifty cards using a new move called the *sky-shuffle* that circumvents casino surveillance cameras from seeing it. The dealer appears to shuffle a slug of cards but un-shuffles the interlaced cards by lifting and pulling them apart under cover of the top card that he slides over the un-shuffling action.

John said, "The casinos rules help create the slug. Dealers pick up the played cards in the exact order that they lie when a hand is over. If a customer claims he won his hand, the dealer will go back and lay out the hands to prove he did or didn't win. Jerry's dealer will make the slug when he picks up the played cards and puts them in the discard tray. After he picks up approximately fifty cards, he will put a 'crimp' in the top slug card to mark the start of it. After the sky-shuffle, he will offer Irwin the cards to cut at the crimp to bare the mini-cooler."

John demonstrated how the computer program worked for Baccarat and 21. He typed 50 random cards into the laptop and pushed a button and a screen appeared showing a series of ten winning baccarat hands. It showed a B for bank, a P for players, and a T for a tie hand. He asked me to record the 50 cards at the casino that would go into the computer program. He loaned me a Radio Shack tape recorder to record the cards. It had a tiny microphone that attached to my collar, and the recorder was smaller than a pack of cigarettes. He said, "After you record the cards, we'll get in my car and enter the cards' values into my laptop to compute the results. It takes about thirty minutes for the dealer to finish dealing the remaining cards in the baccarat shoe after he forms the slug, giving us ample time to compute the winning hands and return to the casino to signal our agents on the game. Jerry, Irwin, and three hustlers John knew from St. Paul will win the money."

I practiced my role several times on day shift at the casino. I whispered the first fifty exposed cards into the microphone, barely moving my lips as I sipped a glass of soda. We would make the play that night.

I followed John to his car after I recorded about 50 cards. I played the recorder and John keyed the cards' values into his laptop. He keyed another button to compute the winning hands. A few blurry lines of script appeared on the screen. He said to rewind the recorder and we tried the process again with the same results. After another try, John gave up and said the sub-freezing temperature affected his laptop. He said, "It's just like in the movies, something always goes wrong."

John explained another neat move to me. He said, "I got another trick in my bag called 'the tunnel.' Irwin had taught Jerry's 21 dealer how to mark his cards as he deals them. When he lays a hit card on the table, he marks it by pressing his thumbnail into it. The big cards are marked in the center of the card and the medium cards are marked slightly off-center. After he deals through a few shoes, most of the cards will be marked. The marks are slight and subtle. Irwin will read them by looking into the tunnel shaped opening of the shoe. He'll maneuver into a position to see the marks reflected off the ceiling lights. He doesn't actually see the nick on the card, but the 'shadow' under the nick. After the play is over, the dealer 'un-marks' the cards as he puts them in the discard tray." We planned to make the play the next night, but John postponed it and said he and Irwin were flying to Canada.

I overheard them talking cryptically about a new invisible ink to mark cards that could only be seen through special glasses or contact lenses. They'd pay $500 to the Canadian inventor for a demonstration with an option to buy it. Their talk intrigued me and I hoped be in on the new trick.

When John and Irwin returned, they didn't mention the new ink. Irwin said he made reservations for him and John to fly to Europe the next day. He said they'd make the tunnel play that night.

The plan was for John and his three shills to bet the big money and I'd play in the last chair to bust the dealer. Irwin would know the dealer's hole card and the top card and would signal us how to play our hands.

The dealer dented the cards, but Irwin struggled to read them as he shuffled around the table looking at the top card. Two bosses huddled-up and appeared to talk about him. One came up to the game and checked the top card in the discard holder while the other one took six new decks of cards from the podium drawer. The play was over. The bosses checked several cards, then put them in a drawer with the other used cards. The next day, I drove John and Irwin to the airport and left for home.

One week later, John phoned me for a mini-baccarat computer play. He had a dealer at Foxwoods Casino in Connecticut whom he had taught the sky-shuffle and he was ready to do business.

John's partner Jerry would record the fifty-card slug and call John in his room with the information. He'd have ample time to compute the winning hands and get to the game with the information. He would signal me what bets to make and our partners would make the same bets as me.

The day before the play, I drove to the casino to surveil it. I could see through the clear strips on the bubble-covered surveillance cameras and none was on the two mini-baccarat tables.

The next day, Jerry hovered around the game as the dealer dealt a new round of hands. He held a drink to his mouth as he whispered into his recorder the order of the cards after each hand. After recording ten hands, he left to call John. I checked to see that the cameras hadn't moved to our game.

When John arrived, I sat down with Jerry and another agent. John stood across the pit where he would signal me how to bet.

After the shuffle, I cut the crimp to separate the slug from the rest of the cards and made my first bet. Jerry and John's shill, Alan, did likewise. After seven winning hands, we won most of the big chips and a boss stopped the game to order a new chip fill.

Two bosses huddled-up and talked about our game. After ten minutes, I surmised surveillance was looking for a videotape of the game to see if it was a cooler. Alan handed a boss his half-empty drink glass and asked for a new drink. The boss spilled the drink onto the cards in the dealing shoe. Jerry bumped me under the table and I bumped him back—it seemed the boss suspected a cooler and spilled the drink on purpose. He called to the other boss to bring him six new decks. The dealer paid us when the fill came and we left the game in different directions and met at John's room. We had won over $30,000 on the botched play. After the play, I headed home to Daytona Beach.

It's hard to keep a good move secret and eventually the mini-baccarat computer move became known. Years later, the FBI busted "The Tran Gang" who had used the move to beat casinos across the United States. According to Wikipedia, they had won around $7,000,000 from twenty-eight casinos, and forty-two persons had pled guilty to the conspiracy.

CHAPTER 11

MARKED CARDS

I rwin phoned me to go on a weeklong cruise aboard the cruise ship, Polaris. He knew a 21 dealer on board who would do business. The plan was for me to switch in a six-deck cooler of marked cards.

We boarded the ship in Miami with over two-thousand passengers. The casino had a full complement of gaming tables and slot machines that opened after one hour at sea. I checked the different ways to get to the casino and found some hiding places for our card marking materials.

The dealer, Bert, came to our cabin with six decks of the casino cards. I demonstrated how I'd swap in the cooler. I said, "I'll set it up for Irwin to win $3,000, and we'll play the marked cards for the duration of the cruise." He agreed and said he would meet us in our cabin after the casino closed.

Irwin asked me to sort the cards while he mixed up a marking solution called nigrosine. He dissolved a match-head-sized amount of the black crystals with hot tap water in a small saucer and mixed in some isopropyl alcohol. The diluted black crystals turned a light grey color. He used a mink artist's brush to *shade* the quadrants of the rose-like design in the center of the card. He painted the aces, nines, and ten value cards on one quadrant and the sevens and eights on the opposite one. He left the deuces through sixes un-marked. I examined the cards by taking my eyes out of focus, and set aside the ones that were shaded too light or too heavy. Irwin re-marked the lighter cards and lightened the darker marks by rubbing them on a towel. When he finished, I set up the cooler.

We sat on Bert's game while the bosses opened other games. He shuffled and when I said, "OK," he set his six decks in front of me. Irwin stood up ostensibly to move an ashtray to the opposite end of the table as he blocked out my left side as I switched in the cooler. Bert used the dealing shoe to cover the right side of the switch. I placed the casino cards in a homemade pouch in my jacket. The casino didn't have surveillance cameras and no one saw the switch. I left to hide the cards then returned to the casino.

Irwin would read the cards and signal me so I wouldn't be seen looking at the top cards of the shoe. We played for two hours and left for our scheduled dinner seating where the maître d seated us at a table with six people. I noticed the ship's photographer stop at every table to take pictures. As he approached our table, I excused myself to avoid having my picture taken as I did when I boarded the ship. Irwin told me I was too paranoid and I realized he didn't have common sense nor understand casino culture.

When we returned to the casino, a new dealer had rotated to our game and I won most of the hands I played. When the dealer shuffled, I'd go to the cashier to cash in some of my chips so I wouldn't have to cash a huge amount at one time and be remembered or pointed out to a boss.

After the casino closed, Bert came to our cabin and we split up $10,000 we had won. He said two other 21 players each lost over $5,000, and the craps table won.

The ship docked in San Juan on Monday, and I hiked to the post office to buy some postal money orders to mail home. Irwin had told me that a friend of his had won over $50,000 playing 21 in the Bahamas, and U.S. Customs confiscated his money because he didn't declare it when he re-entered the U.S. He got most of it back after he paid a fine and was warned that if it happened again he'd forfeit what he didn't declare.

Irwin told me that he and Florida John didn't go to Europe when they left Minnesota, but flew to St. Maarten to use the new invisible ink and contact lenses they had bought in Canada. John knew a boss there who smuggled six decks of Irwin's marked cards into the casino. He said, "We won over $40,000, but took some heat and had to hire a private boat to take us to the Virgin Islands where we caught a plane home."

Irwin asked me how much money I thought we should win and I told him $30,000. I said, "You can wear disguises and use new bettors and take several cruises a year."

After we won $30,000, Irwin said Bert wanted to win $30,000 more so we continued to play and split over $19,000 each after expenses. I asked Bert if there was heat and he said no and that the casino has had bigger losses. We made it through customs with our undeclared cash and rented a car to head home.

Two months after the cruise, Irwin told me Bert wanted to make another play and he asked me to go again. I accepted his offer and he said Gino, who had blocked my sail shot in Atlantic City and Foxwoods, would take his place. I phoned him and we made a plan to meet.

I shaved my mustache, got a short haircut, and headed to the beach to tan my skin and lighten my hair. When we boarded the ship I bought a Polaris hat to wear in the casino and glasses to enhance, my new look so the bosses wouldn't remember me.

Most of Irwin's marks had worn off and we struggled to win $6,000. When Bert came to our cabin, he had a key that opened the cabinet doors where the casino cards were stored. He said he took the extra key off the casino manager's key ring one month earlier when he had helped to close table games. He had a copy of it made in Fort Lauderdale before he returned it. He said the casino's doors always stayed open because of fire regulations, and the cards were kept in a cabinet under each 21 table. We made a plan to "borrow" six decks of cards to mark when the cleaning crew left the closed casino.

Gino watched the entrance while I took the cards and headed to our cabin where we marked them, and then returned them. It was a neat caper and a seed was planted—if I could learn to pick locks, I could snatch cards on other cruise ships.

We spent the next day and night at sea and won over $18,000. When Bert came to our cabin, he said it was Jake. We split our winnings and I returned the key to him.

The next night when we split our winnings, I told Gino that Irwin told me we should win about $50,000. He replied that Irwin told him to win what we could. I said. "The casino manager was beginning to feel the pain and could wake up to the play if we hammered away."

We arrived in St. Thomas, where Gino invited several dealers out to a free lunch and drinks. I bought some money orders to send home and hired a taxi driver to give me a tour of the small island.

Gino said the dealers liked him and the bosses weren't concerned about losing, but I thought differently and when we reached $50,000, I quit playing. Gino said he would try to win some expense money the next night.

I slipped in and out of the casino to cash chips we had hoarded and I spied on Gino. The bosses watched him play and they looked upset.

Gino arrived at our cabin and said he won $12,000 and the casino manager had changed the cards on his game. When Bert showed up, he said the bosses changed decks on all the 21 tables. After we took off expenses, we split over $15,000 each, including Irwin's share. I was happy the cruise was over, but I couldn't relax until we ran the customs gauntlet.

The customs agents asked a couple of softball questions, and no casino bosses were in sight. At the cruise terminal, I rented a car, drove Gino to the airport, and drove to Jacksonville to give Irwin his share. I asked him if he knew anyone who picked locks and he said he had a lock pick gun that he bought in a *Spy Shop*. He said, "Bert said there was no mention of my marked cards on the Polaris, but he had quit his job and was waiting to go to work on the Voyager, a casino boat in Port Everglades near Ft. Lauderdale."

Irwin phoned one week later and said Bert was dealing craps on the Voyager while waiting to deal 21 there. He had stolen six decks of cards and had mailed them to him. Irwin had marked the cards and asked me if I would try to get them into a 21 table with Bert's help.

I met Irwin to pick up the cards and his pick gun and bought several locks to practice with. The pick gun was shaped like a small toy gun with a thin narrow blade in place of a gun barrel. I placed the blade into a lock with a thin bent piece of steel called a tension tool. I pulled the trigger and it made a loud clicking sound as the blade snapped up the lock pins simultaneously. After several tries, the lock opened. After several hours of practicing, I headed to Fort Lauderdale.

The Voyager took daily and nightly gambling cruises. I showed my travel agent ID to a Voyager agent and she gave me a free boarding pass. The *cruise to nowhere* would open its casino when the ship entered International waters and would stay open for four hours.

Bert was dealing craps and I signaled him to meet me on his break. I recognized a dealer I had worked with at the Lucky Casino and I wondered why he was there. In the mid-seventies, he had been the casino manager at the Crystal Bay Club in Lake Tahoe, and a boss at the MGM Grand in Vegas. Bert saw him stealing $100 chips on his game and I told him, "Don't mention it to anyone, someday we might do business with him." My motive was to protect the dealer, maybe he was a fugitive or building a bankroll.

The casino ship had big action and didn't have cameras. One gambler played two hands of 21 for $2,000 each. The casino manager would shuttle back and forth to the two separate casinos to watch the biggest action.

I told Bert on his break that I might be able to pick the locks on the 21 cabinets. He said he could take me into the casino when it was closed to switch in the marked cards. We'd meet in town to go over a plan.

We drove to a copy center in Fort Lauderdale to get an employee ID for me. Bert had previously befriended the manager there and handed him a $20 bill and his employee ID card to make a color copy of it. He pasted a passport-sized photo of me onto the photocopy and made another copy of it, trimmed it, and laminated it in clear plastic. It looked authentic, other than it had Bert's name on it. Bert said the ship's guard would only look at the picture when we boarded the ship.

The crew and employees of the Voyager shared a fenced-in parking lot adjacent to the ship, and a customs officer sat in a shack to challenge anyone that entered the lot. I told Bert I felt a little shaky carrying a burglar tool, the fake ID, and marked cards. He said the guard waves everybody through.

Sure enough, the guard waved us through. The ship's guard at the employee gangway was the next challenge. I wore a white tuxedo shirt to masquerade as a dealer as I followed Bert. He said if someone challenged us, we were looking for the casino manager for a job interview. We took our wallets out, showed our ID cards to the young guard, and went aboard.

Bert escorted me to the casino where he'd be a lookout while I tried to pick open a cabinet lock on a high limit table where a shoe of cards were kept. My pulse throbbed at my temples as I inserted the pick gun end and tension tool into the lock. My hands shook as I pulled the trigger and applied a light turning pressure on the tension tool. I pulled the trigger over ten times before the lock turned. I switched out the cards for our six decks and locked the door. I whispered to Bert, "They're in," and we exited the ship. Bert said he had heard every click of the gun. We left the ship together and I called Irwin to tell him the "tickets" were in. He would drive down the next day.

Irwin said he was barred from playing on the Voyager from a previous play there but he had phoned a crossroader in Knoxville, Tennessee, who would fly in the next day to read the marked cards for me. He said his name is Rick Carter and his specialty is reading marked cards, palming cards, and switching in coolers in poker games.

We picked up Rick and went to Irwin's room where he had some marked cards in a dealing shoe that Rick practiced reading to adjust his eyes.

I shared a room with Rick and we went over the signals we would use that night. We talked about crossroaders we knew and shared some stories, typical of crossroaders when they meet. I showed him a couple of card tricks and he showed me the cooler move he used for poker games. After a legitimate shuffle, he slid a red deck of cards to me to cut. After I cut them, he assembled them and slid them back toward his left hand to square up the deck and he picked them up to deal. The cards were now blue. I didn't see the switch and I asked him to do it again. He explained that he did all his moves by the numbers. On the count of one, he slid the shuffled deck to me to cut as he reached into a pouch in his jacket with his left hand to secure the cooler. On two, he removed the cooler, held it in the back of his left palm, and laid his fingers on the edge of the tabletop while securing the palmed cooler. On three, he assembled the deck I had cut with his right hand, and on four he slid the assembled deck toward his left hand, and let it drop in his lap as his left hand turned up, exposing the cooler. He said he had practiced his sequenced moves in a steady cadence for hundreds of hours and he'd do it the same way in a real game, sometimes switching in six coolers in one night. It was the best explanation and demonstration of a cooler move I had ever seen.

He showed me a jacket that had six separate pouches, which held six different coolers. It was two different-sized denim jackets his tailor had sewn together, one inside the other, and then fabricated the six cooler pouches.

We boarded the ship separately and headed to the buffet. After a snack, I brought two glasses of water to the 21 table, and sat in the first seat on the high limit game where our cards were. I bought in for $500 and asked the boss to call for a cocktail waitress. When she arrived I said, "Two more vodkas over ice, please." When she returned I tipped her $5 and guzzled half of one new drink in front of the boss, the other half I spilled under the table. I pretended I was drunk because of the unusual plays I made. Carter would signal me to stay on fourteen when the dealer had a big card showing and knowing her hole card was a small card. He would leave her a big card to bust.

When the dealer shuffled, I dumped the second glass of vodka in the men's room and filled the glass with water. I kept ordering drinks and winning until the casino closed. I won over $17,000 and Rick won over $7,000. He said he had trouble reading the cards during the last hour of play. I would have to switch in six new decks of marked cards, which I hated to do. Irwin said he'd use a new solvent called Weld-On that would preserve his new marks for several weeks.

Bert said there was no mention of my play. He said the high-limit game in the main casino won big and the bosses were happy. We made a plan to go back to the casino the next night to put in the new set of marked cards.

When we boarded the ship the same guard explained to us in broken-English that he had a wife and four kids that he supported in Costa Rica and he couldn't afford to lose his job. I said "No problem," and we left. He must have read Bert's name on my ID the first night and we were lucky he dummied-up. I told Bert I would board the ship the next night with the other passengers and meet him at the casino when the passengers were at the buffet.

I was the first one to board, with the six decks in my jacket pouch. I met Bert at the casino entrance and entered the casino. I had trouble again opening the lock. Bert whispered, "Try to be quiet." Finally, the lock turned and I switched in the new cards and left the ship.

Next day, I found a spy shop in the Yellow Pages where I bought a standard set of lock picks, two locks, and several manuals on how to pick locks. The lock picks had a variety of wavy tips made of thin narrow strips of steel that inserted into a lock. The idea was to jiggle the pick in-and-out of the lock to line up the pins that would free the lock cylinder to open the lock. A tension wrench was also inserted into the lock and would open the lock as the pins lined up. It was done by feel and after a few hours of practice, I was able to pick the locks I bought and the liquor cabinet lock in my room. It was a silent process and I was elated with my success.

Carter had phoned a friend in California who'd fly into Fort Lauderdale to make the next play with me. His name was Ray Conley and Rick said he was one of the best 21 mechanics to come out of Nevada.

Conley shared a hotel room with me and mentioned some crossroaders whom I had heard about. He was an old timer and liked to tell stories from his past. He said, "When I decided to be a 21 mechanic, I learned to deal left-handed because a lefty has a natural peek. I practiced for six months before I took a job. I worked at several casinos and was on-call 24-hours a day, seven days a week."

He dealt a second for me that was undetectable. He held the deck in his right hand and barely pushed out the top two cards. Simultaneously he slid the top card back and pulled the second card out with his left fingertip and thumb like a regular dealer would do to give a hit card. He said, "The left-handed peek is the easiest because when you turn your right hand over, the thumb automatically slides the top card back just enough to see the card's index." I mentioned that I had dealt 21 at the Lucky Casino and in Searchlight. He asked if I worked for Jack in Searchlight and when I said I did he said, "We had to have worked together because I worked for Jack from his first night to his last night there; I was his main mechanic." I said, "Wow, you may have relieved me when I got on a losing streak."

Irwin put some marked cards in a dealing shoe and asked Ray if he could see the mark. Ray stood a few feet away and called out the top cards as Irwin dealt them off. He didn't miss any and moved farther away from the shoe until he couldn't see the mark.

On the way to the ship, Ray said the best way to make a marked card play was for him to play in the last seat to control the dealer's hand. I said I didn't want to change horses in mid-stream and I explained, "Irwin was a successful card counter and he or someone figured that the take-off man should make his best hand and let the dealer beat the other players so the table wouldn't lose as much." He said he was OK with that.

I went into my drunken act right away and ordered two double vodkas over ice. Ray wore a hat with the name of a U.S. destroyer embossed on it. It covered his eyes from the boss and dealer, and when he peeked at the shoe, he told WWII stories or knocked the ash off his cigarette as he tapped my knee softly to signal me how to play my cards.

The shift boss watched me play for several minutes and walked off unconcerned. Ray made big bets too since the boss was inexperienced and this would be Ray's only play there. We finished winning another big score.

Joey Cartwright would read the marked cards for me on the next play. Irwin told me he was a top-notch card counter who had taught him how to mark cards and his count system. He said, "Joey and I had won big scores card counting and *hole carding* dealers in Israel, South Africa, the Caribbean Islands, Atlantic City, and Nevada. Joey had eagle eyes, and we would find dealers that inadvertently exposed their hole cards. He'd sit low in the last seat where he could see a sloppy dealer's hole card when he put it under his up card. Some dealers, called 'front-loaders,' exposed their hole card to their front. I kept track of when and where the sloppy dealers worked and we played on them accordingly. Most were old-timers who had solidified their bad habits over the years. Many card counters were hole carding and it became so widespread that the Atlantic City casinos quit letting dealers take a hole card."

Bert told us two Cuban customers had lost big in the main 21 pit for the past three nights and they'd be back. Cartwright sat beside me and never made a mistake. Halfway through the cruise I was ahead over $15,000. The casino manager came by and I said, "Hey chief, how about another cocktail waitress." I played on the square, made bets for the dealer and pit boss, and called to the casino manager that I made a bet for him. I won most of my square hands as the casino manager watched me play. He finally walked away shaking his head. I won over $20,000 and Cartwright won $7,000. The pit boss asked me if he could provide a taxi for me in port, and I told him a limo is picking pick me up. As I left the game, I saw Florida John's partner Jerry and his wife spying on me from the slots.

I had won over $55,000 in three plays and needed a break, so I phoned Jessie to take my place. He was with a friend hustling a rich billiard sucker in Atlanta and they'd fly in that night. Jesse's friend Eddie had been a U.S. Open nine-ball champion who also hustled poker and gin and could palm cards.

After a practice session with Cartwright, they left for the ship. When they returned, they said the marked cards were gone and the casino manager pointed Cartwright out to the other bosses. Bert said that the night before, two players had made a suspicious play where our marked cards were and the casino manager removed our cards. I suspected Jerry had made the suspicious play after he saw me leave the game two nights earlier.

Irwin knew two dealers that worked on a casino boat near St.

Petersburg that wanted to do some business. The boat cruised every night and made two trips on Saturday and Sunday. He said it was smaller than the Voyager but it had plenty of action.

The two dealers came to our hotel room. Fred was a 21 dealer, and Harry dealt Caribbean Stud Poker. Fred gave us six decks of red and blue cards to mark. He said about ten minutes before they reached international waters, a boss would come around to each 21 table to unlock the cabinets where the dealing shoes were. I said, "We could switch in a cooler, or I could put the marked cards in a pouch in my jacket and set it on the floor beside the cabinet door if you could switch them for the casino's cards." He said he would try and I said we would block and create a distraction if necessary.

Harry said the Caribbean Stud Poker royal flush jackpot was over $16,000. I told him we could switch cards with each other to make the royal hand in several rounds and we demonstrated how fast we could do it. I sat between Jessie and his friend Eddie as Irwin dealt us each five cards. Jesse had two royal cards and he passed them to me under our biceps, using the transfer. I dropped them into my jacket pocket. After only four hands, we completed the royal flush. Next hand, I slid the five-card royal hand under Eddie's cards and lifted them up into my palm as I dropped the royal flush. I set his cards on top of my original cards and Irwin picked them up and put them aside. Harry said he was surprised we made the royal so fast and he could not see us palm any cards. We made the royal again in five hands and planned to play the next day.

When the boss unlocked Fred's cabinet, I stood at his table and set my coat on the floor beside the cabinet. Fred squatted down and when he stood up, he winked at me. I picked up my jacket that held the casino's cards and led Jesse outside on deck. I wanted to drop the cards overboard and make sure they sank and not float on the surface while the boat drifted. We found a small bucket in a storage locker with some metal bolts and a piece of chain. I stuffed the cards under the chain and bolts and dropped the bucket overboard as we watched it sink into the sea. Back inside, we waited for the Caribbean Stud game to open.

I palmed the queen and ten of diamonds on the second hand and slipped them into my large shirt pocket. Harry, our dealer, put my other three cards in the discard tray. On the next hand, Eddie passed me the ace of diamonds. Two rounds later, I palmed the king and Jesse held out the jack for me. I bumped my partners under the table and signaled Irwin that I had the royal flush and would switch it in on the next hand. Irwin blocked my back as Eddie set his five cards in a neat pile and I switched them for the royal flush. I set his cards on my five cards and Harry put them in the discard tray. Eddie picked up his cards and asked a local player on his right what he had. The player called out, "You hit the Royal Straight Flush!" and he called a boss over to tell him. The boss did not know Eddie but he knew his regular players. When Eddie left, Irwin said the boss asked the local if he saw anything suspicious. The local said he witnessed Eddie pick up the royal hand.

Jesse and I set up on Fred's 21 game with Irwin, to bet the marked cards. We played until the casino closed and won over $27,000 for the trip, including the $16,000 royal flush jackpot. Irwin met with the dealers to give them their end, and made a reservation to fly to Knoxville to meet Rick. I drove him, Eddie, and Jesse to the Tampa airport and headed home.

CHAPTER 12

PIRATES OF THE CARIBBEAN

The Polaris and Voyager cards had been so accessible I wondered if other ships' cards would be too. If so, I could pick their locks open and pirate the seven seas.

I wanted a variety of picks so I phoned a locksmith supplier in Orlando, Florida, to ask them to send me their catalog. Lock picks are burglary tools, but if I was a locksmith, I could get a pass for having them. I found some locksmith logos at a print store and ordered some business cards. In addition, I obtained a county license for my new business, Southern Lock & Key.

When my catalog arrived, I found a variety of picks that would open most locks. I'd buy several picks, tension tools, an Ace lock pick, and waste some money on common locksmith supplies to look legitimate.

I drove to the supplier at lunchtime, when fewer employees worked. I wore a matching brown shirt and pants that looked like a work uniform, and had my list with the name of each item and catalog number. I would pay cash and have my business license and business cards with me. If questioned, I'd say I was new in business and ask for a mail order credit application.

I read my wish list to a clerk and he filled my order. I asked if he had some old locks I could scavenge through and he gave me a box of them and I brought several of them home. I fastened them to a vertical stand and picked them until I had calluses on my fingers. For inspiration, I remembered Wesley telling me that Fat Charley had practiced picking ace locks for so long that he could pick a lock on casino slot machines with his back to the machine.

Irwin phoned and asked me to fly to San Diego to meet with him and Rick to check out a casino boat there. He said he'd been on the boat before and they kept their cards in a locked cabinet under the 21 tables.

We were the first passengers to board the Ocean Pearl, and while the other passengers were at the breakfast buffet we entered the casino. While Irwin and Rick watched the entrances, I picked open a cabinet and found several dealing shoes with cards. I removed six decks from the back shoe and left for the sundeck. I gave Irwin the cards and my picks, and he and Rick exited the ship before it ported. They'd mark the cards at our hotel room while I rode the ship to Mexico to make sure the boss didn't miss the borrowed cards.

It was a beautiful day with more people on the sundeck than in the casino. Most were there to visit Mexico and for the cruise experience. The casino did most of its business on the *cruises to nowhere* on weekends.

A boss opened the casino and removed two dealing shoes from the cabinet for two 21 games he opened. He didn't notice the missing cards.

The casino games closed as we neared Mexico, and the boss returned the two shoes to the cabinet. I disembarked in Ensenada and bought some typical tourists items. When we left port, I waited on the sundeck and watched through a porthole as the boss removed the same two dealing shoes and re-opened the casino.

As we neared San Diego, the boss closed the games and put the shoes back in the cabinet. We'd return the next day with the marked cards.

Rick held the cards until I picked open the locked cabinet and moved the empty shoe from the back to the front. He gave me the cards and I placed them in the shoe and locked the door. We left separately to the breakfast buffet.

We were ahead over $5,000 when the casino manager recognized Irwin from a previous 21 play. Irwin said he and Joey had put in a cooler there with marked cards on a dealer he knew and they took winners heat. The dealer had told him that the boss said he was a professional card counter.

At the hotel, I called some other cruise lines in California and found a cruise ship leaving from Long Beach on a three-day trip to Mexico. It was a new ship called the Renaissance that carried over fifteen hundred passengers. We didn't know where they kept their cards, but we decided to chance finding them.

We paid cash for our tickets at the pier. The ship would stop at Catalina Island, then cruise to Mexico before it returned to Long Beach.

We found the casino and I picked open a cabinet and discovered several shoes with cards. They were plastic Bicycle brand cards that Irwin had a match for in the trunk of our rental car. He left to get them from our car in the cruise ship parking lot.

I borrowed a napkin from a dining room and made a temporary pouch with some safety pins to carry the twelve decks of cards into the casino. While Irwin and Rick played lookout, I unlocked the podium door and switched two decks of our cards, one blue deck and one red deck. We'd return to make our play when the casino opened at dusk.

Irwin found the red marked cards in play and sat down followed by Rick and me. They made maximum limit bets and the bosses talked about them. I signaled them to slow down, but they continued to bet high. I left and waited in my cabin. After twenty minutes, they showed up and Irwin said they had heat and said he wouldn't play again. They won over $5,000 while I had won $500. Rick said after dinner he'd go back to the casino to play craps to see how the boss would react to him. I left to scout the casino.

I didn't want to draw attention to the 21 game where our marked cards were so I played on the square on a different table.

The casino manager asked me, "Where are your friends?" I said, "They were no friends of mine, there was something weird about those guys." It sounded truthful because I believed it. They didn't understand casino culture and resisted taking my advice.

After dinner, I played on the game where our blue cards were. Rick was playing craps to take some attention away from his earlier 21 play and to feel out the boss. The boss conversed with him and didn't seem suspicious. I won over $3,000 and left before the casino closed for the night.

The next morning, I stepped ashore at Catalina Island to jog and hike. I won another $3,000 that night while Rick decided not to play until the last night of the cruise.

On the last night, the casino filled with players who hadn't yet played, and those who tried to get even. Rick played the blue cards and I played the red ones. After we deducted our expenses, we pirates split over $6,000 each for the trip.

Rick and Irwin flew home and I stayed in Los Angeles to visit Sierra and to check out some other cruise ships. Sierra was attending college and renting a house in Manhattan Beach where she and three schoolmates were living the best times of their lives.

At the cruise ship terminal, I learned that cruise ships kept an

officer at the gangway to challenge anyone who boarded. I found a
ship that sailed bi-weekly and I waited near the gangway for an opportunity to board. Several people approached who looked like an
audit team and I fell in behind them at the gangway. A ship officer
greeted the leader and waved everyone aboard. Once inside, I left
the group in search of the casino.

Irwin had asked me to check the lighting in casinos. He said
halogen lights were best for reading marked cards and incandes-
cent lights were next best. Fluorescent or natural light were hard
for reading marks and he marked his cards accordingly. I made a
mental note of the ship's lighting, filled a glass with ice cubes from
a bar, and spilled it in front of a podium cabinet. I dropped down
apparently to pick up the ice cubes and picked open the podium
lock. Inside were some table limit signs and a roulette ball, but no
cards. I left the ship and headed to Vegas.

I bought a variety of used plastic cards in Vegas at the Gambler's
General Store. A clerk told me some had come from cruise ships. I
also bought a dealing shoe, and some books about secret inks and
how to mark cards, then flew home to Florida.

I experimented making *juice* from information I picked up from
Irwin and the books I bought in Vegas. I bought some Gentian Violet and solvents at a pharmacy and I phoned a chemical company
to order some aniline dyes and nigrosine crystals. I used a mink
artist brush and diluted the Gentian Violet to mark some cards to
practice reading. I marked them lightly with the idea that if the
mark was hard for me to see, it would be even harder for anyone
else to see. I put the cards in my dealing shoe and practiced reading them from different distances as Ray Conley had done in Fort
Lauderdale. The farther I moved away from them, the easier they
were to read. I looked at them for ten minutes, and then came back

with fresh eyes every thirty minutes. In time, I trained my eyes to read them effortlessly and then drove to south Florida to check out other cruise ships.

The Caribbean ports were popular destinations because of the calm waters. The Miami cruise ship terminal was the largest in the world and Port Everglades, in Fort Lauderdale, was the second largest. The weeklong cruises departed on Saturday afternoon and would return the next Saturday morning to clean, replenish supplies, and take on new passengers. The three-day cruises left on Friday afternoon and returned on Monday morning, and left in late afternoon for a four-day cruise. The cycle continued year round and after several years, a ship would go into dry-dock to renovate and refurbish. The ships were foreign flagged and the fast growing industry took in several billions of dollars a year. They paid virtually no U.S. corporate taxes but I planned to tax them every chance I could.

I found several cruise line companies in the Yellow Pages and called them for information. I told a receptionist at Fantasy Cruise Lines I was a travel agent and asked if I could get a pass to visit one of their ships. She said to go to the Fantasy Cruise Ship pier in Port Everglades with my travel agent ID and driver's license, and the guard there would give me a pass to inspect the ship.

I approached the security guard at the gangway of the Fantasia, said I was a travel agent, and was there to inspect the ship. He asked for my driver's license and he traded it for a pass that I clipped to my sports coat. Once on board I removed the pass and hunted for the casino. The casino entry doors had high security locks that I couldn't pick and I couldn't find an alternate way into the casino so I settled for a free lunch on the sun deck. Two other Fantasy Cruise ships would leave from Miami the following day that I would check.

The Jubilation and Exhilaration casino doors also had high security locks. There was a Diamond Cruise Line ship beside the Exhilaration, and I asked a uniformed woman at the gangway for a pass. She said I had to arrange for a pass at corporate headquarters in Miami. I flashed my travel agent ID and said I had just inspected the Exhilaration, was leaving town that night for home, and asked her to make an exception for me. She asked for my driver's license, handed me a pass, and said to be off the ship at least thirty minutes before departure.

I found a secluded 21 pit and scattered some ice cubes, but I couldn't pick the lock open. I noted the name on the lock and headed topside for lunch.

The next day, I boarded The Tropic Star for a one-day cruise to Freeport, Bahamas. It traveled there during the week and like the ship out of San Diego to Mexico, most of the weekday passengers wanted to shop in Freeport and to enjoy the cruise experience. It took *cruises to nowhere* on weekends for gamblers.

I skipped the breakfast buffet to search for the casino. I found two casinos on the main deck separated by several passenger cabins and a duty-free gift shop. I couldn't unlock the cabinet locks and headed to the buffet to wait for the casino to open.

A casino boss unlocked a podium door and removed a key ring to open the 21 table cabinets where the card shoes were stored. I would try to pick the podium lock in port, when the casino was deserted.

From the top deck, I watched as the captain and crew smoothed the ship into its berth at Port Lucaya in Freeport. As the passengers departed, I entered the casino and picked open the podium lock. I removed the key ring and headed to the smaller, secluded casino. I found the key that opened the 21 cabinets, removed it from the ring, and returned the key ring to the podium and left the ship.

I hired a taxi and asked the driver to take me to a locksmith. On the way, we were stuck in traffic due to a politician's daughter's wedding. The driver said it was a holiday. When we arrived at the locksmith shop, it was closed. The driver said he knew another locksmith and we hurried there. It was a small shack that was someone's home. The owner made a copy of the key and we rushed back to the ship so I could return the key before the ship departed.

The new key worked and I put the original key back on the key ring in the podium cabinet. In Miami, I phoned Irwin and asked him and Rick to meet me the next day.

We boarded the ship early and rented a cabin. I opened a cabinet in the back casino and removed six decks of cards. We marked them on the way to Freeport and I returned them to the cabinet. We'd make a play on the ship's gambling cruise to nowhere, on Friday night.

In the meantime, Rick accompanied me to Carnival Cruise Line corporate offices to try to get visitor passes for the Ecstasy and the Neptune. The Ecstasy left on Saturday for a weeklong cruise and the Neptune left out of Port Everglades for bi-weekly cruises to the Bahamas.

A receptionist phoned an executive to meet with us. I showed him my travel agent ID and said we were travel agents in Miami for unrelated business, but would like an opportunity to inspect the Ecstasy and Neptune before we left town. He wrote our names down and would call the cruise ship pier and arrange for us to pick up our passes for a self-guided tour.

I easily picked open the cabinets on both ships while Rick watched my back. Both casinos cards had logos so we'd have to borrow them to mark when the casino was closed at a future date.

We played on the Tropic Star cruise to nowhere on Friday and Saturday and won over $30,000. Irwin said the marks on our cards wouldn't wear off for two months.

At home, I prepared for the trip on the Ecstasy. I realized I was most vulnerable when I removed and switched the six decks of cards; it was noisy removing and replacing the shoes roller and cards, and time consuming. It would be easier and safer to remove the whole shoe to take to my cabin. I brought my brown locksmith uniform and a gym bag that resembled a worker's bag. To passengers, it would look like I worked there and I could even fool an employee since various private contractors worked on ships when they were in port between cruises.

The Ecstasy would be hosting the Tahitian Tropic Suntan Lotion beauty pageant. Don Tice, the owner of Tahitian Tropic, would be there with his celebrity friends from Hollywood and Florida. Tahitian Tropic headquarters was in Daytona Beach, Florida, where I lived. At the company gift shop, I bought a hat and shirt with the Tahitian Tropic logo to masquerade as a member of Tice's party.

We were the first passengers to board. I changed into my worker's uniform and we headed to the casino. I opened a cabinet and put a six-deck shoe into my bag and we left for our cabin. Irwin and Rick marked the cards while I scouted the casino.

We returned the marked cards before we left port and would play that night. I wandered around the deck to meet people to learn their names and hometowns to use in the event a boss would ask me my name. I wanted to stay below the casinos radar and I didn't think using someone's name could hurt him and it might earn him some comps.

When the casino opened, the tables filled up with celebrities, tourists, and us pirates. Some were big bettors like us, but no one was winning. After a play, I'd go to the bar and mingle with Tice's guests and friends, some of whom I'd met earlier. I wore my Tahitian Tropic hat and shirt and made sure the casino bosses saw me.

When the cruise was over, we split up another big score with no heat. It had been another exciting cruise making a score and mingling with the beauty contestants.

We played on the Tropic Star on Sunday, and won big again. On Monday, we left for a four-day cruise on the Neptune.

In the casino, I put a piece of black duct tape over the clear strip of a black plastic camera dome. It hung from the low ceiling and faced the podium—the tape would block the camera if it were recording. I found a 21 table with a high-limit sign and removed the shoe of cards from the cabinet beneath the table. Irwin and Rick would mark them while I observed the casino. They finished the cards and I returned them while they distracted the ship photographer and some tourists.

Thirty minutes after the ship departed, a casino boss showed up in the main pit and opened a cabinet to remove some equipment for the table games. She left the pit and I followed her to an office outside the casino. After several minutes, she came out with some paperwork.

Five dealers showed up to open 21 games. A dealer opened the high-limit game where I had put our cards. She called to the boss and said one of the decks was missing the deuce through six of spades. The boss questioned the dealer who had closed the game the night before. He said all the cards were there when he closed the game. The other dealers reported all their cards were there. She left for the office with a dealer, and returned with a case of new cards and replaced the cards on every game.

The casino manager left our shorted marked cards on a pit

podium. I told Rick and Irwin we'd have to take turns observing them to find out what would happen to them so I could try to snatch them before we returned to Miami.

On Rick's watch, the casino manager took our cards to the office. I sat in a lounge across from it and watched as dealers entered and left.

The office door lock was pickproof. I explained to Rick and Irwin that the casino manager left the office unlocked earlier and she might leave it unguarded the next day. I could look for our cards if they could watch her and warn me if she headed back to the office. I told them to meet me in the lounge across from the office at four-fifty.

Rick showed up late and I asked him where Irwin was. He said he ordered some sandwiches to the cabin and would be down later—I was shocked but composed myself. I told Rick the boss had already opened the office and was in the casino. I asked him to watch her and if she left to hurry to the office and bang on the door.

I found the cards and put them under my jacket. I called to Rick and we left for my cabin. I put the cards and several ashtrays into a pillowcase that I knotted and pitched overboard. I asked Rick to go back to the casino with me to listen for any buzz about the shorted cards.

There was no talk about the cards. The boss may have thought it was an inside job and I hoped she wouldn't report it to the front office in Miami. I too was confused and wondered if Irwin or Rick misplaced the six cards and didn't want to admit their mistake. I was the mechanic in the crew and should have checked the cards before I switched them.

I suggested we make another play on the Tropic Star on the weekend. Rick said he had to be somewhere else. Irwin and I would play without him and meet on Saturday. Meanwhile, I would check out some other ships. On the Monarch, I unlocked a cabinet and discovered four dealing shoes. I phoned Irwin and we made a plan to take a four-day cruise on the Monarch after our play on the Tropic Star.

I called Irwin on Saturday morning and he said he woke up with the flu and vertigo and he couldn't make it. He suggested I play on the Tropic Star by myself and he'd be ready to ride the Monarch on Monday.

The Tropic Star had Halogen lights and it was easy to read our cards. I made descent scores on Saturday and Sunday.

Irwin arrived late for the Monarch cruise so we had to wait until the casino closed and the cleaning crew left before I removed the cards. We marked and returned the cards and played that day and night. The casino manager was inexperienced and we won over $10,000 the first night. When the casino closed, I could only cash in $3,000 of my winnings. Irwin had already cashed-in $5,000 and the cashier said she didn't have enough cash to pay me until morning, but said she'd give me a receipt for my chips. I didn't want to give up my name so I told her I'd keep the chips to show my friends and would play with the chips the next day.

We played the next two days and nights. On the last night, the boss asked me my name and I told her the name of a passenger whom I'd met on deck when we left port. Near closing time, I noticed the man whose name I had given the boss playing on the table next to me. He didn't notice me and when he left, I cashed-in.

We flew to LA to play on the Renaissance again where we assumed our marked cards were still in play. I asked Irwin to call Rick and he said we didn't need him—so much for loyalty.

We found our marked cards, but waited until after dinner to

play. The casino manager recognized Irwin and conversed with him. Irwin left the casino and I followed him to our cabin. He said the boss told him he could play, but he put a $25 maximum limit on him. Irwin thought we had heat and he wouldn't play again. I headed to the casino to pump the boss.

I had grown a beard, and had longer hair since our first trip, and I wore glasses and a hat. The boss didn't recognize me and I said to him, "My friend said he wouldn't play anymore 21." The boss replied, "Your friend played here two months ago with another professional card counter named Rick Carter and the front office said if they came back they could only bet $25 per hand." I was happy no one suspected foul play. We were up $4,000 and I decided to quit and save my face for a future play.

At home, the *Official Cruise Guide* and a maritime trade magazine I had ordered had arrived. The cruise guide listed most of the world's cruise ships with a picture of their deck plan, including the casino layout. I studied the pictures with a magnifying glass to see which ships had twenty-four-hour open access to the casino. Some ships' casinos were throughways that always stayed open due to fire regulations. I noted the ships that looked promising and phoned the purchasing agent for each one. I pretended to be a playing card sales representative like Florida John's friend Gino had done in Baltimore. I said I will sell them any brand of playing card, with or without the ship's logo, for less than wholesale prices. I quoted them some prices, and several told me the brand of cards they use, and if they had logos. The purpose of my call was to find out that information so we could board the ship with their cards pre-marked.

I planned to continue pirating gambling ships on the high seas, but a phone call from Carlo put those plans on hold.

CHAPTER 13

BILOXI

Carlo phoned me and said a friend of his needed a marked card expert and there was a chance to make some big scores. I told him a public pay phone number where his friend could call me at a designated time.

Carlo's friend, Johnny Bitaro, specialized in putting up huge jackpots on slot machines that included a world record jackpot of over two million dollars that cost him jail time. Bitaro told me he knew some people in New Orleans who needed someone who can read marked cards to take off a riverboat casino in Biloxi. He said, "I know a casino boss there who will put marked cards on 21 games and your crew can keep half of the money you win if you decide you want in." I told him I needed to check with a partner and to call me back that night.

I had to decide whether I wanted to use Irwin. He had a bad work ethic but I didn't have enough experience to risk blowing this opportunity. I couldn't go to the Yellow Pages to find someone who could mark and read cards so I threw caution to the wind and called him.

I asked him if he'd like to go for a jog. It was a pre-arranged code meaning to go to a designated pay phone. He said he'd be ready to jog in fifteen minutes. I called him back and told him about the play and he said we could use the new invisible ink he had re-ordered from Canada.

I told Bitaro I was in and he gave me a phone number to call in New Orleans. Joe Galiano said he'd meet me at the airport the next day and I described myself and what I'd be wearing.

Galiano confirmed what Bitaro had told me. He said, "We got a boss who wants to make some big numbers. He works at a Biloxi casino and controls the casino's cards. Two other guys from Nevada made a play at the casino, but had trouble marking the cards and the boss nixed them. Johnny said you guys were pros, so I don't expect any noise from the boss. He's a little cocky, but I control him." Joe was about forty years old and seemed sure of himself. He wore fancy clothes and jewelry and had a gangster persona. I would find out his father was the underboss of the Carlos Marcello crime family in New Orleans, and Joe was being groomed to take over his father's position.

We drove to a restaurant in the French Quarter where he introduced me to a man who had worked in Nevada with Bitaro. I told him we could mark any cards and win the money. He asked me if our marked cards could be seen by a "black light" (ultraviolet). I explained we would use a new invisible ink only seen with special tinted glasses or tinted contact lenses.

Joe gave me a bag containing seven decks of cards. He said the boss included the extra deck so he could examine it before he put the other six decks into play. They were Gemaco brand paper cards with the Star Casino Riverboat logo. I said we'd be ready to play in one week.

I met with Irwin to explain the conversation I had and we agreed to split our half of any money three-ways with the take-off man. I asked if he had anybody in mind we could trust and he said Joey

Cartwright, whom I had worked with on the Voyager cruise ship in Fort Lauderdale.

We used a steam iron and Exacto knife to unseal the seven decks of cards. Irwin said he would *flash* the cards. With his mink brush he painted the crisscrossed white diagonal lines on the cards with a coat of lightly tinted green ink and left the centerline unpainted so it stood out or flashed when you looked at it. The nines, tens, and aces were flashed in one direction and the sevens and eights were flashed in the opposite direction. We resealed them and I reached Galiano on his cell phone to tell him I was on my way.

I met Joe and his driver, Nick, at a sports bar and we left there to drive to the casino boss' house. Nick was a big guy about three hundred pounds, about thirty years old, and was likable.

John Ritini had worked as a pit boss in Las Vegas, where he met Bitaro who had put him in touch with Galiano. He was about forty years old and living in a rented house in Biloxi. He said, "I run day shift at the Star Casino and I control the casino cards that are kept in my office. It's easy for me to smuggle out and returen twelve decks of cards weekly. At the start of day shift, I bring the cards to the podium and they stay down for 24-hours. I work with a boss who will put the marked cards on hi-limit games." I handed him the seven decks of cards and he opened one to examine. He said he had a ultra-violet light in his office to test the cards before he would put them in. I asked him how much money he wanted to win; he said $10,000 on day shift and $10,000 on swing shift and the cashiers wouldn't call the pit for cashing in under $10,000.

I picked up Irwin at the airport in Gulfport and filled him in on what the boss had said. He said Joey Cartwright would drive in that day.

At noon, we left for the moored riverboat casino. The Mississippi casino boats didn't cruise open waters, but stayed moored to land. Joey would play in the first seat and Irwin would sit where he could best read the cards. I'd look for a trap and watch the bosses reactions to the play. Nick would sit at the bar in case I needed him.

Irwin played for thirty minutes, and left the casino to an outside deck. He said he couldn't read the cards because of the glare from the sun, and the boss needed to put the cards on a table facing away from the windows. Nick said he'd tell the boss. In the meantime, we would wait to play at night.

Joey won his quota on swing shift and I drove Irwin to the airport and gave him twelve new decks of cards to mark that I'd pick up from him on Thursday.

Joey invited me to make a 21 play with him at the Gulfport Grand Casino the next night. He said he found a 21 dealer there who inadvertently tipped-off his hole card and he could beat the game.

I followed Joey to a 21 table at the Grand casino where the dealer dealt a double-deck game. Joey said when the count was right he would raise his bet and he wanted me to do likewise. He sat in the end seat and I sat beside him. He'd bump my leg if he wanted me to take a hit card, insurance, double down, or split my hand.

Joey wore a baseball hat and slumped low in his seat. I kept a dialogue going with the dealer and he never noticed Joey spying his hole card. He bet from $25 up to $200 and I bet $10 to $100. After two hours, we left the game separately. When we met at his room, I told him I won over $2,200 and I asked him how much I owed him. He said, "I won too, so you keep what you won." He invited me to play again the next night.

On the next play, I noticed two security people hovering around our game. A boss approached the game and said, "Joey, your play is over." He replied, "What're you talking about?" The boss said, "Joey you know the score and your friend has to leave too." He answered, "This man's not with me!" The boss said, "We watched you two play here last night." We cashed-in and left. Joey said the boss had recognized him from Las Vegas. He was driving home and said to stay in touch with him. I asked him where I could buy a stinger and he gave me a phone number of a guy in Atlanta who made rigged gaming equipment for magicians and crossroaders.

On my drive home, I stopped in Atlanta to call Butch Roberts. I told him who I was and he invited me to stop by his shop.

Butch's shop was a miniature version of Tex's shop in San Francisco. He made every type of dice I asked him about and he had a thorough knowledge of marked cards. He was about my age and personable. I bought a stinger from him and he invited me back again.

At home, I called Irwin to check on the cards and he said he had some trouble marking them. He would have them finished by midnight.

I picked up the cards and headed to Mississippi. When I arrived, I realized there were only ten decks of cards in the bag. I examined each deck and they were sloppily sealed. I called Irwin and he said he messed up two decks.

I told Ritini about the cards. He said he had planned to put in two sets of cards on two different games and he wasn't happy. He said to win $10,000 on day shift and the same on swing shift. He gave me a pay phone number to call him one hour after the day shift play.

Rick and an army friend of mine living in Florida would take off the money on the two plays. I Picked up Irwin and Rick at the airport and explained to them the game plan, and emphasized not to win more than $10,000.

I sat down at a poker machine on the second floor overlooking the casino below. Irwin and Rick were the only players on the game and it looked like they were struggling. The pit boss looked relaxed so I sat at a bar to look for outside men.

I cruised by the game to count Rick's chips and was shocked that he had over $20,000. I brushed them out and asked Irwin what happened. He said, "When you make a juice play you have to win what you can because you don't know if it's your last play." I said, "That's insane. I told you we have *inside* help and we might be able to play here indefinitely. This could be our last play."

Rick won over $23,000 and Ritini was hot. He told me not to cash in any chips until I talked to Galiano. He said the cards were hard to take out of their boxes and luckily, his partner told the boss who opened them that they sometimes get stuck because of the Gulf Coast humidity. I didn't like to talk shop on an unknown phone so I didn't respond and said goodbye.

My army friend had driven in from Florida, and I explained to him what happened and I would call him in the future. He said, "No sweat," and I gave him $500.

I explained to Galiano what happened and he said Ritini wanted to deal with Irwin in the future. He said he had to occasionally give in to the boss and he asked me to try to keep everybody happy, and for me to bring in the bettors. He said his driver Nick would give Irwin twelve new decks of cards to mark and he could overnight them back to an address in New Orleans. We could play on the weekend, and two bettors could each win $10,000 on day shift and $10,000 each on swing shift. I told him I'd stay on a temporary basis, but if anything else went bad again, I'd be gone.

I told Irwin a boss had a hard time taking the marked cards out of their boxes and he said he'd spray the cards in the future.

I realized I was working with a bunch of amateurs and I'd have to be careful. I wanted to get away from them all, but the potential to make several decent scores kept me there.

I called a friend in Jersey City who had been around gambling hustlers and bookies all his life. He would fly to Gulfport on Friday. Irwin said Joey would come back to play.

I met Lenny at the airport and told him the plan on the way to the Isle of Capri Casino where we had a mock 21session. He sat in the first seat and I sat beside him. I bumped him with my knee when to hit, double down, split his cards, and take insurance. We practiced for an hour and he never made a mistake. We drove to the Star casino to make a dry run of entering and leaving the casino. I pointed out the exit doors, the cashier's cage, and a place to talk, if necessary. On the way to our room, I pointed out two places we could meet if we had trouble or separated. I reminded him to quit after he won $10,000, and to cash it in after the play.

I'd use Irwin's purple tinted glasses to read the marked cards for Lenny. I would know the dealer's hole card and the top card of the shoe and make the best percentage plays. After I played Lenny's hand, I would guess what the players on the end might do considering the dealer's up card. If it looked like they'd stay on their hand I could take off a hit card, or leave it, to control the dealer's hand.

Lenny won his quota in less than an hour. Rick and Irwin played after us and won too. We came back on swing shift and each won another $10,000. After expenses, the bettors, Irwin, and I cut up over $6,000 each for the day's work.

Ritini told Irwin he could see some marks on the cards. Irwin told him he would use o[a new ink from Japan made from animal fat that disappeared in twenty-four hours—just another botched move and a lie to cover it up.

For several months, we used several bettors to win over $400,000, in spite of Irwin's sloppy card marking. I'd seen some of his pathetic marks on cruise ships where he needed to mark the cards quickly, but there was no excuse here. When I mentioned it to him, he said he'd spray them in the future—the same excuse he had used after the cards were stuck in their boxes.

Ritini wanted to quit for two weeks, so I headed to Miami to check some cruise ships. When I got home, I had phone messages from Cap and Nick.

Cap said a judge dismissed our Laughlin case. Ironically, the casino's surveillance videotape of our play proved the casino manager had perjured himself, which caused the dismissal. The tape didn't show any cards being switched but it did show the casino manager had his back to us when we switched to make the blackjack, which contradicted his eyewitness statement and court testimony that he saw us switch our cards to make the blackjack. I should have considered I was a free man, but I slept that idea.

I called Nick who said that Galiano was in a hospital recovering from a gunshot wound he received as he exited the Grand casino in Gulfport. He didn't have any other information except the newspapers speculated it was a mob hit. He said he would take Joe's place until he returned.

Irwin called me and said Ritini wanted to make two more plays on the weekend. Lenny sent a friend down and I called my army comrade and schooled them what to do. Nick told me Ritini said there was heat on betting $100 chips and he wanted the bettors to bet $25 chips. When I told Irwin, he said he was leaving and I told him he wouldn't be coming back. I told Nick and he told Irwin the bettors could still bet $500 a hand, but not with $100 chips. Irwin said he'd make one play. The bettors won their quota, but I told

Nick he needed to nix Irwin or I was gone. He asked if I could find someone else to mark cards and I said I could.

Galiano was out of the hospital and he called me to say Ritini told Irwin that he had heat playing and nixed him. I called Joey Cartwright and explained the situation and he said to count him in. We drove to Atlanta to see Butch Roberts.

Butch set us up for an eye test with an optometrist and we ordered the same tinted eyeglasses and contact lenses Irwin had bought in Canada. Butch said he had given the Canadian the formula for making the ink. He gave us a small bottle of green powder called IR-125 and told us the solvents to use for the various types of cards.

Joey told me Irwin had told him about the ships in Long Beach, Ft Lauderdale, and San Diego, and that he had played on them and gave half of his money to Irwin. He said Rick Carter had played there too. The betrayal had never occurred to me but now it made sense.

We practiced wearing our contact lenses as I watched Joey "dry brush" our cards. He wet his brush with the ink and patted it lightly on a Kleenex before he applied it to the cards. They were perfect.

Joey called a dealer he did business with in Tunica, and Lenny sent another bettor from Jersey. We schooled them and they each made two plays and won their quotas.

We shared our concerns about safety, and stayed at a motel in Mobile to mark the cards. Joey suggested we use conventional juice so we wouldn't be in jeopardy wearing the tinted contacts lenses or glasses in case of a trap—it was a no-brainer. At Wal-Mart, we bought red and blue "Rit" dye, rubbing alcohol, nail polish remover, and rubber gloves. We marked the cards, wiped off our fingerprints, and re-sealed the decks.

After two successful plays, Ritini wanted to give the casino a rest for several weeks. I told Joey about several cruise ships we could play on and I made reservations for a four-day cruise on the Monarch.

Joey stood by the deserted casino entrance as I picked open the cabinet lock, and removed a six-deck shoe. We marked the cards with the IR-125 and returned them. The beauty of the invisible ink was we could use Q-tips to *shade* the cards quickly and not so precisely.

We took turns playing, and each won over $10,000 for the four-day trip. The next week we took a four-day cruise on the Neptune out of Ft Lauderdale. I told Joey about the past trouble on the ship when our marked-cards came up short. He suggested that if we couldn't get to the cards, we could fly home from our first port-of-call.

We were the first passengers on the ship and I easily picked open a lock and removed a six-deck shoe that we marked and returned. A real estate group from Florida created a lot of action and we easily made a big score for the trip. We flew to Long Beach to play on the Renaissance, the sister ship to the Neptune.

The 21 boss who told me Irwin and Rick Carter were professional card counters was gone. But on our second day of playing, we felt a draft as the bosses huddled-up and whispered. Joey left to cash in his chips and someone in the cashier's cage took his picture.

We speculated we had winners heat from the play on the sister ship the week before. We hoped the front office thought we were professional card counters, but we played it safe and pitched our juice and contacts overboard. We made it through customs OK, but as we left the port in a taxi, a man a tried to take our picture. We ducked down and belly-laughed halfway to the airport at the drama.

Everything seemed normal at the airport. We flew home and I made reservations for a weeklong cruise on the Ecstasy. It was hosting a special "Baseball Cruise" with baseball players, celebrities, and souvenir dealers.

It was business as usual, and a fun cruise talking to the baseball players in the gym, the restaurants, and the 21 games. We won a decent amount after four nights of playing and decided to quit early.

On Monday, we boarded a ship called the Royal Goddess. We marked the cards and returned them before we ported. We played conservatively on the first night, but the bosses looked concerned. The next morning, I played on the square to see if there was heat. Two new dealers arrived and I overheard them talk about our play the night before. One mentioned a card counting system using a laptop computer. I was ahead $700 when the casino manager arrived and he told me that Joey and I could only bet $25 per hand. I pretended to be upset and asked him if we could play four hands at $25 each and he said no.

I told Joey I won $700 on the square and the dealer gossip about card counting with a laptop computer and we had a good laugh. We decided to get off the ship in Puerto Rico and fly home. We packed our suitcases and waited to arrive in San Juan.

The cabin steward knocked on our door and asked if we needed anything. I tipped him and told him what happened in the casino, assuming he'd be questioned later. Joey had a 21strategy sheet showing when to take insurance and when to surrender that he left it on the nightstand. We expected the cabin steward to turn it in to casino personnel, suggesting we were professional card counters that the casino manager must have already thought.

We watched the gangway from a porthole as an officer reminded departing passengers to have their boarding passes with them so they could re-board the ship. We walked past him with our suitcases and hustled down the gangway. He ran after us and said it was illegal to get off with our bags, and he asked us to wait one minute. Another officer arrived and I told him what happened in the casino, and we were going to the Puerto Rico casinos. He said we had to go through U.S. customs because the ship had stopped in Nassau, a foreign port. We followed him to a customs office and the officer apologized to us and left.

We told the customs agent why we were leaving and he asked if we had anything to declare. We said no and we didn't get off the ship in Nassau. He asked us to open our suitcases. He looked into one of Joey's shoes and dismissed us.

I called Galiano from the airport and he asked us to play on the weekend. Joey would bring a take-off man from home.

Joey and his friend left their room for the Casino. A half-hour later, I left and as I backed my car out, a car blocked me in. Several men approached me and identified themselves as FBI agents. They showed me a search warrant for a personal search, looking for marking pens, inks, contact lenses, tinted glasses, or any information related to a cheating scheme. No worries since I always worked sterile except for personal ID, money, and chips. We walked to the motel breezeway where they searched me and confiscated my cash and chips. One agent asked me if the address on my license was current and said they'd be in touch with me and I could go. Two FBI agents would visit me twenty years later to return my cash and chips that were worthless because the ship went out of business.

When I met Joey, he said several FBI agents had surrounded the 21 game and confiscated his chips and the cards. They searched him and one agent shined a flashlight into his eyes looking for contact lenses. He asked me to call Galiano for any information.

I decided to meet Galiano in person at his brother's restaurant in New Orleans. On the way, I stopped in a wig store and bought a baseball cap with a ponytail attached. Galiano had told me the restaurant had been under FBI surveillance in the past. I walked into the busy restaurant with a couple I pretended to know. I sat at the bar and asked Joe's brother for a beer. I wrote on the napkin I needed to talk to Joe. Thirty minutes later, he showed up and I followed him out a back door. He told me FBI agents had questioned three casino bosses, and searched Ritini's house. They found a journal he kept, detailing the plays we made. I told him I was going on the lam and he gave me a safe phone number where I could call him.

I made a beeline for home to get some money and clothes as I planned a long vacation. I told Joey the news and he said he had hired a top-notch lawyer from Texas.

After skiing for two weeks and sightseeing at Acadia National Park and New England, I headed home and called Galiano. He said Ritini was a British citizen and he had eluded the FBI, flew to London, and would fight extradition.

I didn't have any mail from the Justice Department, or any news from the grapevine. I called Jesse and he asked me to meet him in St. Louis to meet with Joe Smalley to make some *sail* plays.

Smalley would shoot his shot right-handed and I'd shoot left-handed. We'd block the stickman for each other and Jesse would bet from the end of the table and *turn* the boxman and bosses. We went over some signals and headed for the new riverboat casino near the airport.

The casino help and the players were inexperienced. We killed several shots and left the boat before it departed.

The riverboat casinos in Davenport, and Bettendorf, Iowa, were huge and were moored to land. I saw Gerry, the boss from Biloxi who put our marked cards on the hi-limit 21 games. He was working as a boss and I wondered if he was hiding out from the Feds or Galiano.

We beat several other casinos. Before leaving the state, we stopped at an Indian Reservation and it looked like security was waiting for us. We left in different directions and met at the car. Three men approached us and one showed his sheriff deputy ID and asked for our ID. He wrote down our names and we left the state. We stopped in Tunica, Vicksburg, and Natchez, and several casino boats in Louisiana. Smalley and Jesse had been squabbling since leaving Iowa, and Smalley flew home to Vegas.

Jessie and I played two-handed and always found a way to get in at least one winning play. After several plays, we quit and made a plan to meet in LA in one week. Jessie would be visiting his friend Marty there and I would be picking up Sierra's car to drive it to Boston where Sierra would be attending medical school. I drove him to the airport in New Orleans and drove the rental car back to Florida. We had driven over 8,000 miles in two weeks.

While in LA, we stopped at the Australian consulate for visas to visit Australia to check out their casinos. We planned to go after our upcoming road trip starting in Chicago.

After leaving Boston, I flew to Chicago, rented a car, met Jesse, and we headed to Joliet to check their two riverboats. After a few plays we left for Iowa. The dealers and a boss in a Dubuque casino recognized Jesse and we left the craps game in opposite directions. I headed for the rear stairway and removed my outer shirt, hat, and glasses, and stuck them between two slot machines. I cut into two older couples at the gangway and walked off the boat with them as if we were together. We passed two security guards who were handcuffing Jesse. In the excitement, no one noticed me drive away.

I waited at our meeting spot in East Dubuque, Illinois, until the bar closed. I got a hotel room and asked for a wake-up call. I called a bondsman in the morning who said Jesse had just bailed out.

When he showed up, I assumed someone followed him and I told him to have a beer at the adjacent bar that had a back door leading to a small parking area where I'd be waiting.

Jesse said he had called Marty who wired him bail money. He was charged with cheating at gambling from the play we made in Clinton, Iowa, one month earlier. In addition, a cop told him there was a warrant out for Smalley and me.

I'd been living as a fugitive since the FBI had questioned me, but now it was official. I'd need to get some fake ID if I were to stay free.

Jesse had a friend in Illinois who owned a poolroom who said he knew some crooked politicians in Iowa. We made a beeline to his poolroom and he put us up at a friend's farmhouse. After a few days, he told us he couldn't help us.

We headed to Chicago to visit a friend of Jesse's who verified through a police friend that Iowa had a warrant out for me. He introduced me to someone who fixed me up with some solid ID. It cost $3,000 but I needed it. I got a legitimate birth certificate, social security card, and driver's license with my picture on it. He said the documents were in the name of a person who was in a psychiatric institution and had never been fingerprinted.

Jesse drove me to the train station and he would drop off my rental car. I boarded a train to New York, to visit with Lenny. The train ride gave me a chance to do some soul searching and figure my best strategy. If I turned myself in, I would be at the mercy of federal and state authorities; if I stayed out in the cold I could watch the case against the others go forward so staying free seemed the best strategy. Two years later, seven people including myself were indicted in the case. The Biloxi *Sun Herald* reported on February 10, 1996 that five defendants were found guilty and sentenced to prison, and Joey was acquitted while I remained a fugitive.

Lenny picked me up at Penn Station and offered me to stay at his house. He helped me find a car, a beeper, and a secured credit card in my new name, and I traded in my Illinois driver's license for a New Jersey license. Too many people knew me in Jersey City so after two weeks I decided to head south.

CHAPTER 14

A LONG VACATION

I thanked Lenny for his help and hospitality. I needed to rent a place by the month to keep my *nut* down. I had enough money for Sierra's medical school and living expenses, but I'd be on the road indefinitely and would have legal expenses eventually.

In Florida, I found a furnished beachfront condo for rent. I drove home to get some clothes and a neighbor told me a FBI agent had asked him if he had seen me. My mother and Karen had a FBI visit too.

I took several cruises to nowhere and visited Butch who lived just outside of Atlanta. He invited me to live with him and to keep him company while he worked on several projects. I told him my legal status and he said, "I'm not concerned and this is a safe place to hide out."

Butch had stores of gambling paraphernalia, tools, and machines for making dice and card gaffs, including *deuce shoes* and sophisticated camera systems. He bought most of it from gaming supply houses that went out of business, and from estates of dice makers or crossroaders who had died or retired. The rest he had made.

He was a master carpenter and mechanical genius. If someone needed a specialty item, he'd build it in his mind as the customer was explaining what he needed; he would buy the materials he needed and make it from scratch. I watched him fabricate a covert camera system for reading invisible ink on marked cards. It transmitted a card's image to a monitor up to one-hundred yards away. He manipulated the small camera and transmitter into a fancy light fixture he made that would hang over a card table in a customer's bar.

Another bar owner delivered an electronically controlled craps table called a *juice-joint* for repair. Inside the table was some wiring and electronic parts that Butch tested, repaired, and replaced. At each end of the table was a copper coil that created an electromagnetic field when an electric current passed through it. Magnetically charged dice passed over the field and would stop on a predetermined number controlled by a hand-held clicker. Another customer from St. Louis dropped-off a pool table for Butch to turn into a juice-joint. He said he owned a bar, and after-hours his customers would block the pool table holes with bar towels and play craps on it. Another guy left his pickup truck and Butch built a juice-joint into the truck bed. The owner said he planned to drive it to clambakes and picnics throughout the south to hustle craps. He would lay a sheet of plywood on the bed of his truck, cover it with a thin blanket, and start a craps game.

Butch asked me to deliver a *deuce shoe* he made for Ben Potter, a customer in Columbia, South Carolina. He said, "Potter is a bookmaker who hosts 21 and poker games at a nightclub. He's a betting legend in Myrtle Beach, and when he shows up at a golf course there, gamblers followed him around in a caravan of golf carts making bets with him. He's in with the smartest hustlers and handicappers including a top golf pro, and when a *dump* goes down, he's on the winning side of it.

I drove to Columbia to meet Potter and he invited me to stay with him. He was in his 60's and had some health issues. Potter had a lot of country in him and was a good cook and storyteller. He told me he once trapped hall of fame golf pro Raymond Floyd. He said, "I gave Floyd six strokes to play par on a golf course he usually plays under par. He had to tee off twice and finish playing both balls, and his worst score counted. The trap was he usually had one long chip or putt to make. After losing, he asked me for more strokes. I checked with my handicapper, I call 'the figurehead,' who said I could give Floyd eight strokes; he lost again and quit. I trapped another pro by giving him ten strokes using another method. After teeing off, the pro had to walk backwards for the entire game. His caddie held his arm to guide him to his next shot. The pro was so disoriented by the fifteenth hole he gave up the game and his cash."

Potter was handy with a deck of cards, but hustling proposition bets in backroom craps games was his long suit. I chauffeured him to small southern towns that had a craps game one or two days or nights each week where Potter was always welcome because he was so colorful. The players knew him and he got a lot of action on sucker proposition bets from the suckers because he gave them action, or so they thought. They'd bet on long-shot bets they thought were fair bets. And he'd pick up *sleepers* in the fast-paced "shoot-and-fade" games. He'd show up with handfuls of five and ten-dollar bills to salt the game so when he won his first bet, he would claim he had been overpaid. He would give $10 back to the loser to set everyone up for future bets. Afterwards, he'd shoot $100 in small bills but only put down $90. When he lost the bet, the excited winner picked up the money never counting it. Potter won a lot of money after several hours and hundreds of bets and gave me part of his winnings.

Potter said, "Gambling was more widespread until the FBI closed most operations down cold. They raided every gambling operation in the south searching for information about who killed the federal judge John Woods. Any two employees who operated a game on two or more occasions were charged with the RICO statute so most operators quit. I only run my 21 game on special occasions now." According to Wikipedia, the FBI arrested and imprisoned gambler and drug dealer Jamiel Chagra for the murder. He had hired actor Woody Harrelson's father to assassinate the judge. Potter continued bookmaking and gambling, but eventually became ill and had to stay in bed. I headed back to Atlanta to visit with Butch.

I called Lenny in Jersey who said the FBI interviewed him about Biloxi, and he and his lawyer had a meeting with the federal attorney in Newark. He told the attorney he had traveled to Mississippi to party with me and we played 21 in three different casinos there. He said I was a good card counter and he had played 21 with me in Connecticut and Atlantic City. The federal attorney told him he might have to go to Mississippi as a witness before a federal grand jury.

Lenny said, "I wound up going to Mississippi but wasn't called to testify at the trial. Joey Cartwright was acquitted and five others were convicted. The FBI found out about Biloxi while conducting surveillance and wire-tapping the New Orleans mob and some politicians for a slot machine and video games license-fixing scheme in Louisiana. Galiano made a deal to plead guilty in the Louisiana and Biloxi case and sentenced to two years in federal prison."

I called Joey who said he was on his way to Nevada and Oregon to do some 21 counting and he invited me to go with him. I reminded him he would be harboring a fugitive, but he didn't care. He said if I would drive, he would pay all the expenses and give me 20 percent of his winnings. I'd meet him in Reno.

Most of the casinos in Reno dealt single deck 21 and most dealers were keeping track of the aces and shuffling when the deck was ace rich. It was quasi-cheating Joey couldn't overcome so we left for Oregon.

Joey said, "The FBI had played forty wiretap tapes during the Biloxi trial, and that Ritini's partner Gerry had flipped and interpreted our code words from the tapes. He said we wore special tinted glasses or contact lenses to read the marked cards. My lawyer asked him if he could positively identify me and he said he couldn't. The cards that were confiscated from the game were rushed to the FBI forensic lab in Washington by an FBI agent on the first flight out of Gulfport." I told Joey Irwin had lied to Galiano and Ritini that he had used a new substance for marking cards made from animal fat from Japan that would disappear in twenty-four hours. Apparently, the FBI had picked up the tale on a wiretap. Joey said, "My lawyer asked me to talk to the bailiff during the lunch recess and to try to touch our cards on the evidence table so if the prosecutor surprised us and said my fingerprints were on them the bailiff would be our witness that I had touched the cards during the recess. So I picked up a few cards and asked the bailiff, 'Are these the marked cards?' the man said the court bailiff was at lunch and he didn't know. I could still see our Rit dye on the cards we had marked two years earlier. An FBI forensic chief testified he found marks on the cards while examining them with a spectrophotometer at his lab in Washington. My lawyer asked him how much the spectrophotometer weighed and he said about 400 pounds. He asked the FBI agent who had approached me on the game if I was wearing contact lenses or tinted glasses. He said, 'No,' and my lawyer asked him if there was a 400-pound spectrophotometer under my 21 chair. I was acquitted and the others got prison time."

We stopped at an Indian casino in Coos Bay, Oregon, where Joey found a $50 maximum limit 21 game he could beat. We rented a room and would play there until we were barred. After two days, a boss who had worked in Vegas had recognized Joey and said he had to bar him from playing to protect his job. We drove to Lincoln City, Oregon, to check the two casinos there. They were dealing six-deck shoes and cutting off two decks of cards to discourage card counters. Joey couldn't overcome the cut so we left. The other Northwest casinos were cutting off one-third of a shoe so we headed back to Nevada.

Joey knew a boss in Vegas who gave him a room, food, and beverage comp. Joey said he could play there until they were tired of him winning. I felt I was a distraction to him because of my status and told him I was leaving for Florida. He advised me to call his lawyer, Dill Durham, who he said was one of the top criminal lawyers in the country.

Durham lived in Dallas, Texas. I phoned him with Joey's recommendation and he said he'd represent me and he charged me a conservative fee. I asked him if I was breaking any laws by living incommunicado. He said a judge could declare me a fugitive since I hadn't maintained a residence, nor communicated with my family. He added there was no statute of limitations for an indictment. I told him I wanted to remain a fugitive until the prosecutor offered me a good deal and he asked me to stay in touch with him.

I realized I could have a long wait before my troubles in Mississippi would be over. I flew into LA, rented a car, and visited Sierra. She knew me well and said she was confident I would come out of my trouble OK. On my way out of town, I stopped at a bank to withdraw some cash with my legitimate credit card. I spent several months visiting Death Valley, the Grand Canyon, and Yosemite

National Park. I drove up and down the California Coast Highway and throughout the Northwest before heading back to Florida.

Bill Durham had phoned the federal attorney in Biloxi, who offered me a deal. If I turned myself in, he'd ask for a three-year jail sentence. And he wanted me to tell about the casino scheme and the people involved. I told Bill that was a non-starter, but I'd stay in touch with him.

After returning home, I drove to Atlanta to visit with Butch. He was working with two gambling hustlers who had come to Atlanta to beat a local bookmaker named Bennett. Butch said the hustlers had already beaten him for $50,000. Bennett would hustle them playing golf during the day and they'd hustle him playing gin at night. They played in a conference room at the full-service hotel where the card hustlers stayed. Butch had installed a covert camera system in a light fixture in the conference room, and could see Bennett's cards from a monitor in a hotel room and would transmit the information to the hustlers through a tiny earpiece. The earpiece was so small that Butch attached a piece of transparent monofilament fishing line to it so it wouldn't get lost in the hustler's ear.

I had accompanied Butch to the hotel to test the camera equipment and earpieces and to meet the hustlers. I had met one of them around the time I dealt 21 in Las Vegas, over thirty years earlier— another small world meeting. His name was Lenny Moore, and he had done business with Bill Douglas and other old-time crossroaders. Lenny was the real-life boyfriend of Gerry McGee portrayed by Sharon Stone in the movie "Casino." Actor James Woods had played his part. I asked him if the producers paid him and he said they offered him a free lunch with Sharon Stone that he had turned down.

On the next play with Bennet, I sat with Butch in his hotel room and could see Bennet's cards that Butch transmitted to his partners.

After the play Butch told us about a similar system he had installed in the card room at a country club in Myrtle Beach. He said the day after he flew home, his customer phoned him and said while playing golf and changing the channels on his golf cart TV, he saw the poker table in the card room on the golf cart screen. Butch said he flew back on the first available flight to change the frequency on the transmitter to correct the near disaster.

Butch asked me to drive to Houston to pick up some dice equipment from Crush, a retired crossroader. He had talked to Crush's wife on the phone and agreed to buy all of his dice and equipment sight-unseen for $1,000. I had never met Crush, but we had mutual friends who had referred to him as a legend. Florida John had told me Crush had hustled craps in Fort Worth, as a teenager and went on the road as a dice and card mechanic with Clayton Gatterdam when he was fifteen-years old. Gatterdam was later caught switching dice at a Lake Tahoe casino.

I drove for ten hours, and checked into a motel. I still had another five-hour drive and I wanted to be fresh when I arrived in Houston. I hit the TV power button as I opened my overnight bag and halted when John Walsh of "America's Most Wanted" mentioned my name. Walsh said the New Orleans mafia had infiltrated a casino in Biloxi, and were cheating 21 games there using marked cards. He said I had marked the cards and had taken large sums of money from the casino. An FBI surveillance videotape showed me leaving my motel room in Biloxi with Joe Galiano. An FBI agent said I was the ringleader and described how I operated. Walsh said I failed to show up for the Biloxi trial where five other people had been convicted. He described me incorrectly as 6 feet 3" tall with light hair and said to watch for me in casinos and on cruise ships.

I wondered why I was on such a seamy program. My hyper-analytical mind figured viewers were tired of seeing violence on the program, and millions of people were fascinated by casinos. Some would find an interest in the story and some would be glad to see the casinos being ripped off. For the FBI and U.S. Marshals, having my picture out there was free advertising.

I phoned Jesse and he said several of our friends saw the show, and that he and I were shown allegedly switching cards on a variety of TV programs from clips taken from the Reno-Hilton Casino surveillance videotapes.

I wondered about the motel clerk who had checked me in. The FBI videotapes showed me with a mustache, sideburns, and medium-length hair. Now, I was clean-shaven with short hair, and two years older. I wore a plain gold wedding band to square up my image and John Walsh said I was three inches taller than I was. When checking in I had posed as a travel agent to get the 50 percent discount for the room, but that had gone smoothly as usual.

I should have seen the trouble coming in Biloxi. In the past, I had warnings before a potential disaster and averted trouble, but then I had worked with loyal handpicked partners and stayed away from rings and organized crime figures that always have heat.

The next morning, Crush's wife gave me directions to their home. Crush was in his 70's and jovial. We talked about mutual friends and shared gambling experiences, and he showed me some impressive dice and card moves I had never seen before. He said he had learned a lot of his moves from Clayton Gatterdam. I mentioned a friend of mine had worked with Gatterdam when he was caught busting-out craps players at The Lake Tahoe Casino. Crush said, "Clayton also got busted in London and did time for beating a casino there. And he had been captured at the Battle of the Bulge during WWII and was busted at a POW camp with several sets of tees."

I gave Crush the $1,000 Butch had given me, and he helped me carry his dice paraphernalia to my car. He had a cigar box full of brass dies for monogramming dice, a Kingsley embossing machine, numerous packets of tungsten discs and other heavy metals for loading dice, and his dice kit was a custom-made alligator skin suitcase with drawers lined with a multiplicity of tees, weight, and *fronts*. He had boxes of celluloid dice stock and a heavy die press for making dice. After his wife fixed us a sandwich and a milk shake, I gave her the $1,000, said goodbye, and drove straight through to Atlanta.

Butch already knew I was a movie star. His girlfriend and one of his workers had seen me on America's Most Wanted. I told Butch I would be going Europe.

I phoned an old friend I had worked with at the Lucky Casino who lived outside of Amsterdam, and he invited me to visit with him. I couldn't use my own passport so I asked a cousin to loan me his passport; we looked alike and were close to the same age. He didn't hesitate and wished me good luck. I bought some American Express travel checks and made a reservation to fly to Amsterdam.

I visited Sierra to say goodbye. She said two FBI agents had stopped at her house the day after I had last seen her. They told her I used my credit card to withdraw some cash from an LA bank, and asked her if she had seen me. She told them she wouldn't make any statements. She said the female agent stopped back an hour after the first visit to verify her phone number. I told her it sounded like she was tipping her off that her phone was tapped. Sierra was likable and anyone who met her wanted to be her friend. I apologized for the FBI visit, told her my plans, and she wished me luck and asked me to stay in touch with her.

I was used to dealing with customs agents from my cruising

days and made it to Amsterdam with no problem. My friend Terry picked me up at the airport and I filled him in on my latest adventures. He suggested I write a "Life and Times" book while I was killing time.

After we toured Holland and Belgium for several days, Terry went back to work and I continued sightseeing. I played in the European Holdem Poker Championship at the Amsterdam Casino where I met an American player who told me about a poker casino in Bregenz, Austria where full-time players had their meals and room comped.

I decided to give Terry a break and told him my plans. He made me a couple of sandwiches for my ten-hour train ride.

I arrived in Bregenz and registered at the casino hotel just outside of town. After unpacking my bag, I headed to the poker casino to find out about the free room and board. I played in a holdem poker game and befriended an Austrian player named Martin who explained the requirements for the comps and local customs. He was a rounder and he pointed out the best players, and the easiest games. Some of the players were locals and some were from other places in Europe. The main game was a pot-limit Omaha poker game. Martin pointed to a player in the game and said, "That's Tom Cruise's younger brother and he's the main draw. He came here to ski in nearby Switzerland and to play hi-stakes poker at night, as he had the previous winter. The other players are a Swiss Ski champion, a European Backgammon champion, a Chess champion, and some businessmen. Cruise had been skiing and playing poker with the skier all week. He will win or lose several thousand dollars in one night." I spied on the game and didn't detect any hidden cameras or other cheating, but I assumed something crooked was happening.

A German ran the poker room and cut the hotel owner in for

a percentage of his profits in exchange for using his facilities. The poker players kept the hotel full and the restaurant busy.

I was there to kill time so it was a perfect situation for me. I went sightseeing in the daytime and played poker at night in the $100 buy-in holdem tournament. There were enough players in the tournament to make the payoffs decent. I finished in first place one night and collected over $2,000.

On Christmas Eve Day, Martin knocked on my door and said the poker was over. Austrian government officials had just served notice to the hotel owner to cease operations. Half of the dealers had already left and the rest were arranging transportation home. The sudden closing came as a surprise to everybody. Martin said it was political because of the competition to the government-run Bregenz Casino.

Martin and I joined the poker boss and his family for lunch. He told the boss I had no plans to leave Bregenz. The boss said he'd honor my comp at the hotel for one week and would ask the hotel owner for a special rate if I stayed longer.

The Captain used to say, "When in doubt, the best move is no move at all," so I decided to stay where I was indefinitely. My nut was small and my hotel room was quiet and cozy. I started a "Life and Times" book.

A food store was several blocks away and my room had a deck to keep my milk and other perishables fresh. Lake Constance, a huge alpine lake bordering Germany, Austria, and Switzerland was two-hundred yards from my hotel and I could catch a five-minute bus ride into Bregenz to get a hot meal and haircut. The Bregenz Casino had a small one-man craps table, but it was bouncy and my *air ball* wouldn't work.

Writing was pleasant and easy for me. Most of my past had been fun so I relived those good times. After dinner, I wrote and fell asleep with a pen in hand. When I awakened, I continued writing. After a light breakfast, I wrote before my daily walk through the woods to Lake Constance. During my walks, I recalled past experiences and made short notes.

I got a notion to phone Butch who suggested I call a customer of his who was living in Berlin. His name was "Fast Jack" Kelly and he invited me to meet him in Frankfurt. He would be there with two friends who planned to rip off an illegal casino.

I met Jack and his friends and we checked into a fancy hotel. Jack's friends left, saying they would call if they needed us. Jack and I stayed up for several hours sharing stories and various moves.

Jack woke me in the morning and said his friends were in the hotel restaurant having breakfast. They had played all night and didn't say if they won or lost, but they were going back to Berlin and Jack invited me to go with them. He was living with a friend who was visiting his family in Greece. I could stay with him at his friend's condominium and there was a chance to make some money in underground casinos there. I had no obligations and decided to go.

Jack told me he had worked in mob-run illegal casinos in the Northeast U.S. and had met his Berlin friend in a crooked gambling supply store in New York. He said they had made some big scores playing gin and poker working with a ring of Berlin gamblers.

Jack was sporty and wouldn't let me pay for anything. We'd eat in the best nightclubs and he would talk to everybody he saw to hustle up a game—any game. It wasn't the life for me and after doing some sightseeing, I caught a train back to Bregenz.

I was happy to be back to my routine of writing and taking walks in the woods. One spring day, while hiking in the Alps foothills above Bregenz and Lake Constance, it dawned on me I didn't need to be around hustlers and crossroaders. I knew some tricks to beat casinos and I could shoot my air ball on hundreds of craps games. I made a reservation to fly into Orlando the following week.

I made it through customs and felt relieved to be home. I started my new odyssey on Interstate 95 playing on gambling boats from South Florida to Maine. The boats were free with my travel agent ID or my VIP card, and they had free buffets. Most of them spread 21, craps, roulette, Caribbean Stud Poker, slots, and Holdem poker, and some boats were cheating.

On one boat, I saw some 21 players who looked suspicious. They were playing with marked cards and when they left, I played on their game and made a nice score. Since then I always look for marked cards when I pass a 21 game in a casino.

I had an advantage with my dice shot and I was able to press my Caribbean Stud bets, and I'd find defective slot machines to beat. They were $1 machines that accepted quarters. A faulty worn-out mechanism would recognize a quarter as a dollar and pay off in dollars, the quarters returned with the dollars in a free-fall. On a boat out of Miami, I found a $5 machine that accepted $1 tokens. After winning over $800, an observer approached me and said he had watched me on a surveillance camera putting in $1 tokens. I said emphatically, "I don't know the denominations; I'm playing whatever tokens the machine pays me." He said he had to shut the machine down. I cashed-in and hid out for the rest of the cruise.

Some boats would give VIP players an extra $100 in VIP chips for buying $1,000 in regular chips—it was a marketing tool to attract new customers, and to keep loyal customers from playing on other boats. The extra $100 was four $25 chips that could be bet but not cashed-in. Half of the time, I would lose betting them, and half the time I would win; basically, it was a $50 gift that covered my nut. On a boat in Savannah, I befriended a hi-rolling craps player who might lose or win $20,000 on one cruise. When he lost big, the ship owner would refund ten percent or more of his losses back to him to keep him from playing on other boats. When he won, he'd slip me chips to cash in for a five percent fee. Six other boats were within a three-hour drive of Savannah, so I stayed in the area for one month before moving on.

I'd call the motel chains for the best travel agent rates. Most offered a free continental breakfast that I loaded up on before leaving; I had learned well from old-time crossroaders how to keep my nut down.

Some mornings when I woke, I didn't realize where I was or what state I was in, but it was comforting to know no one else knew where I was. I enjoyed the solitude, freedom, and the opportunity to read some classic literature I had never found time for in the past.

I was passing through the time barrier, waiting for the best deal my lawyer could get me. I phoned him every several weeks and he would tell me the latest offer.

In Atlantic City, I met an old girlfriend whose family was friends with my family. Linda had learned about my trouble from my mother and invited me to stay with her on weekends. In less than an hour, we were doing "the wild thing" as she called it, and became close again. We talked about my legal situation and she pleaded with me to turn myself in.

Bill Durham told me if I surrendered, the prosecutor would accept a plea of Interstate Travel in Aid of Racketeering (ITAR). He would ask the judge for a one-year prison sentence and I'd be released on my own recognizance while awaiting sentencing. Bill said he had seen some FBI notes Ritini had written explaining the whole operation in Mississippi. I realized I had no chance of beating the case. I had been a fugitive for over four years and couldn't run forever. I phoned Bill and we planned to meet in Biloxi in two weeks.

I met Bill in Biloxi and he dropped me off at the U.S. Marshall's office where I opened the door and waited at a counter where I heard some men talking in the next room. After waiting several minutes, I wondered if someone in the past had wanted to surrender and waited like me and changed his mind and left. I re-opened the door and closed it. Three men came out and I told them who I was and my situation. One of them took me to a jail cell and said he would call the prosecutor. After some paperwork, he said we'd meet my lawyer and the prosecutor within the hour.

At the courthouse, Bill introduced me to Ray Gold, the Federal Prosecutor who had tried the primary case several years earlier. He was friendly and told me he'd have me out of there in less than one hour. Bill had become friends with him and the judge during the main trial that lasted two-and-a-half weeks.

At my hearing, the judge proceeded in an informal and friendly manner. He addressed me by my nickname, Bobby, and asked me how I wanted to plea. I said guilty and the prosecutor told the judge he had promised me he wouldn't ask for bail while I awaited sentencing. The judge set me free on my own recognizance and told me to meet the probation people when I left the courtroom. A marshal objected saying I had an outstanding warrant in Iowa. The judge asked my lawyer if he would call the state attorney in Iowa to take care of it. He said he would and the judge told the marshal I was free to go.

I met my Probation Officer and she recorded my personal history. She told me not to enter any casinos and to call the Federal

Probation Officer in Orlando when I arrived home. I phoned Linda and several friends and relatives before heading home.

Linda flew down to celebrate with me and I rented a beach condominium in Daytona. After one week, we decided to get married. We met my new probation officer in Orlando and then honeymooned at Amelia Island, Florida. We decided we would commute with each other until after I was sentenced.

Linda and her business partner were planning to build several houses on an elite parcel of land she owned in New Jersey. When she arrived home, she was surprised that permits to build the first two houses were approved, and her partner would begin building. I obtained a pass to visit her to find that she was overwhelmed dealing with the building department, buyers, and sub-contractors. After a few visits, and not knowing when I'd be sentenced to prison, we realized our relationship was not what it should be and we were divorced in less than one year.

I spent my time fixing up my house, playing golf with new friends, and working on my air ball while I awaited my sentencing hearing.

Over a year later, I left for Biloxi, to be sentenced and said goodbye to my mother and friend, telling them I'd see them in one year. I rented a car in Daytona, dropped it off at the Gulfport airport, and took a taxi to a Holiday Inn. At noon, I taxied to the courthouse to meet Bill.

The judge sentenced me to one year in a Federal prison, followed by three years' probation and a $2,500 fine. He asked me when I wanted to begin my sentence and I said right away. He said I could turn myself in after the Christmas holidays if I liked. I said, "Judge, I've held up my daughter's wedding long enough and I'd like to start serving my sentence today." He asked the U.S. Marshal if he could take me and he said he could.

Gold asked the judge if he and Bill could confer at the bar. After a short conference, the judge told me he was going to amend my sentence. He suspended my one-year prison sentence, the other sentencing stood.

Bill told me the probation officer had misinterpreted the federal sentencing guidelines and recommended to the judge the one-year prison sentence. Luckily, Gold knew the guidelines and corrected the mistake. I made some phone calls and rented a car in Gulfport to drive home.

Bill called me to tell me he phoned the state attorney in Iowa, who said there was still an outstanding warrant for my arrest, but it was a non-extraditable warrant and there was no jeopardy for me unless I returned to Iowa, where I would be arrested.

I met a new probation officer in Florida who explained the conditions of my probation including working. I found an easy job as a sales rep for a water treatment company. The owner of the company trained me well and I worked when I wanted. I soon found out business people were as crooked as the casinos and I looked forward to a better future.

CHAPTER 15

PARTING SHOTS

The day my probation expired, I quit my job and drove to West Palm Beach to visit Florida John and check some cruise ships in Miami, and Ft. Lauderdale. John had a visitor who had worked in casino security in the Bahamas. John told him I was caught switching dice there years earlier. I told him a boxman nailed me shooting tees in 1965, at the Lucayan Beach Hotel-Casino where I scurried out of the casino and was tackled by Joey Maxim. John's friend Mike said, "Bobby, I was the guy who tackled you, Maxim said, 'Hold him while I hit him.' I told him wait a while and we took you to the back room." I said, "Thanks Mike," and shook his hand again. We were all surprised at the small-world coincidence and had a good laugh. He said the boxman who caught me switching dice was the sharpest in the casino and had just retired from a casino in Atlantic City.

John had just returned home from a six-month prison sentence for violating his federal probation. His probation was for a gaming conviction at an Indian casino in Minnesota. He said, "Somebody tipped-off the casino and a trap had been set." He played a copy of the casino's surveillance-videotaped evidence used at his trial. It showed him purposefully spilling a drink on several cards and the dealer calling to a boss who was in on the play. She told the dealer to stop dealing as she left to the podium to get six new decks of cards. While the dealer was assembling the old cards, the boss held the six new decks of cards below the surface of the 21 table where John's partner Jerry, sitting in the last seat, swapped them for the marked cards. The boss gave the marked cards to the dealer for the old cards. After they won several hands, five FBI agents took the cards, the boss, and John and his crew into custody.

John said he had quit beating the casinos because the sophisticated surveillance cameras shut down the sleight-of-hand moves he used to use. He said, "Modern crossroaders are using computer technology to beat poker and 21 games. They wear miniature spy cameras with special filters that can read marks on cards that can't be seen by the naked eye. The information is sent to a cell phone monitor, then transmitted to the hustlers wearing earpieces. Some cameras can read the DNA of cards as they are being shuffled. The information is transmitted in real time to a small computer that deciphers the shuffled cards and the order they will be dealt, revealing the outcome of any card game." He said the creator of "The Simpsons" claimed he had been cheated playing online poker. And a friend of his who is a well-known poker professional had lost $4 million when someone burgled his home and installed a ceiling spy camera overlooking his computer screen where he played high-stakes online poker. The scammers would play on line with him and knew the cards he held. John said some crossroaders were using the *transfer* to beat poker games and the designer card games Let it Ride, Three Card Poker, and Caribbean Stud.

I took a three-day cruise on a cruise line ship I had played on before. Every game now had a surveillance camera targeting it, and the casino cards were kept in the cashier's office. And I checked two *cruises to nowhere* gambling ships I had previously cruised that now had cameras. It appeared my pirating days were history, and other crossroaders were burning up the *transfer.*

The transfer was special when no one knew it existed. There was only one 21 dealer out of several hundred that I respected and wouldn't play on, and only two bosses. My partners and I had used the transfer for tens of thousands of 21 hands and never got caught in the act of palming a card, switching it, or returning it. We had a great run with it over a sixteen-year period. The transfer was truly a million-dollar move.

In 2005, I flew to Vegas to take a trip down memory lane. I visited the new super-casinos and had fun challenging the craps crews with my air ball that is legal according to the rules in Nevada. I increased my skill level and discovered new gems on each play. On some tables, I could hit the table end with both dice and my air ball would "stick and stay" on the base of the table's rubber backing.

I stood at 21 tables in some casinos I had played on in the past and reflected on the beauty of the transfer. Some dealers and bosses who I had played on were still working and I'd watch them and re-call details of past plays with them.

Because time and distance prejudice relationships, I lost contact with some of my friends and partners. I heard on the grapevine that Mack had died prematurely. Tony Paxon, who I had worked with in Minnesota, was ninety-years-old and still hustling Super Bowl parties and winter guests at the Caribbean hotels. I spent one week with Jesse in Reno watching the Masters Golf Tournament on TV just one month before he died at sixty-four-years-old—if he had only quit drinking a few years earlier... Jesse had a unique personality and style that he owned, and he affected everyone who knew him.

Carlo, Joey, and Wesley have retired, while Cap and I are semi-retired taking occasional fun trips to Atlantic City and Nevada shooting our air ball. We see scores of *dice dominators* playing craps who think they're controlling the dice and we always have a good laugh watching them. They set and toss the dice the same way and imagine they're succeeding.

I googled "dice dominators" and found numerous web sites explaining how to throw a controlled dice shot. Some sites are selling books, DVDs, and teaching suckers live classes. They have no chance of succeeding and the casinos welcome their business. They re-enforce the casinos belief that it's impossible to throw a controlled shot.

Some Vegas casino executives think differently. They suspect that Archie Karas, a famous gambler, has some kind of dice shot and barred him from their casinos after he had won millions of dollars. According to Wikipedia, Archie won $40,000,000 playing craps and poker. He had beaten the top poker players in the world including Doyle Brunson, Stu Unger, and Chip Reese, among others.

Archie told me he had used a high velocity spin shot that had ruined his shoulder. He said he had overcome the craps odds by *killing* just one die in ten shots. Meanwhile, Cap and I are a floating craps game—we're the casinos and the casinos are the suckers.

I have run into friends from my youth who have master's degrees and careers that never matched up to their expectations. When I compare my life to theirs, I feel I have had the best of it, and have no regrets that I left home early and did what I did.

The End (Maybe)

GLOSSARY

The glossary focuses on key words in the story.

agent: A person who works with a casino employee to beat a casino.

air: Degree of attention from a casino boss or dealer: lots of air means a lack of attention.

air ball: An airborne dice throw to control one die.

apron: Worn by dealers to cover their waistband and pockets to prevent stealing.

baloneys: Any type of crooked dice, e.g., *tees, weight, flats.*

bend, the: A technique to mark cards by bending them while playing.

bet the money: To *take-off* the money on a shady gambling play.

blackball: To ostracize someone preventing him from working.

boxman: Craps game supervisor who puts incoming cash into the table money box.

brush, the: A signal to an accomplice to leave an area by brushing-off a forearm or the back of one's head—the quicker the brush, the quicker the exit. Also, a poker room employee.

bust: To go over 21 playing blackjack.

card counting: Keeping track of cards dealt in a 21 game and using that information for an advantage. A 2008 movie drama titled "21" is about the successful MIT card counting team.

carny-speak: Language carnival people, pool hustlers, and cross-roaders use to communicate.

catwalk: A walkway above a casino floor where a surveillance operator observes employees and players through one-way mirrors or plate glass. See *eye-in-the-sky*.

chop, the: A sleight-of-hand card palming technique using two hands.

clean up: To return a held out card in a card game, to remove crooked dice from a dice game, or to toss or hide any item such as a slot machine key that can be used as evidence in a criminal case.

coffee cup move: A move used by dealers to steal chips by dropping them into an abandoned glass of Coke or coffee cup that an accomplice retrieves.

cold deck: A pre-arranged deck of cards, secretly switched into a card game.

collector: Someone who collects a fixed slot machine jackpot.

comps: Short for complimentary meals, drinks, and/or rooms, given to habitual gamblers and hi-rollers.

cooler: Same as cold deck above.

count, the: A count of all chips on all gaming tables taken during the last hour of a casino shift change.

crew: A team of casino craps employees, or a team of crossroaders.

crossroader: Modern term for people who beat casinos. The name may have originated in the Old West where at major "crossroads" could be found a saloon, a restaurant, and some form of gambling. Travelling gamblers frequented these places to beat the players and the house, and became known as crossroaders.

cruises to nowhere: Gambling ships that cruise in international waters.

daub: A colored waxy substance used by crossroaders to mark cards with a faint smudge while playing.

dead aces: *Loaded dice* weighted to favor aces to roll.

dead fives: *Loaded dice* weighted to favor fives to roll.

dealing shoe: A plastic box used to hold multiple decks of cards for dealing 21 and baccarat. It is supposed to prevent cheating. See deuce shoe.

deuce dealer: A card *mechanic* who covertly peeks at the top card, and if it will help his hand, he saves it for himself and deals the "second" card to the players.

deuce shoe: A rigged dealing shoe that enables a *mechanic* to peek at the top card, and deal seconds.

dice dominators: People who try to shoot a controlled dice shot.

doing business: A casino employee who rips off a casino is said to be doing business.

double down: A 21 strategy used to double one's bet when it's to his advantage.

dump shot: A controlled dice shot done by dumping dice from a cup onto a set die to *kill* a desired number. The set die is held in the middle three fingers that cover and shake the dice cup. The set die appears to be poured out of the cup with the other dice that drop on the controlled die to stop it.

even splitters: Crooked dice with one die having double aces, treys, and fives, the other die having double deuces, fours, and sixes. The dice will roll odd numbers, mostly losing sevens, and are used to beat craps players who bet even numbers. See *odd-splitters*.

eye: Same as *eye-in-the-sky* below.

eye-in-the-sky: An observer who surveils casino games and slots casino through one-way mirrors, tinted plate glass, or through a casino surveillance video camera system; same as the *peek*, the eye, the *catwalk*.

face down: A dealing style in 21 where the players are dealt two cards face down instead of face up. Dealing face up prevents players from marking cards, *hand mucking,* and *pressing* bets.

field: A place on a craps table to make a one-roll proposition bet. The numbers 2, 3, 4, 9, 10, 11, and 12 are winning numbers; the 5, 6, 7, and 8 are losing numbers.

field splitters: Crooked dice used to beat field betters. One die has double aces, deuces, and treys; the other has double fours, fives, and sixes. Field bettors lose eight bets in nine rolls on average.

fill: Chips brought from the cashier's cage to replenish casino table games.

flashing: A *move* used by a 21 dealer to expose the top card to his agent. He slides the top card out with his thumb exposing the index between his separated first and second finger. A crooked poker dealer will flash the top few cards to his agent by lifting them up with the tip of his forefinger. Also, a method used to mark cards by painting the card's surface except one area that stands out or flashes.

flat or *flat store:* A crooked game or casino.

flats: Altered dice that are more brick-shaped than square and tend to land on the "flatter," bigger surfaced side of the dice. Six-ace-flats roll more aces and sixes to make more craps and sevens.

floorman: A casino boss who supervises table game employees.

flop, the: A poker term for the first three community cards dealt simultaneously in a *holdem* and *Omaha* poker game. The succeeding two dealt cards are the "turn card" and "river card."

fronts: Legitimate dice.

gaming agents: State employees with police authority who enforce gaming regulations to protect the public and casinos from being cheated.

George: A positive term used by crossroaders to signal their confederates verbally, or by touching their chin, forehead, etc. Dealers use the term for big tippers. See *Jake*.

Griffin Book: A book with mug shots, names, associates, and M.O. of crossroaders and card counters. Casinos who subscribed to the Griffin Detective Agency received a copy of the book. The agency also provided undercover agents to casinos to look for crossroaders and crooked employees.

hand mucking: The act of palming and switching cards to improve one's hand.

hard way bet: A craps game term for betting double deuces, sixes, eights, or tens.

heat: Unwanted suspicion or attention.

heat score: A risky play or play that goes badly.

hit card: A card given by the dealer to a 21 player when she *scratches* or asks for a card.

holdem: A poker game where two cards are dealt to each player and five community cards are dealt face up, intermittently, followed by rounds of betting. The best five-card poker hand wins. See *flop*.

hole card: In blackjack, a dealer deals himself two cards: one up, and one down. The face down card is the hole card. The other card is the up card.

hole carding: Seeing a 21 dealer's hole card by peeking at it from the front, side, or behind. Some crossroaders use hidden mirrors or spy cameras to see the card.

hustle, hustling: To scam someone. To zealously push oneself to ply his trade.

hustler: Someone who scams casinos or people; a pool, poker, or golf hustler, a hooker, a crossroader.

inside: To work the inside means to beat a casino with inside (employee) help. See outside.

Jake: Hustler lingo meaning everything is OK. Same as *George.*

juice: A liquid substance used to mark cards. Also, someone who has influence for a job, a promotion, etc., is said to have juice.

juice joint: An electro-magnetically controlled roulette table, craps table, or backgammon board.

junket: An all-expense paid trip to lure VIP gamblers to a casino, usually for three days. The gamblers are normally required to play for a certain amount of time each day and bet a minimum amount.

kill: To successfully control a dice shot. Or to see an opponents cards in an underhanded way.

layout: An area of a gambling table where players place their bets.

leak: When cards or dice are exposed in the act of *palming,* or *switching.*

light: A mirror glued to a palm, finger, or under a fingernail for spying a card's value as it is dealt.

loaded dice: Dice weighted with tungsten or another heavy metal to favor certain numbers.

marked cards: Cards identified by sight or feel to disclose their value.

mechanic: A crooked dealer proficient at sleight-of-hand with cards or dice.

mini-baccarat: A version of the French game Baccarat, popularized in James Bond movies.

money plays: When a player bets cash, or large denomination chips, the dealer calls out, "Money plays" or "Black plays" to alert a boss.

moves: A hustler term for techniques to switch dice, palm, mark, or switch cards, confidence games, etc.

muck: To *palm* a card to use to improve one's hand.

Nevada Black Book: A blacklist maintained by the Nevada Gaming Commission listing the names of crossroaders and mobsters banned for life from entering Nevada casinos.

nut: Living expenses.

odd-splitters: Crooked dice with one die having double aces, fours, and fives; the other having double deuces, treys, and sixes. The dice will roll even numbers, or losing sevens. They're used to beat craps players who bet odd numbers. See even-splitters.

Omaha: A poker game similar to *holdem* except each player is dealt four cards instead of two, and the winner must use "exactly" two of his four cards to qualify.

on the muscle: To beat a casino without inside (employee) help.

on the square: To play a game fairly.

outside: To work the outside means to beat a casino, without inside help, *(on the muscle.)*

outside-man: A casino employee who prowls the floor looking for crooked employees or crossroaders.

palm: To conceal and secure cards or dice in the palm of the hand to improve one's winning chances.

pass line: A place on a craps table to make a bet; the most popular place to bet in a craps game.

past-post: To place a bet after an event, guaranteeing a win.

pat and pay: A dealer will pat or pay his agent's losing hand like it was a tie or winning hand.

peek: A slight-of-hand move enabling a card mechanic to see the top card's index (value). Also, a place to spy on a card game, backgammon game, or chess game through a light fixture, a vent, a one-way mirror, a camera system, etc. The spy sends the information to his confederate electronically.

pit: A walkway enclosed by gaming tables where bosses and dealers enter to supervise or deal the various games.

pit boss: The chief boss in a casino pit.

pitch, the: A backhanded sleight-of-hand move used by a casino dealer to pass chips to his agent.

podium: A freestanding cabinet in the center of a casino *pit* where playing cards, phones, etc., are kept.

press move: A subtle sleight-of-hand move to increase the amount of a bet.

prop bet: A proposition bet. A sucker bet offered in a casino game.

river card: The last card dealt and acted upon in a *Holdem, Omaha,* or stud poker game.

rounders: Poker hustlers and other gamblers who "make the rounds" looking for action.

runner: When a crossroader has *heat* and has to hurry away from a casino.

sail shot: A dice shot slid on a craps table surface instead of thrown in the air. Same as scoot shot.

sand: Marked cards sanded during play using a hidden piece of sandpaper to sand the edges of cards in different places to signify different values.

scratch: When playing 21, a player will scrape his cards on the table to let the dealer know she wants a hit card.

second: A devious dealing move also called a *deuce*, wherein a dealer peeks at the top card, and if it will help his hand he deals the second card to players to save the top card for himself. Or, he'll deal it to a high roller if it will ruin his double down or split hand, or bust his hand.

selective shuffling: When a 21 dealer shuffles prematurely to offset a players advantage when the deck is heavy with aces and big cards, lessening the chance of a player making a blackjack or twenty. It is Quasi-cheating employed by some casinos and tolerated by some state gaming authorities.

shade: A method to mark cards by tinting areas of the card with *daub* or *juice*. Also, a person who blocks his partners' backs during a 21 or slot play.

shift boss: A supervisor in charge of a casino for an eight-hour shift.

shill: A member of a team of crossroaders posing as a legitimate player, and used as a lookout or to distract someone. Also, a casino employee used as a decoy to lure a player to a game.

shotgun-chair: A large tall chair used for observation in some casinos. It originated in illegal gambling joints in Texas, where a man sat with a shotgun across his lap to protect the game from a heist.

sky-shuffle: A false-shuffle used to fool the eye-in-the-sky. After the cards are shuffled (interlaced), they are pulled apart under cover of the top card that is slid over the deck to cover the unshuffling action, returning the cards to their original position.

sleepers: Bets that players forget to pick up.

slick-sleeve: A jacket sleeve lined with mohair for sliding cards in-and-out of a card game.

slug: A group of known, unshuffled cards created during a card game; a mini-cooler.

spill-shot: When a dice mechanic loses control of his dice in the middle of a dice switch.

split hand: When a 21 player is dealt two paired cards (8,8), he has the option to separate the cards and asks for a hit cards on each card. He then would be playing two hands.

splitters: Crooked dice—a player has no chance to win vs. splitters. See *odd-splitters, even-splitters.*

spy shop: A store that sells lock picks, covert surveillance cameras, listening devices to bug someone's house or car, and a variety of books describing their use.

steer: To lug, or bring someone to a crooked gaming venue.

stickman: Craps dealer who returns the dice to the shooters and calls out the numbers they roll.

stinger: A battery-operated remote-controlled transmitter and receiver unit used to send electronic signals (shocks) from one crossroader to another.

strippers: Certain cards that are sanded, cut, or shaved on the sides and identified by feel during a shuffle and pulled to the top to set up a good hand to beat an opponent.

sub: A pouch, or anything used to conceal stolen chips.

switching cards: To exchange cards with a confederate to improve one's hand.

take off: To win money on a gambling play. A takeoff man is an agent who wins the money.

tees: Crooked dice with double numbers on the tops, sides, and bottoms. They make specific numbers, e.g., ace-four-five tees will roll the numbers two, five, six, eight, nine, and ten. They can't roll a losing sevan and are used by crossroaders to beat casinos. Crooked casinos also use tees to beat honest players, see *splitters.* Tees are also called tops and mis-spots.

tipping a hole card: When a 21dealer signals his hole card to his agent.

tired: A code word meaning time to leave a game or casino; real tired means leave quickly.

Tom: A negative verbal signal used by crossroaders to tell their confederates there is *heat.* A hustler will touch his nose, or make a fist, etc., to give an animated signal.

transfer, the: A card switch between two players—the "million-dollar move."

T.R. Kings: A gambling supply store in Los Angeles that sold legitimate and crooked gambling items.

turn: To distract someone or turn his head away from a *move.*

turn card: The fourth community card dealt and acted upon in an *Omaha* and *Texas Holdem* game.

weight: Dice loaded with heavy metal discs that favor certain numbers to roll.

Made in the USA
Monee, IL
14 February 2021

60510208R00163